NEW HOME PLANS For 1997

TABLE OF CONTENTS

GARLINGHOUSE

Cover photograpy supplied by
Bob Shimmer, Henrich Blessing Studios
Cover design by Paula Mennone

Publisher James D. McNair III
Library of Congress No.: 95-81709/ISBN: 0-938708-68-6

Submit all Canadian plan orders to:
The Garlinghouse Company
60 Baffin Place, Unit #5
Waterloo, Ontario N2V 1Z7

Canadians Order Only: 1-800-561-4169
Fax#: 1-800-719-3291
Customer Service#: 1-519-746-4169

Single Level Convenience — No. 24701

This home features a well designed floor plan, offering convenience and style. The roomy living room includes a two-sided fireplace shared with the dining room. An efficient U-shaped kitchen, equipped with a peninsula counter/breakfast bar, is open to the dining room. An entrance from the garage into the kitchen eliminates tracked-in dirt and affords step-saving convenience when unloading groceries. The private master suite includes a whirlpool tub, a double vanity and a step-in shower. A large walk-in closet adds ample storage space to the suite. The secondary bedroom and the den/guest room share use of the full hall bath. A materials list is not available with this plan.

Main floor — 1,625 sq. ft.
Basement — 1,625 sq. ft.
Garage — 455 sq. ft.

Total living area — 1,625 sq. ft.

Alternate Foundation Plan

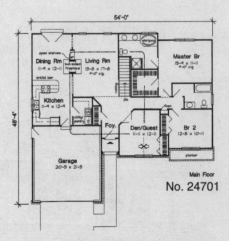

Main Floor
No. 24701

Refer to **Pricing Schedule B** on the order form for pricing information

Please note: The cover photo has been modified to suit individual tastes.

COMFORTABLE COUNTRY EASE

A sprawling front porch gives way to a traditional foyer area with a half bath and a graceful staircase. A tray ceiling adds elegance to the dining room, which directly accesses the kitchen. A large country kitchen with a center work island includes plenty of storage and work space. A tray ceiling accents the family room. A fireplace in the center of the rear wall of the family room adds cozy warmth to cool evenings. A vaulted ceiling and a private bath highlight the second floor master bedroom. Two additional bedrooms share the use of a full hall bath. There is a fourth bedroom option. No materials list is available for this plan.

**First floor — 1,104 sq. ft.
Second floor —
960 sq. ft.**

*Total living area:
2,064 sq. ft.*

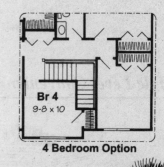

**Alternate Crawl
Space/Slab Option**

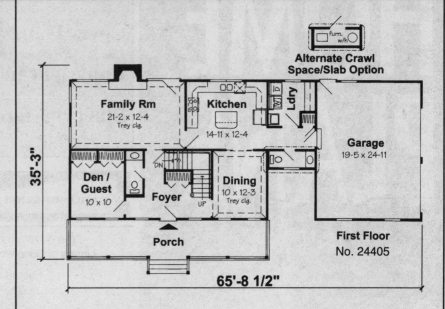

**First Floor
No. 24405**

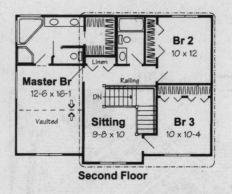

Second Floor

4 Bedroom Option

An
EXCLUSIVE DESIGN
By Upright Design

Refer to **Pricing Schedule C** on
the order form for pricing information

ELEGANT YET ECONOMICAL

The elegant bay window and porch detailing combine to create a cozy home that is actually economical to construct. A 42" high wall separates the dining area from the fireplaced living room with it's 9' sloped ceiling and expansive corner windows. The efficient kitchen has plenty of cabinets, along with a pantry and a corner sink. The master bedroom has a 9' sloped ceiling, private master bath and a large walk-in closet. The secondary bedrooms share the full bath in the hall. No materials list available for this plan.

**Main living area —
1,198 sq. ft.
Garage — 431 sq. ft.
Width — 43'-4"
Depth — 50'-0"**

*Total living area:
1,198 sq. ft.*

Refer to **Pricing Schedule A** on the order form for pricing information

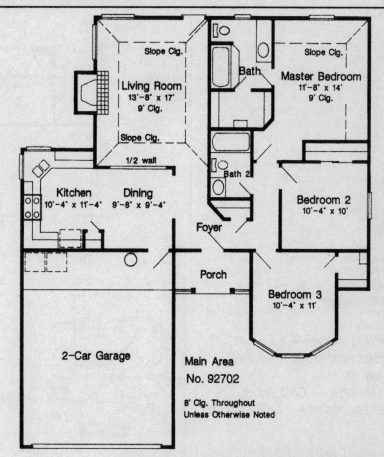

Living Room
13'-8" x 17'
9' Clg.
Slope Clg.

Bath

Master Bedroom
11'-8" x 14'
9' Clg.
Slope Clg.

1/2 wall

Bath 2

Kitchen
10'-4" x 11'-4"

Dining
9'-8" x 9'-4"

Bedroom 2
10'-4" x 10'

Foyer

Porch

Bedroom 3
10'-4" x 11'

2-Car Garage

Main Area
No. 92702

8' Clg. Throughout
Unless Otherwise Noted

CLASSIC FRONT PORCH

Stone and columns accentuate the wrap-around front porch of this home, hinting of times gone by. Inside, columns are repeated in the entrances of the adjoining living room and dining room. Directly accessing the dining room, the island kitchen efficiently serves both the informal and formal eating areas. A large snack bar island dominates the kitchen which features plenty of cabinet and storage space and a walk-in pantry. The breakfast room flows into both the kitchen and the family room creating a terrific family living space. A corner fireplace and a built-in entertainment center are featured in the family room. Four bedrooms are located on the second floor. The lavish master suite includes a decorative ceiling and a private ultra bath. A full bath serves the three additional bedrooms. No materials list available.

First floor — 1,584 sq. ft.
Second floor — 1,277 sq. ft.
Garage — 550 sq. ft.
Basement — 1,584 sq. ft.

Total living area: 2,861 sq. ft.

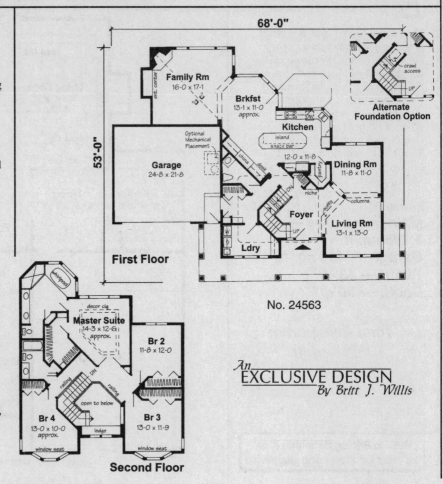

No. 24563

An EXCLUSIVE DESIGN
By Britt J. Willis

Refer to **Pricing Schedule E** on the order form for pricing information

GRANDEUR WITH COLUMNS AND BRICK

As you enter this gracious home, the turned staircase and 21' high ceiling make quite an impression. The formal dining room and the living room/parlor both contain beautiful, brick fireplaces and the parlor also boasts a bar. The expansive family room features cathedral ceilings and the largest fireplace of the home. The spacious, island kitchen has room for several counter stools, as well as a large breakfast room. Off the utility room is a entry, which leads to the workshop and golf cart storage area. The master suite exceeds all expectations and spans the entire width of the home. It boasts a vaulted 12' ceiling, two walk-in closets (one of which is a room sized L-shape), and a plethora of bathroom amenities. The upper floor claims three large bedrooms, a balcony, and two full baths in a creative shared arrangement. home is a dream that came true. No materials list available for this plan.

Main floor — 2,432 sq. ft.
Upper floor — 903 sq. ft.
Basement — 2,432 sq. ft.
Garage — 742 sq. ft.

Total living area:
3,335 sq. ft.

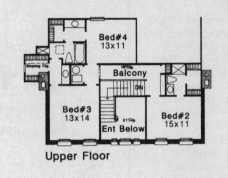

Upper Floor

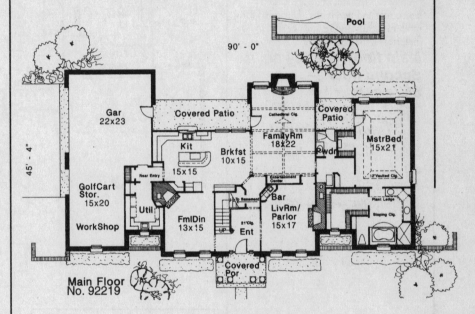

Main Floor
No. 92219

Refer to **Pricing Schedule F** on the order form for pricing information

Design 92207

COUNTRY FRENCH STYLED

This country french home has a hipped roof with dormer accents. The spacious entry is open to the living room and formal dining room. The island kitchen opens to the breakfast nook and the cathedral ceiling family room with a fireplace. This area of the home is wonderful for gatherings and opens to the patio. The master bedroom has a vaulted ceiling and private master bath with walk-in closets. Convenient to the master bedroom is the study that features a fireplace. Upstairs there are three bedrooms and two baths. Designed for modern family living at its best. No materials list available for this plan.

Main floor — 2,304 sq. ft.
**Second floor —
852 sq. ft.**

*Total living area:
3,156 sq. ft.*

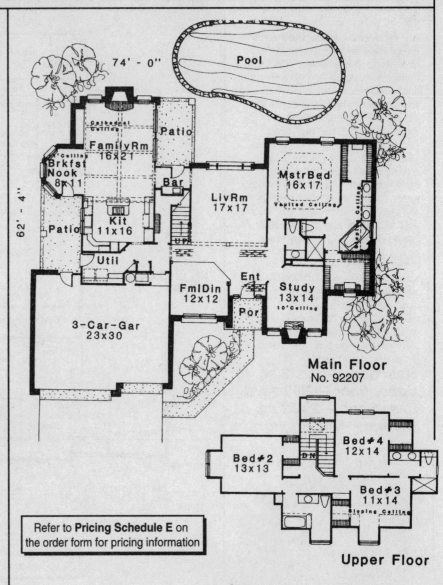

Main Floor
No. 92207

Upper Floor

Refer to **Pricing Schedule E** on the order form for pricing information

GREAT ROOM WITH FIREPLACE

This home is highlighted by a Great room that lives up to its name. A large fireplace on the rear wall serves as a focal point and provides warmth and coziness to this expansive room. There is direct access to the sun deck. An elegant dining room flowing from the Great room promotes successful entertaining. The galley kitchen has been efficiently laid out. A large master suite with a private bath and a walk-in closet has been provided. Two additional bedrooms share a full hall bath. A materials list is not available with this plan.

First floor — 1,261 sq. ft.
Entry (lower level) —
20 sq. ft.
Basement — 600 sq. ft.
Garage — 552 sq. ft.

Total living area:
1,281 sq. ft.

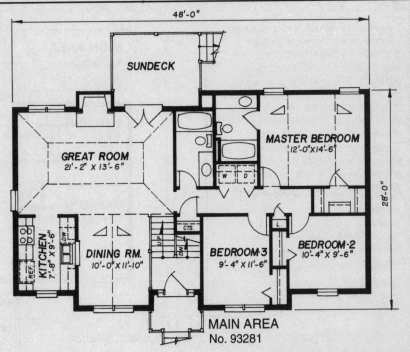

An
EXCLUSIVE DESIGN
By Jannis Vann & Associates, Inc.

Refer to **Pricing Schedule A** on the order form for pricing information

VACATION RETREAT

An attractive elevation to be placed in your dream environment, perhaps perched on a mountainside or by a lake. A deck expands living space outdoors. The open layout between the dining and living room is accented by a central fireplace. An efficient U-shaped kitchen includes a corner double sink surrounded by three windows providing a great view. Two bedrooms are included, one with a private bath and a walk-in closet.

Main floor — 950 sq. ft.

Total living area:
950 sq. ft.

MAIN AREA
No. 94300

40'

26'

53'

RAIL

DECK

Roof O.H.

BEDROOM
9'X11'

KIT.
8'X9'

LIVING
14'X17'

EATING

W. D.

BEDROOM
11'X14'

Clearstory Wdos.

ENT.

STORAGE

OPTIONAL CAR PORT
14'X18'

An
EXCLUSIVE DESIGN
By Marshall Associates

Refer to **Pricing Schedule A** on the order form for pricing information

A PICTURESQUE FRONT PORCH

The lovely front porch of this home is just waiting for a porch swing. The entry hall inside, is graced by a staircase. A formal living room is to the right, featuring a focal point fireplace. A formal dining room, flowing from the living room, is convenient for entertaining. A large, efficient kitchen is directly accessed from the dining room. A cooktop island, built-in pantry and desk add to its efficiency. A second fireplace enhances the family room, and can be enjoyed from the kitchen or the nook. A spacious master suite that includes a lavish bath and walk-in closet is on the second floor. Four additional bedrooms share the full bath in the hallway.

First floor — 1,200 sq. ft.
Second floor — 1,339 sq. ft.

Total living area: 2,539 sq. ft.

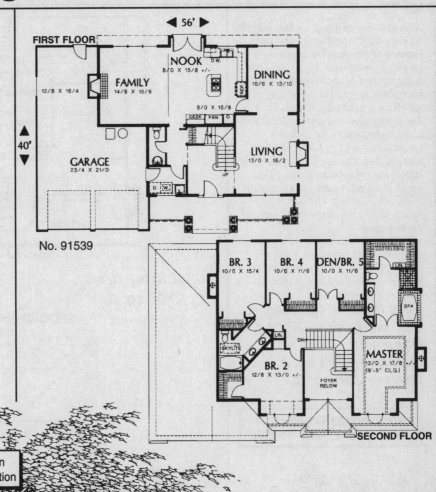

FIRST FLOOR

◄ 56' ►

40'

NOOK
8/0 X 15/8 +/-
FAMILY
14/6 X 15/8
12/8 X 16/4
DINING
10/6 X 13/10
9/0 X 15/8
DESK PAN.
GARAGE
23/4 X 21/0
LIVING
13/0 X 16/2
UP

No. 91539

BR. 3
10/0 X 15/4
BR. 4
10/6 X 11/6
DEN/BR. 5
10/0 X 11/6
SPA
SKYLITE
LIN.
DN
BR. 2
12/8 X 13/0 +/-
FOYER BELOW
MASTER
13/0 X 17/8 +/-
(9'-5" CLG.)

SECOND FLOOR

Refer to **Pricing Schedule D** on the order form for pricing information

Design 93228

SMART STUCCO

A large living area with a warm fireplace makes a terrific first impression upon entering this home. The openness in the layout of the active living areas of the home create a spacious feeling. The formal dining room is served easily by the efficient kitchen, just steps away. The double sink and ample cabinet and counter space make the kitchen a pleasure to work in. A built-in pantry area and direct access to the sun deck are featured in the breakfast room. The wonderful master suite will pamper the owner. A private master bath with two basins, corner tub, separate shower and walk-in closet will certainly be appreciated by any parent. The two additional bedrooms share a full hall bath. A loft area with three skylights will become a special area customized to the family's needs.

First floor — 1,678 sq. ft.
Second floor — 282 sq. ft.
Basement — 836 sq. ft.
Garage — 784 sq. ft.
Deck — 288 sq. ft.

Refer to **Pricing Schedule C** on the order form for pricing information

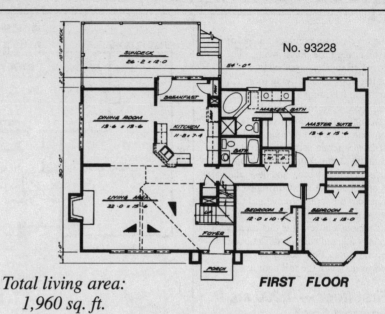

No. 93228

FIRST FLOOR

Total living area: 1,960 sq. ft.

SECOND FLOOR

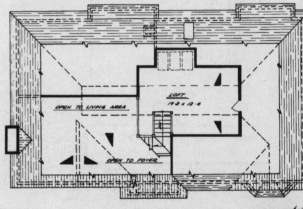

An EXCLUSIVE DESIGN
By Jannis Vann & Associates, Inc.

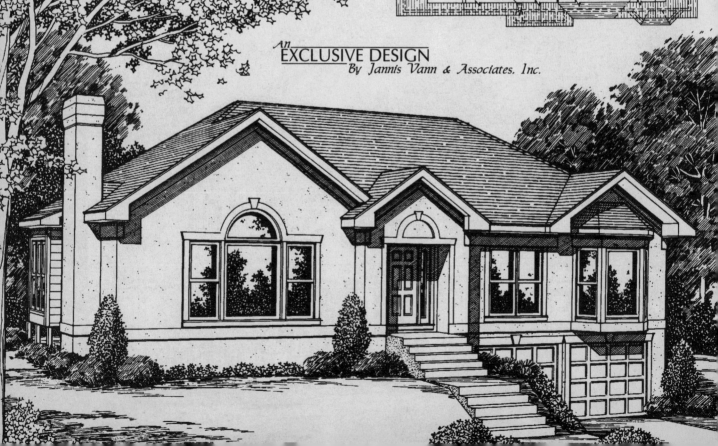

DESIGNED FOR UP-SLOPING LOTS

This home features multi-paned windows and high ceilings, giving a feeling of spaciousness to what may be considered a smaller home. Upon entering the home, you step up to enter the dining room which is separated from the kitchen by only a peninsula counter, again adding to the spaciousness. The elegant living room makes quite an impression; the tall, multi-paned window seems to climb to the roof, since the room is two stories in height. A fireplace completes the picture and adds to the ambience of the room. Informal family gatherings will be comfortably accommodated in the large family room. There is a convenient half bath located to the rear of the family room. Sleeping quarters are located on the second floor. The master suite has a vaulted ceiling and French doors. There is a walk-in closet and a full lead to a small private deck.

The two additional bedrooms have ample closet space and easy access to a full bath.

First floor — 1,022 sq. ft.
Second floor — 813 sq. ft.

Total living area:
1,835 sq. ft.

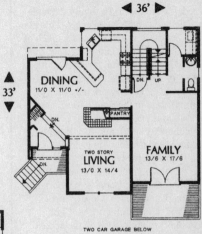

◄ 36' ►

33'

DINING
11/0 X 11/0 +/-

DN. UP

PANTRY

TWO STORY
LIVING
13/0 X 14/4

FAMILY
13/6 X 17/6

TWO CAR GARAGE BELOW

1st Floor
No. 91517

BR. 2
10/2 X 13/0

TUB

DN.

BR. 3
10/8 X 11/8

LIN.

LIVING RM.
BELOW

VAULTED
MASTER
13/6 X 12/6

2nd Floor

Refer to **Pricing Schedule C** on the order form for pricing information

Design 93216

CONVENIENCE WITH A TOUCH OF CLASS

In today's busy world a family depends on efficiency and convenience. This plan will meet those needs and add a touch of class. The informal family areas of this home conveniently run together adding a feeling of space, added efficiency and convenience. Homework may be accomplished in the family room under the watchful eye of the dinner preparer. After-dinner conversations will continue uninterrupted as clean-up is done. Family togetherness is easily sustained with this open layout. Of course, the formal areas of the home are important and this plan includes a lovely formal living room and dining room. The bedrooms are all located on the second floor. The master suite has a touch of class with a decorative ceiling and private master bath. The two additional bedrooms share the full hall bath. There is a convenient second floor laundry and a bonus room to accommodate your changing needs. No materials list available for this plan.

First floor — 986 sq. ft.
Second floor — 932 sq. ft.
Bonus room — 274 sq. ft.
Basement — 882 sq. ft.
Garage — 532 sq. ft.

Total living area:
1,918 sq. ft.

Refer to **Pricing Schedule C** on the order form for pricing information

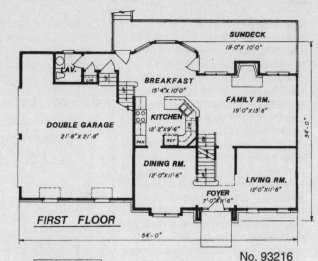

FIRST FLOOR

No. 93216

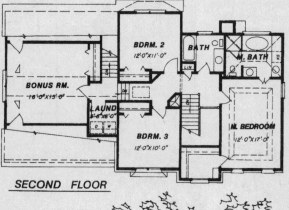

SECOND FLOOR

An EXCLUSIVE DESIGN
By Jannis Vann & Associates, Inc.

SPACE EFFICIENT STYLING

The elegant styling of this very space efficient plan features the charm and elegance of brick and stucco. As you enter the foyer, you find the spacious dining room to your right and to the rear of the foyer is a very large den. The dining room has eleven foot ceilings and palladian windows. A large country kitchen is located to the rear of the dining area and features built-in double ovens, cooktop, and vent hood, double sink and disposal, as well as a dishwasher and desk. The breakfast bar opens into the large breakfast room. The den is entered from this area and features ten foot ceilings and a brick fireplace with two sets of double French doors that open onto the patio area. The bedrooms are designed to split the master bedroom away from the other two. From the den there is a very short hall that leads to two smaller bedrooms, both with walk-in closets. The master bedroom features a ten foot trey ceiling and large walk-in closet. The master bath has double vanities, linen closet, whirlpool tub, separate shower and private toilet compartment.

**Main living area —
1,959 sq. ft.
Garage — 512 sq. ft.**

*Total living area:
1,959 sq. ft.*

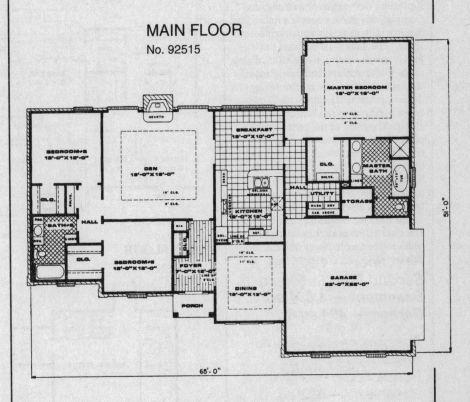

MAIN FLOOR
No. 92515

Refer to **Pricing Schedule C** on the order form for pricing information

FARMHOUSE COLONIAL

Design 99632

Reflecting the warmth of a farmhouse Colonial, this home is surely a house for the 90's with its flexible arrangement of space. The main floor contains the family activity areas: living room, dining room, kitchen/dinette and family room, while off the foyer in a private setting are three bedrooms. Upstairs is multi-use space with its own full bath and walk-in closet. The motif of the front porch is carried inside with two decorative columns placed between the living and dining rooms. There are two heat-circulating fireplaces; one in the living room and one in the family room. A large terrace extends along the rear with access from the dinette and family room. The large efficient kitchen has a full-width bay letting in plenty of light.

First floor — 1,925 sq. ft.
Second floor — 549 sq. ft.
Basement — 1,854 sq. ft.
Garage — 494 sq. ft.

Total living area:
2,474 sq. ft.

Refer to **Pricing Schedule D** on the order form for pricing information

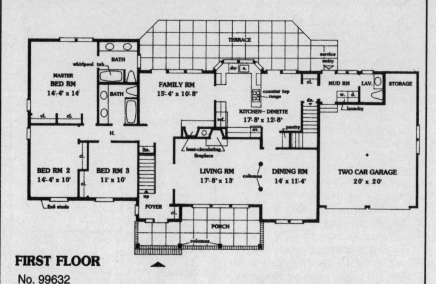

FIRST FLOOR

No. 99632

Width — 80' - 8"
Depth — 41' - 6"

SECOND FLOOR

FOR AN UPWARD SLOPING LOT

This plan is designed for a lot that slopes upward. A sheltered entrance leads to a small entry hall. The sunken family room, to the left, features a two story ceiling, built-in shelves, and a two-sided fireplace. To the right of the entry hall is the formal parlor. One step up from the parlor is the formal dining room. A spacious kitchen is equipped with an island/eating bar, a cooktop and an informal eating nook. On the second floor, the master suite includes a decorative ceiling, terrific private bath and a walk-in closet. Two additional bedrooms have private access to a full bath.

First floor — 1,713 sq. ft.
Second floor — 998 sq. ft.
Lower floor — 102 sq. ft.

◄ 56'-6" ►

38'

Total living area: 2,813 sq. ft.

NOOK
10/0 X 15/0
(9' CLG.)
13/8 X 13/6 +/-

DINING
11/0 X 13/7
(9' CLG.)

PARLOR
13/8 X 15/5
(10'-1" CLG.)

DEN
13/10 X 12/0 +
(9' CLG.)

2 STORY
FAMILY RM.
15/10 X 20/6 +/-

DECK

STOR.

LINEN

FIRST FLOOR
No. 91538

3 CAR GARAGE UNDER

BR. 2
10/0 X 12/8

BR. 3
11/0 X 12/8

WINDOW
SEAT

LINEN

SPA

DN.

MASTER
15/2 X 15/8 +/-
(9'-8" CLG.)

FAMILY RM.
BELOW

DECK

SECOND FLOOR

Refer to **Pricing Schedule E** on the order form for pricing information

COUNTRY CHARM

The warm, welcoming flavor of this one-story, sprawling country home gains its charm from the expression of its separate masses. The lower portions build up pleasantly to the center, the focus, which contains the large space rooms such as the 10 foot high living room and family room/dinette with its bay window and heat circulating fireplace. The mass to the left contains the dining room enhanced with a huge bay window. Right of the center is the bedroom wing. The master bedroom has a private bath with a separate stall shower and whirlpool tub. Both full baths have double basins. The plan exemplifies the comfortable life style of today, separating the formal from the informal everyday spaces, yet allows these areas to spatially flow together.

Main living area — 1,650 sq. ft.
Garage — 491 sq. ft.

Total living area: 1,650 sq. ft.

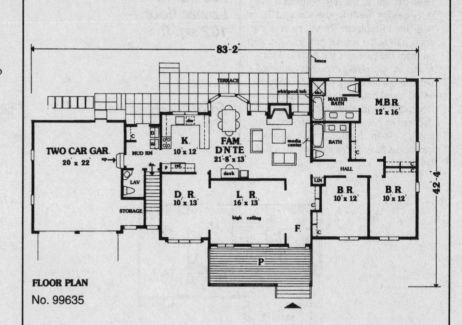

FLOOR PLAN
No. 99635

Refer to **Pricing Schedule B** on the order form for pricing information

MAGNIFICENT ELEVATION

An
EXCLUSIVE DESIGN
By Jannis Vann & Associates, Inc.

From the attractive facade, to the design inside, this home keeps your attention. The dining room and the living room have bay windows illuminating the room with natural light. The informal family area is an open format. The kitchen includes two islands and a built-in pantry. The breakfast area is illuminated with natural light through the use of skylights. The sunken family room has a large fireplace and direct access to the rear yard. A large master suite is located on the second floor. A private sitting area and lavish master bath pamper you with luxury, while two walk-in closets take care of storage needs. Three additional bedrooms, one with a private bath, area of a good size and have ample closet space. No materials list available for this plan.

First floor — 1,695 sq. ft.
Second floor — 1,620 sq. ft.
Basement — 1,695 sq. ft.
Garage — 572 sq. ft.

Total living area: 3,315 sq. ft.

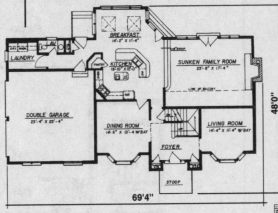

FIRST FLOOR
No. 93273

Refer to **Pricing Schedule F** on the order form for pricing information

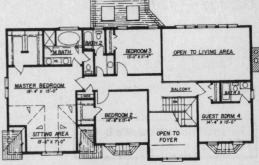

SECOND FLOOR

THREE BEDROOMS AND MORE

A sheltered entrance leads to a tiled foyer. To the right is the dining and kitchen area. Straight ahead is the roomy living room with a cozy fireplace. The master suite, privately located, includes a vaulted ceiling, compartmented bath and a walk-in closet. At the opposite end of the home are two additional bedrooms, one with a cathedral ceiling the other with a walk-in closet, sharing use of the full bath in the hall. The utility room serves as a mudroom entrance from the garage. No materials list is available with this plan.

Main living area — 1,653 sq. ft.
Garage — 420 sq. ft.

Total living area: 1,653 sq. ft.

Refer to **Pricing Schedule B** on the order form for pricing information

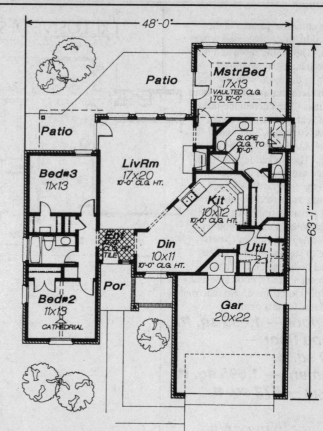

Main Floor
No. 92283

LARGE CONTEMPORARY

At the heart of this home is a combined kitchen and family room with a sunny eating nook nestled into a bay window. The L-shaped center island, which houses both a range and a vegetable sink, also doubles as an eating bar. Plenty of counter and storage space is here to feed and serve a small platoon of family and friends. Sliding glass doors provide access to a deck that wraps around the entire back of the house, a natural for summertime entertaining. The master suite is downstairs, separate from the other bedrooms. It features a large walk-in closet and double vanities located outside the water closet. A raised nook could either hold a spa, or serve as a small, bright sitting room. The utility room has plenty of cupboards, counter space for folding clothes, and a fold-down ironing board. Clothing, bed linen and towels, from upstairs, arrive via a laundry chute.

First floor — 2,484 sq. ft.
Second floor — 972 sq. ft.
Basement — 2,440 sq. ft.
Garage/storage — 990 sq. ft.

Total living area:
3,456 sq. ft.

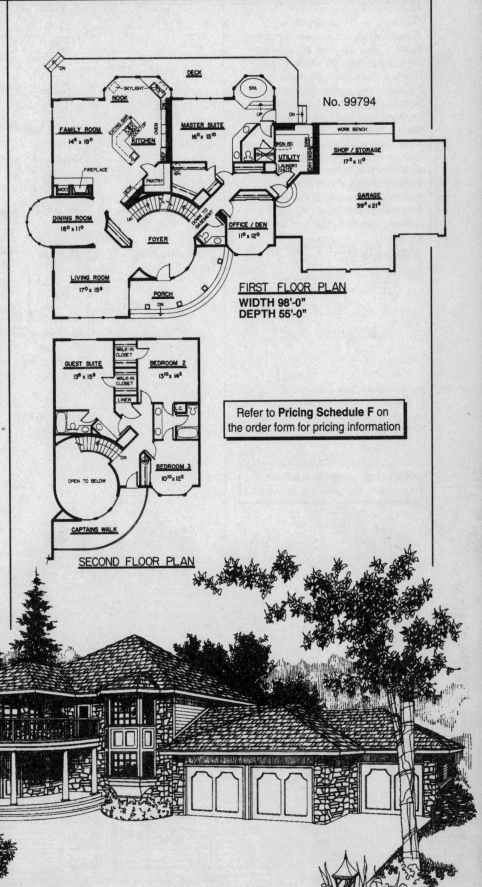

No. 99794

FIRST FLOOR PLAN
WIDTH 98'-0"
DEPTH 55'-0"

Refer to **Pricing Schedule F** on the order form for pricing information

SECOND FLOOR PLAN

AFFORDABLE BEAUTY

Simple clean lines make this home affordable to build, without sacrificing beauty. The tiled entry advances into the living room, which features a gas fireplace that adjoins the dining room. An efficient U-shaped kitchen is separated from the dining room by a breakfast bar. Sliding glass doors add light and give access from the dining room to the rear deck. The master suite includes ample closet space and a private bath with a shower. A full bath in the hallway serves the two additional bedrooms. One of the bedrooms is crowned by a vaulted ceiling. No materials list available for this plan.

Main floor — 1,250 sq. ft.

Total living area:
1,250 sq. ft.

Refer to **Pricing Schedule A** on the order form for pricing information

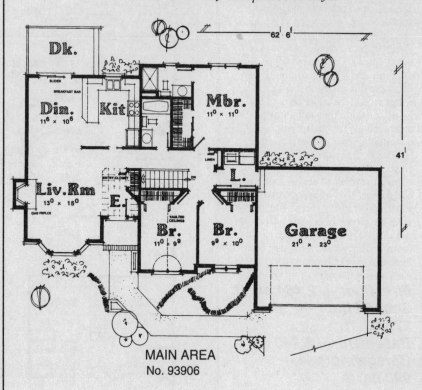

An
EXCLUSIVE DESIGN
By Independent Designs

MAIN AREA
No. 93906

No materials list available

FIT FOR THE FAMILY

This three bedroom ranch provides abundant family living space with traditional exterior styling. The arched entry porch and the living room featuring large windows add to the curb appeal of this home. Vaulted ceilings extend views and the natural light from the transom windows. The kitchen is spacious and opens to a bowed breakfast and family room. A nice feature of this home is that the secondary bedrooms are zoned for privacy. The generous master suite is on the other side of the house, and has a compartmented bath and separate closets. The secondary bedrooms share a bath.

Main area — 1,700 sq. ft.
Garage — 393 sq. ft.
Total living area:
1,700 sq. ft.

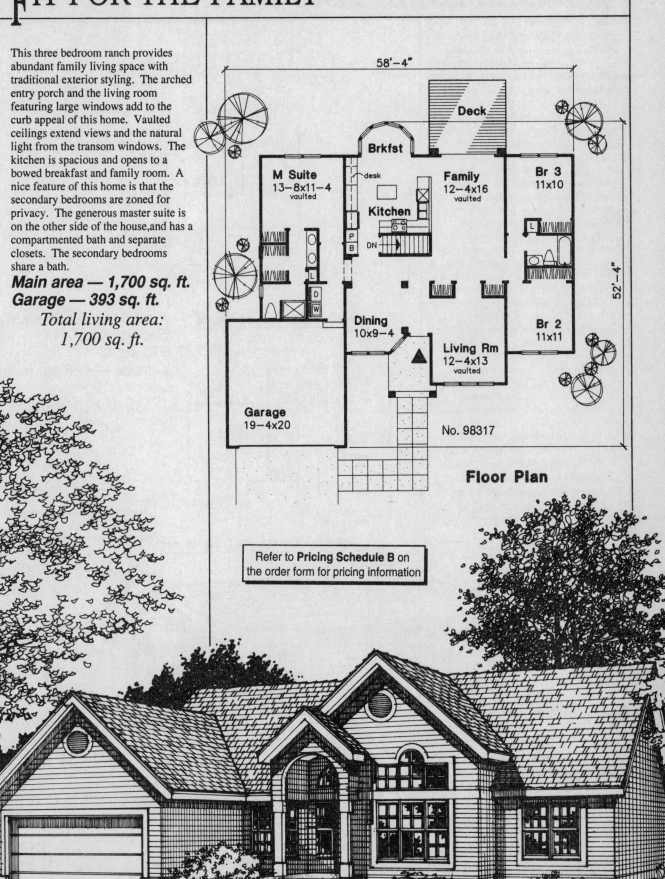

58'-4"

Deck

Brkfst

desk

M Suite
13—8x11—4
vaulted

Family
12—4x16
vaulted

Br 3
11x10

Kitchen

L

P
B

DN

Br 2
11x11

52'-4"

Dining
10x9—4

Living Rm
12—4x13
vaulted

Garage
19—4x20

No. 98317

Floor Plan

Refer to **Pricing Schedule B** on the order form for pricing information

FOR THE FIRST-TIME BUYER

With its gable, dormers and covered entry, this two-story plan has great curb appeal and is the perfect size for a first-time buyer. This home has all the amenities of a larger home including formal and informal areas, two and a half bathrooms, and a master bedroom. The main entry offers a convenient coat closet, immediate access to the upper level, and a direct view through the sunny windows in the dinette. A half bath is located off the entry hall and a formal living room is situated to the left of the entry, with bay windows at the front. The country kitchen features a corner sink with two windows offering a double view. The kitchen merges with the dinette and flows into the family room to create an open feeling. This informal room includes a raised hearth fireplace, three windows to the rear and access to a patio. A central hall on the upper level separates the master suite on one end from the two bedrooms on the other end. The master suite boasts a full bathroom, a large walk-in closet, and a sitting area by the front windows. Bedrooms two and three share a full bathroom and a linen closet off the hall. Both have ample living space, and the front bedroom offers a window seat. No Materials list available with this plan.

An
EXCLUSIVE DESIGN
By Gary Clayton

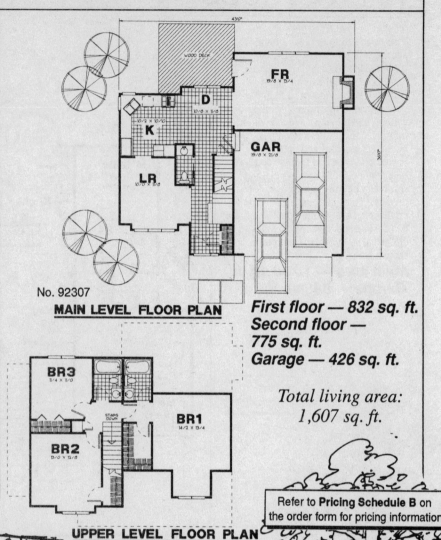

No. 92307
MAIN LEVEL FLOOR PLAN

UPPER LEVEL FLOOR PLAN

**First floor — 832 sq. ft.
Second floor —
775 sq. ft.
Garage — 426 sq. ft.**

*Total living area:
1,607 sq. ft.*

Refer to **Pricing Schedule B** on the order form for pricing information

OPEN SPACES

The family room, kitchen and breakfast area of this home all connect to form a great space. A central, double fireplace adds warmth and atmosphere to all the rooms. The efficient kitchen is highlighted by a peninsula counter that doubles as a snack bar. The master suite includes a walk-in closet, a double vanity, separate shower and tub bath. Two additional bedrooms share a full hall bath. A wooden deck that can be accessed from the breakfast area expands living space in the warmer weather.

Main living area — 1,388 sq. ft
Garage — 400 sq. ft.

Total living area: 1,388 sq. ft.

Refer to **Pricing Schedule A** on the order form for pricing information

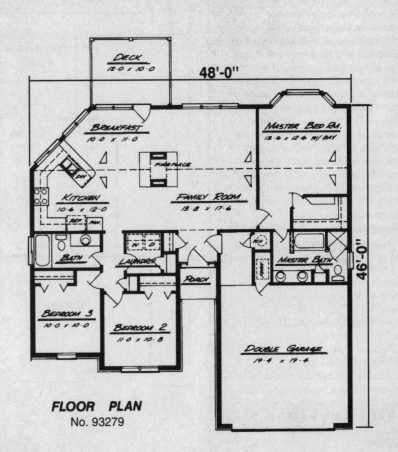

FLOOR PLAN
No. 93279

An
EXCLUSIVE DESIGN
By Jannis Vann & Associates, Inc.

Design 24588

GREAT ROOM WITH A VAULTED CEILING

The view from the foyer is the captivating Great room with a focal point fireplace. The dining room has direct access to the screen porch, and is an annex to the kitchen. A center work island contributes to the counter space in the kitchen, offering an eating bar. A pantry and a planning desk add built-in conveniences. The master suite also boasts a vaulted ceiling and includes a walk-in closet and a private bath. An additional bedroom has use of the full bath. The study may easily be turned into a bedroom, as it sports a closet. No materials list is available for this plan.

First floor — 1,786 sq. ft.
Lower floor(Finished) — 718 sq. ft.

Total living area: 2,504 sq. ft.

An EXCLUSIVE DESIGN
By Britt J. Willis

64'-0"

60'-4"

Opt. Screen Porch
13-8 x 13-8

vault clg

Master Suite
13-0 x 16-2
vault clg

Dining
10-0 x 14-10

Great Rm
15-0 x 14-10
flat clg

Kit
10-0 x 12-10

pantry

desk

bench

DN

DN

open to below

1/2 wall

columns

railing

niche

Foyer

niche

Br 2
11-0 x 10-0

window seat

Study/Br 3
13-1 x 9-5

W

D

Garage
33-5 x 21-8

MAIN AREA
No. 24588

Refer to **Pricing Schedule D** on the order form for pricing information

INVITING WRAP-AROUND PORCH

A warm and inviting welcome is the feeling brought home by the wrap-around porch in this elevation. A skylight illuminates the entry area. The Great room features a corner gas fireplace and includes two skylights overhead. Flowing directly from the Great room, the dining room receives natural light from sliding glass doors to a rear deck and a skylight. The well-appointed, U-shaped kitchen includes another skylight and a breakfast bar separating it from the dining room. The bedrooms are clustered to the right of the home. A luxurious master bath and a private deck highlight the master suite. Two additional bedrooms share use of the full bath in the hallway, and receive light from the dormers, acting like clerestory windows above. No materials list available for this plan.

Main floor — 1,716 sq. ft.
Width — 72'-0"
Depth — 46'-0"

Total living area:
1,716 sq. ft.

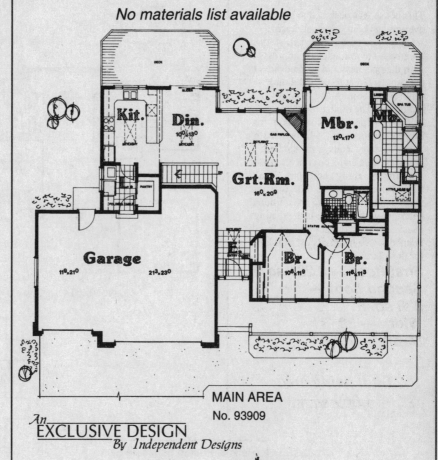

No materials list available

MAIN AREA

No. 93909

An
EXCLUSIVE DESIGN
By Independent Designs

Refer to **Pricing Schedule B** on the order form for pricing information

Design 92614

Spacious Style and Elegance

This house was designed to provide everything desired in your dream home. Upon entering the two-story foyer you are immediately impressed with the openness and spaciousness of the sunken Great room and dining room with columns and custom moldings. The dining room has an alcove providing additional room for furniture placement. A hallway with a butler's pantry leads to the kitchen, breakfast area and a cozy hearth room for intimate family gatherings. The second floor offers two bedrooms that share a tandem bath and an additional bedroom with a private bath creating a guest suite or a retreat for older family members. No materials list available for this plan.

First floor — 2,231 sq. ft.
Second floor — 838 sq. ft.
Width — 59'-8"
Depth — 72'-0"

Total living area: 3,069 sq. ft.

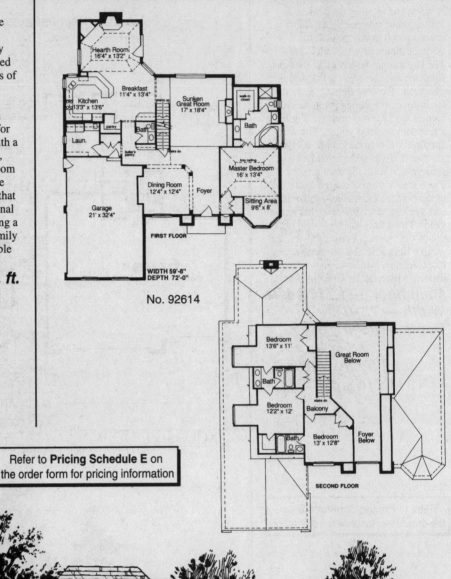

No. 92614

Refer to **Pricing Schedule E** on the order form for pricing information

WELL DESIGNED PLAN

Enter this well-designed Traditional style home from a cozy covered porch to an open, inviting two-story entrance with lavish window details. The vaulted, bayed living room and dining room are together on one side and the open living areas to the rear of the house, make this an excellent family home. The open kitchen, with cooktop island and corner windows, makes this an enjoyable feature for the family. The winding staircase leads you to an "open to below" landing, welcoming you to the second floor bedrooms. Three good-sized bedrooms join the master suite to make this home suitable for any family. The generously sized master suite has a lovely master bath with a whirlpool tub, a double cornered vanity, and a large walk-in closet. All of this is enhanced with a great exterior. No materials list available for this plan.

Main floor — 1,026 sq. ft.
Upper floor —
965 sq. ft.
Garage — 594 sq. ft.
Width — 52'-0"
Depth — 40'-0"

Total living area:
1,991 sq. ft.

An
EXCLUSIVE DESIGN *By*
CRANE DESIGN inc.

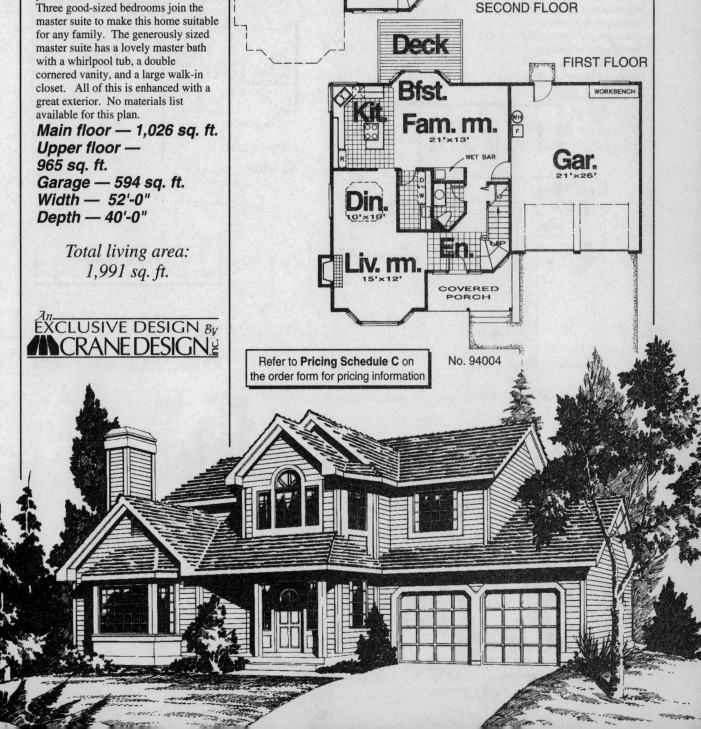

Refer to **Pricing Schedule C** on the order form for pricing information

No. 94004

WELCOMING STYLE

The two-story entrance welcomes you to this traditional home. With the angled staircase and the sunken bayed living room that invites you to the formal bayed dining room, any guest would feel welcomed. Along with the formal style comes warmth and efficiency for a living style you can't miss. This well designed four bedroom home gives you the maximum house in the minimum square footage. The generously sized master suite, enhanced with a window seat and a large walk-in closet, leaves you separated yet close enough to the three additional bedrooms. The exterior of the home lends itself the diversity and street appeal to fit well into any neighborhood. No materials list available for this plan.

**First floor —
947 sq. ft.
Second floor —
752 sq. ft.
Garage — 440 sq. ft.
Width — 40'-0"
Depth — 40'-0"**

*Total living area:
1,699 sq. ft.*

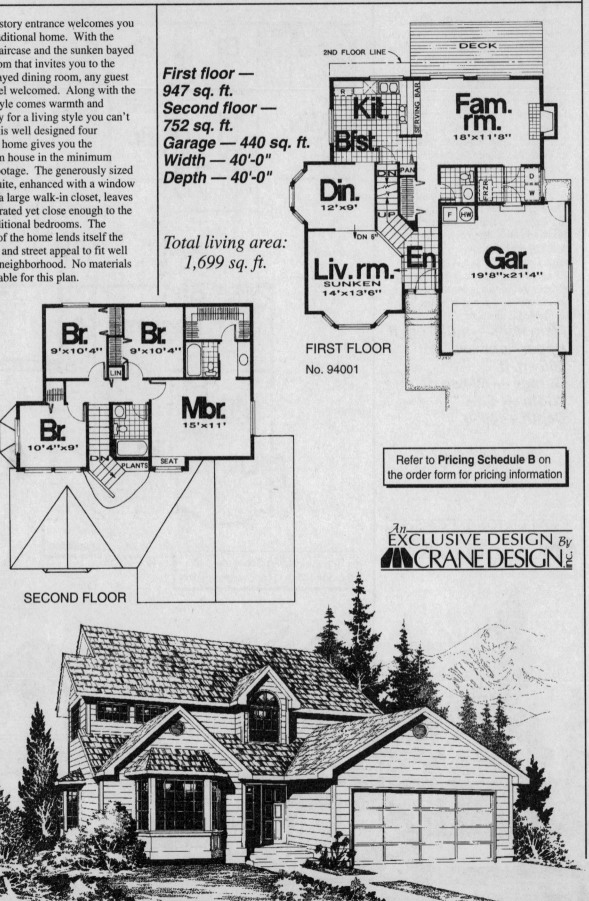

FIRST FLOOR

No. 94001

SECOND FLOOR

Refer to **Pricing Schedule B** on the order form for pricing information

An
EXCLUSIVE DESIGN *By*
CRANE DESIGN. inc.

ATTRACTIVE BRICK ELEVATION

The brick facade of this home is accented by quoins at the corners, creating a decorative touch that enhances the entire home. A sheltered entrance leads to the entrance hall and the living room. A sloping ceiling and a fireplace in the center of the rear wall highlights the living room. The master suite also includes a sloping ceiling and has two walk-in closets as well as a private bath. The island kitchen, which includes a dinette area, is well-appointed. The two additional bedrooms share the use of a full hall bath. No materials list available

**Main floor —
1,415 sq. ft.
Garage — 440 sq. ft.**

*Total living area:
1,415 sq. ft.*

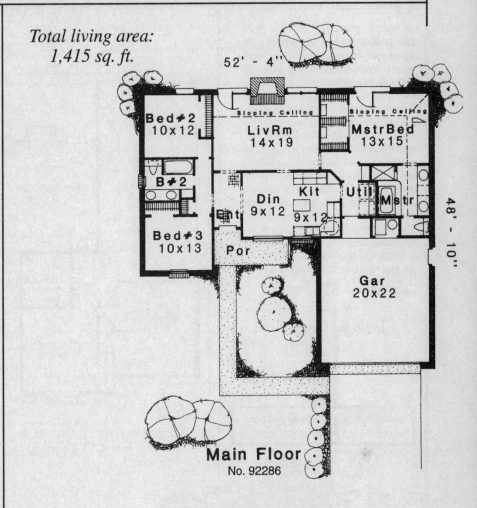

52' - 4"

48' - 10"

Bed #2 10x12
LivRm 14x19
Sloping Ceiling
MstrBed 13x15
Sloping Ceiling
B #2
Din 9x12
Kit 9x12
Util
Mstr
Ent
Bed #3 10x13
Por
Gar 20x22

Main Floor
No. 92286

Refer to **Pricing Schedule A** on the order form for pricing information

COZY TRADITIONAL

This homey Traditional plan has all the amenities of a larger plan in a compact layout. The ten foot ceilings give this home an expansive feel. An angled eating bar separates the kitchen and the Great room while leaving these areas open to one another for family gatherings and entertaining. The master bedroom includes a huge walk-in closet and a superior master bath with a whirlpool tub and a separate shower. A large utility room and an oversize storage area are located near the secondary entrance to the home. Two additional bedrooms and a bath finish the plan. No materials list available for this plan.

Main level — 1,862 sq. ft.
Garage — 520 sq. ft.

Total living area:
1,862 sq. ft.

Refer to **Pricing Schedule C** on the order form for pricing information

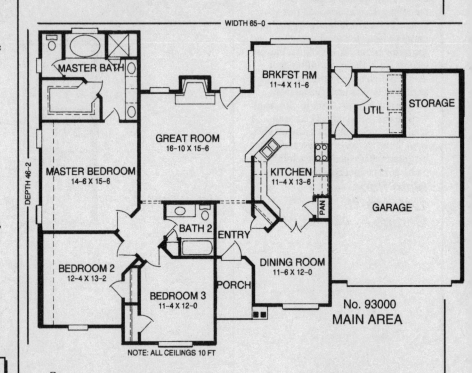

WIDTH 65-0

DEPTH 46-2

MASTER BATH

GREAT ROOM
16-10 X 15-6

MASTER BEDROOM
14-6 X 15-6

BRKFST RM
11-4 X 11-6

UTIL

STORAGE

KITCHEN
11-4 X 13-6

PAN

GARAGE

BATH 2

ENTRY

BEDROOM 2
12-4 X 13-2

BEDROOM 3
11-4 X 12-0

PORCH

DINING ROOM
11-6 X 12-0

No. 93000
MAIN AREA

NOTE: ALL CEILINGS 10 FT

An
EXCLUSIVE DESIGN
By Belk Home Designs

MAJESTIC PRESENCE

A varied roof line and detailing around the windows and corners of this home create quite an impression. That impression continues once inside. A grand staircase graces the center of the foyer. Columns accentuate the entrance to the living room, while a decorative ceiling and a fireplace further enhance the room. The elegant formal dining room also includes a decorative ceiling. A cooktop island kitchen efficiently serves both the dining room and the informal nook area. A huge family room provides a relaxing atmosphere. A den with built-in bookcases provides privacy. The second floor includes the master suite and three additional bedrooms.

First floor — 1,746 sq. ft.
Second floor — 1,396 sq. ft.

Total living area:
3,142 sq. ft.

Refer to **Pricing Schedule E** on the order form for pricing information

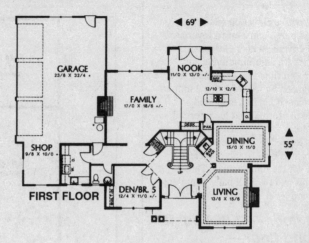

No. 91532

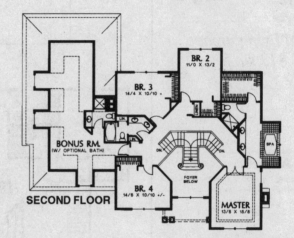

Design 94104

BAY WINDOWS HIGHLIGHT LIVING ROOM

This attractive elevation features a sheltered porch entry into a foyer area with a convenient coat closet and a staircase. An adjoining living and dining room flow into each other and are enhanced by the front bay window. The L-shaped kitchen is located between the formal and the informal dining areas. An expansive family room is topped by a cathedral ceiling and accented by a fireplace located directly off the dinette area. Three bedrooms and two full baths complete the second level. No materials list available.

First floor — 1,094 sq. ft.
Second floor — 719 sq. ft.

Total living area:
1,813 sq. ft.

FIRST FLOOR
No. 94104

FAM RM
19'8 x 13'4
cath cl'g

DIN
10' x 11'4

KIT
9'10 x 11'6

DIN RM
10'8 x 11'6

LIV RM
14'4 x 11'10
plus bay

GARAGE
19'8 x 21'8

Porch

36'

52'

BR3
10'10 x 10'4

MBR
12'2 x 14'

BR2
11'11 x 10'7

SECOND FLOOR

Refer to **Pricing Schedule C** on the order form for pricing information

LUXURIOUS ELEGANCE

This appealing facade and an impressive entrance through a double door entry leads into a two-story foyer. A curved staircase graces the foyer that is flanked by the formal living and dining rooms. The Great room, crowned in a cathedral ceiling, includes a massive fireplace and a built-in entertainment center and shelves. The dinette area flows easily from the spacious island kitchen. The master bedroom includes a vaulted ceiling and a lavish bath with a huge walk-in closet. Three additional bedrooms are located on the second floor, each with private access to a full bath and a walk-in closet. This plan is available with a basement or slab foundation only. Please specify when ordering. No materials list is available for this plan.

First floor — 2,190 sq. ft.
Second floor — 920 sq. ft.

Total living area: 3,110 sq. ft.

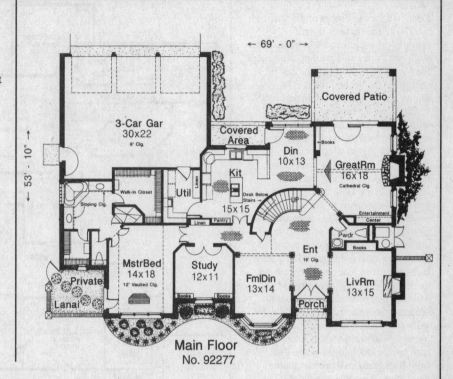

Main Floor
No. 92277

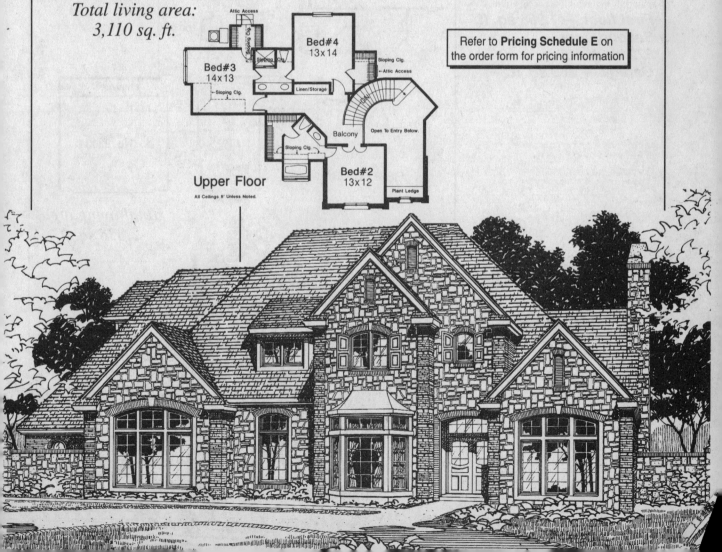

Upper Floor

All Ceilings 8' Unless Noted.

Refer to **Pricing Schedule E** on the order form for pricing information

Design 93034

FOR PIE SHAPED OR CORNER LOT

Designed for the corner or pie shaped lot, this home features mirror elevations on right and left that make it a winner from any direction. Entering the foyer, a lovely split stair moves upward to the second floor. The dining room opens the right and features an elegant entrance flanked with square columns. The kitchen with cooktop work island features a pantry and angled window sink. A vaulted ceiling gives the breakfast room a distinctive look and adds character to the kitchen wing. A private study opens to the left of the foyer and can be used as bedroom five if needed. The master suite is located at the rear of the home with access to an outdoor covered porch. The master bath provides a sumptuous retreat for the homeowner. Separate his-n-her vanities, a corner whirlpool tub and separate showers are standard. Two walk-in closets complete this luxury bath. Upstairs, three bedrooms and a bath are included in the plan. The third bath features a private double vanity area for convenience. No materials list available for this plan.

First floor — 1,966 sq. ft.
Second floor — 872 sq. ft.
Garage — 569 sq. ft.

Refer to **Pricing Schedule E** on the order form for pricing information

SECOND FLOOR

BEDROOM 3
12-6 X 12-6

BATH 3

BEDROOM 2
12-6 X 11-6

LIN

BALCONY

OPEN TO GREAT ROOM BELOW

BALCONY

OPEN TO FOYER BELOW

ATTIC

BEDROOM 4
11-4 X 13-6

WIDTH 79–10

MASTER BATH
9 FT CLG

HIS

MASTER BEDROOM
16-0 X 13-6
9 FT CLG

COVERED PORCH

HERS

STUDY/ BEDROOM
12-6 X 11-6
9 FT CLG

LIN

BATH 2

BOOKCASE

GREAT ROOM
17-0 X 18-6
2 STORY CLG

FP

PATIO

FOYER
2 STORY CLG

PAN

KITCHEN
12-0 X 13-0

FRZ

STORAGE

PORCH

DINING ROOM
11-4 X 13-0
9 FT CLG

9 FT CLG

UTIL
5-8 X 6-0

GARAGE
No. 93034

BRKFST RM
11-4 X 10-0
CATHEDRAL CLG

FIRST FLOOR

DEPTH 63–10

Total living area:
2,838 sq. ft.

Design 92632

GOOD TASTE AND FLEXIBILITY

Designed to provide the most efficient use of square footage, this home personifies good taste and flexibility. The foyer features an elegantly styled split staircase, providing depth and excitement to the entry. In the extra large kitchen, an abundance of counter space and cabinets are available, making cooking and clean-up simple and even enjoyable. A few steps away is the sunny breakfast area, which flows easily into the oversized Great room. A fireplace is the center of this favorite gathering place, while strategically placed windows and a separate entry door provide a favorable indoor/outdoor spatial relationship. A dining room with a box window extends the dining area for large crowds, or more formal entertaining. A loft is highlighted on the second floor, adding an element of drama. The master bedroom is fully equipped with a private bath, double vanity and a large walk-in closet. The additional bedrooms and a compartmented bath round out the second floor. No materials list available for this plan.

First floor — 934 sq. ft.
Second floor —
850 sq. ft.
Basement — 831 sq. ft.
Garage — 229 sq. ft.

Total living area:
1,784 sq. ft.

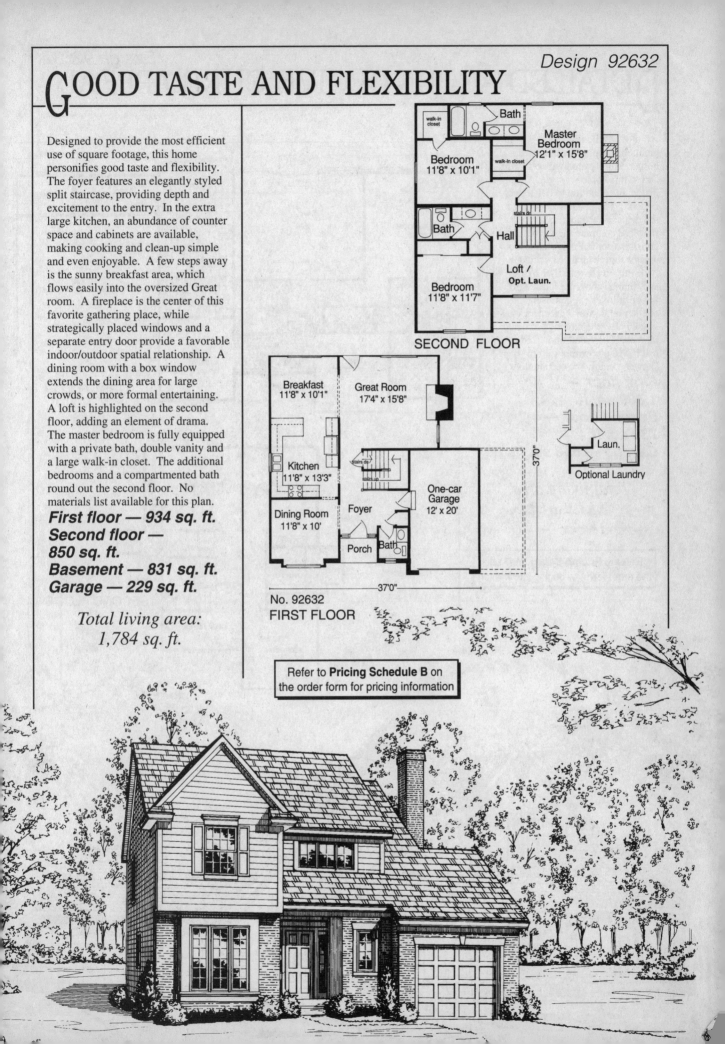

SECOND FLOOR

Bath

Master Bedroom 12'1" x 15'8"

walk-in closet

Bedroom 11'8" x 10'1"

walk-in closet

Bath

stairs dn.

Hall

Loft / Opt. Laun.

Bedroom 11'8" x 11'7"

37'0"

Breakfast 11'8" x 10'1"

Great Room 17'4" x 15'8"

Kitchen 11'8" x 13'3"

stairs dn.

stairs up

Dining Room 11'8" x 10'

Foyer

One-car Garage 12' x 20'

Porch

Bath

Laun.

Optional Laundry

37'0"

No. 92632
FIRST FLOOR

Refer to **Pricing Schedule B** on the order form for pricing information

Design 92537

DETAILED ACCENTS GIVE CURB APPEAL

All those "little touches" result in great curb appeal for this terrific home. Multi-paned windows also add to this home's appeal. Once inside, the attention to detail does not end. The decorative ceiling in the den and the large focal point fireplace continue the theme. A lavish master bath highlights the master suite which also includes two walk-in closets. The living and dining rooms are located off the open foyer. A peninsula counter adds work space and a snack bar to the already efficient kitchen. Three bedrooms and two full baths, one with a step-in shower, occupy the second floor.

**First floor —
1,809 sq. ft.
Second floor —
730 sq. ft.
Garage — 553 sq. ft.**

*Total living area:
2,539 sq. ft.*

Refer to **Pricing Schedule D** on the order form for pricing information

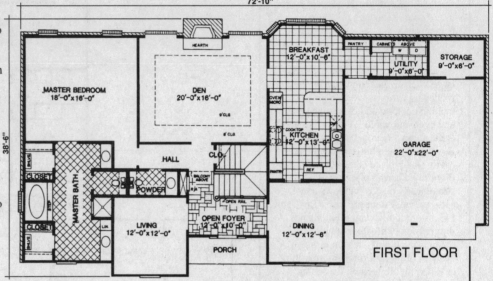

FIRST FLOOR

SECOND FLOOR

COLONIAL ADAPTATION

Working on a tight budget? This Colonial adaptation provides a functional design that allows for expansion in the future. Notice the cozy fireplace in the living room and the roomy L-shaped kitchen with a breakfast nook space. The upstairs holds two bedrooms, a full bath and a master bedroom with an attached bath. A large storage area over the garage can become a bedroom or an office/study in the future.

First floor — 624 sq. ft.
Second floor — 624 sq. ft.

Total living area: 1,248 sq. ft.

Refer to **Pricing Schedule A** on the order form for pricing information

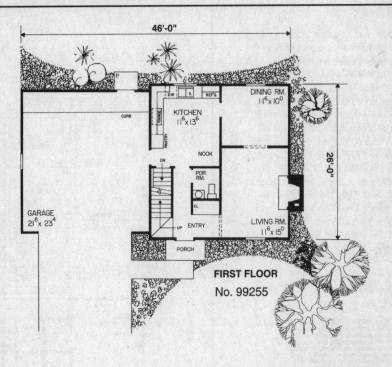

46'-0"

26'-0"

GARAGE
21'8" x 23'4"

CURB

RANGE

DW S. REF'G.

KITCHEN
11'6" x 13'6"

DINING RM.
11'6" x 10'0"

PANTRY

NOOK

DN

PDR. RM.

CL.

UP ENTRY

LIVING RM.
11'6" x 15'0"

PORCH

FIRST FLOOR
No. 99255

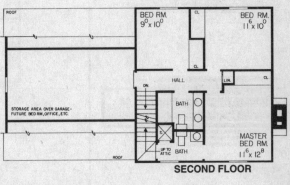

ROOF

BED RM.
9'0" x 10'0"

CL.

CL.

BED RM.
11'6" x 10'0"

CL.

HALL

DN

LIN.

CL.

BATH

STORAGE AREA OVER GARAGE -
FUTURE BED RM., OFFICE, ETC.

UP TO ATTIC

BATH

MASTER
BED RM.
11'6" x 12'8"

ROOF

SECOND FLOOR

EARLY AMERICAN COLONIAL

A sheltered entrance leads to a foyer area that includes a coat closet. A large bow window and terrific fireplace with a raised hearth, highlight the sunken living room. The elegant dining room is enhanced by a bay window with a window seat and charming French doors to the rear yard. An efficient U-shaped kitchen is large enough for an informal eating area. Isolated from the living area, the sleeping area consists of three large bedrooms. The master bedroom includes a French door to the rear porch. Two additional bedrooms share the full bath in the hallway.

Main floor — 1,598 sq. ft.

Total living area:
1,598 sq. ft.

Refer to **Pricing Schedule B** on the order form for pricing information

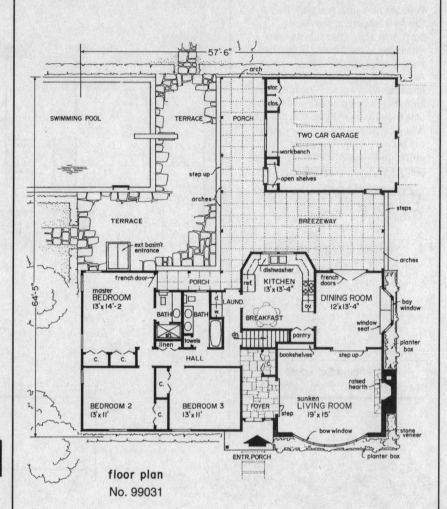

floor plan
No. 99031

FOUR-BEDROOM WITH ONE FLOOR

A distinguished brick exterior gives this home attractive curl appeal. The entry hall leads to a gallery area and into the expansive living room with a focal point fireplace. The well-appointed kitchen is separated from the breakfast room by a peninsula island with a double sink. Each of the four bedrooms have ample closet space. The master suite includes a vaulted ceiling and a large private bath with a huge walk-in closet. No materials list is available for this plan.

Main floor — 2,675 sq. ft.
Garage — 638 sq. ft.

Total living area:
2,675 sq. ft.

Refer to **Pricing Schedule E** on the order form for pricing information

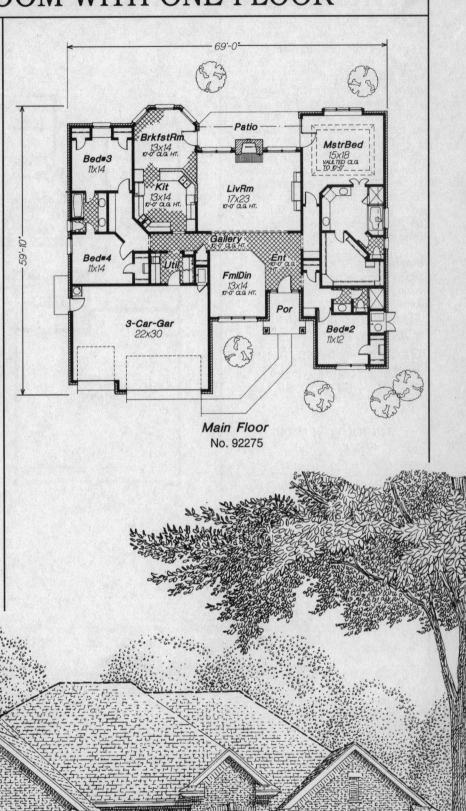

Main Floor
No. 92275

Design 99710

STATELY AND SPACIOUS CONTEMPORARY

Lofty brick columns flank the high, gabled entryway of this home. The brick facade and cultured stone sill on the front window positively exudes solidity and permanence. The vaulted entry area is warm, and filled with natural light. The kitchen features an angled extension on the eating bar that creates more seating while giving a unique shape to the basically U-shaped kitchen. There is also ample storage in the cupboards and pantry. The master suite, located on the opposite side of the family living area, is situated away from the other two bedrooms for added privacy. Each sleeping area has its own bathroom. The Great room features a corner fireplace in the living room section and sliding glass doors to a covered deck.

**Main living area —
1,459 sq. ft.
Garage — 567 sq. ft.
Width — 56'-0"
Depth — 54'-0"**

*Total living area:
1,459 sq. ft.*

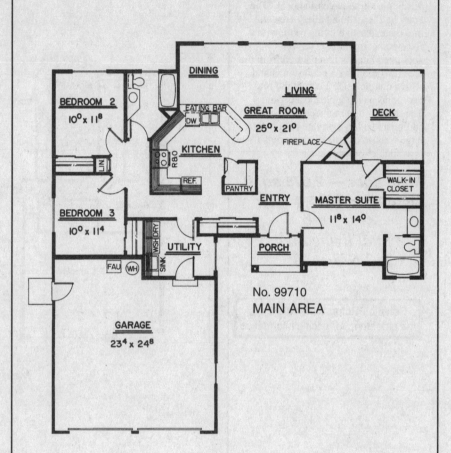

No. 99710
MAIN AREA

Refer to **Pricing Schedule A** on the order form for pricing information

WITH ATTENTION TO DETAIL

It's the little details that make a home so much more. A window is a window, yet with the detailing around the windows of this home it becomes a multi-paned looking glass to the outside world. A door is just an entry way, yet with the curved glass crown above and detailing around the door, it becomes a grand entrance. Paying attention to details continues inside the home. Decorative and vaulted ceilings "dress-up" many of the rooms. These little touches add to the elegance and spaciousness. There is a formal living room and dining room for entertaining. Privacy is the theme of the master suite. The master bath pampers the owner in luxury. An island kitchen is waiting for the gourmet of the family to personalize. Three second floor bedrooms will accommodate the rest of the family members. Two of the bedrooms have direct access to a full bath with a double vanity. The third bedroom has access to a full hall bath. No materials list available for this plan.

First floor — 2,115 sq. ft.
Second floor — 914 sq. ft.
Basement — 2,155 sq. ft.
Garage — 448 sq. ft.

Refer to **Pricing Schedule E** on the order form for pricing information

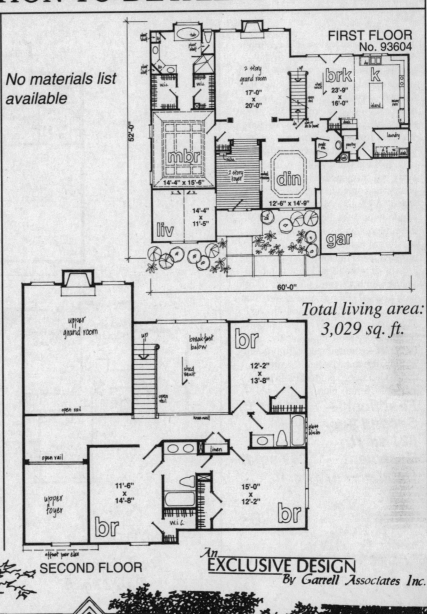

No materials list available

FIRST FLOOR
No. 93604

Total living area:
3,029 sq. ft.

SECOND FLOOR

An
EXCLUSIVE DESIGN
By Garrell Associates Inc.

QUALITY AND DIVERSITY

The warmth and texture of the exterior of this home is an indication of the quality and diversity found inside. The sloped ceiling above the foyer ties into the two-story ceiling over the Great room offering an impressive view from the stairway and second floor balcony. A corner fireplace and triple glass French doors set the mood for the luxury of the Great room. A few steps away is a spacious kitchen with a pantry, and an abundance of counter space. A breakfast bay surrounded by windows enables the family to enjoy the outdoors without leaving the comfort of home. A formal dining room expands the dining area for large crowds or more formal entertaining. The master bedroom suite earns its title with a raised ceiling, large closet, dual vanities, a whirlpool tub and shower. The powder room and convenient first floor laundry room complete the main level. Three additional bedrooms and a compartmented bath are located on the second floor. No materials list available for this plan.

First floor — 1,401 sq. ft.
Second floor — 621 sq. ft.
Basement — 1,269 sq. ft.
Garage — 478 sq. ft.

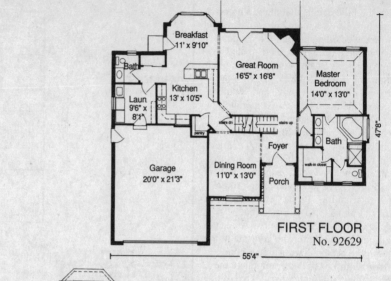

FIRST FLOOR
No. 92629

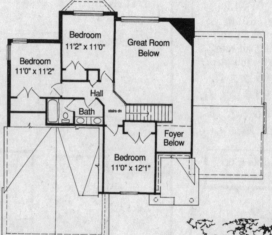

SECOND FLOOR

Total living area:
2,022 sq. ft.

Refer to **Pricing Schedule C** on the order form for pricing information

RESIDENCE FOR THE EXECUTIVE FAMILY

The main floor of this luxurious residence is zoned into three main living areas: formal, informal, and the master suite. The master suite is a bevy of pampering elements. With it's double walk-in closets, exercise area, sitting area and grand master bath, you couldn't ask for much else. The angular kitchen is a cook's dream — the large center island and planning desk are added bonuses. If your a book fanatic the grand library with a warming fireplace will be a relaxing retreat for rainy days. This home has everything you could possibly need and dream of.

First floor — 3,798 sq. ft.
Second floor — 1,244 sq. ft.
Basement — 3,798 sq. ft.
Garage — 3-car

Total living area: 5,042 sq. ft.

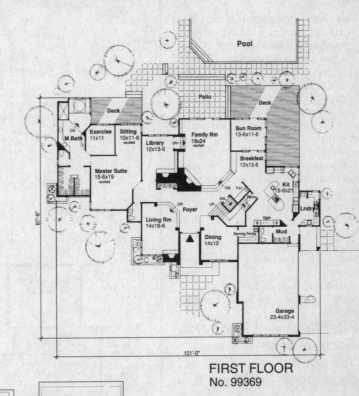

FIRST FLOOR
No. 99369

Refer to **Pricing Schedule F** on the order form for pricing information

SECOND FLOOR

SMART LOOKING LEISURE HOUSE

This smart looking leisure house can nicely fit a ski area, a beach front or a wooded area. One of its many features is a gear and equipment room. The spacious and imposing living and dining rooms look even larger due to the openness of the foyer and kitchen. The large expanse of windows offers a commanding view from any orientation. A partial wrap-around deck allows for outdoor living. In the rear are two bedrooms and two baths. The master bedroom has its private bath equipped with a separate stall shower and double basins. Upstairs, the broad balcony overlooking the living/dining rooms can serve many purposes. In the rear, the third bedroom can also serve as a studio. The exterior is a combination of natural vertical wood siding, interesting glazing and stone chimney which features a rustic stone fireplace on the interior.

First floor — 1,292 sq. ft.
Second floor — 368 sq. ft.
Basement — 694 sq. ft.

FIRST FLOOR
No. 99645

Total living area:
1,660 sq. ft.

Refer to **Pricing Schedule B** on the order form for pricing information

LOFT FLOOR

SMALL AND TASTEFUL

This attractive elevation includes a covered entrance into a small tiled entry area that leads to either the formal dining room or the bedroom area. The living room adjoins the dining room which has direct access to the kitchen. This layout offers smooth transitions in entertaining. The efficient U-shape kitchen is equipped with a peninsula counter/eating bar and a built-in desk. There is ample work and storage space and the peninsula counter is all that separates the kitchen from the family room. A fireplace and direct access to the rear deck are highlighted in the spacious family room. A double vanity, private full bath and a wall length closet are the amenities offered in the master suite. The two additional bedrooms share a full hall bath. No materials list available.

Main floor — 1,581 sq. ft.
Garage — 473 sq. ft.

Total living area:
1,581 sq. ft.

Refer to **Pricing Schedule B** on the order form for pricing information

MAIN FLOOR
No. 94033

Deck

Mbr.
13'8"x10'8"

Din.
10'x15'

Kit.

Fam. rm
17'x15'

Br.
10'8"x9'6"

Liv. rm.
15'6"x13'8"

Gar.
19'4"x20'4"

Br.
14'x9'4"

COV. PORCH

R   DESK   W D   F   WH   LIN

Width — 55'-0"
Depth — 42'-0"

An EXCLUSIVE DESIGN By
CRANE DESIGN inc.

A MODIFIED "A" FRAME

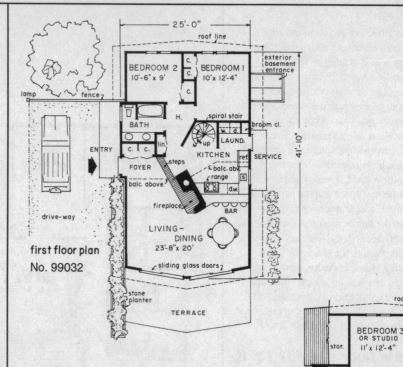

Design 99032

The entry foyer steps down into the living/dining area, which is highlighted by a fireplace and two sliding glass doors to the terrace. The kitchen is small, yet efficient. Two first floor bedrooms share a full bath in the hall. A spiral staircase leads to either a studio or a third bedroom. A balcony overlooks the living/dining area.

First floor — 994 sq. ft.
Second floor — 366 sq. ft.

Total living area: 1,360 sq. ft.

Refer to **Pricing Schedule A** on the order form for pricing information

**first floor plan
No. 99032**

25'-0"
roof line
BEDROOM 2
10'-6" x 9'
BEDROOM 1
10' x 12'-4"
exterior basement entrance
c.
c.
c.
BATH
H.
spiral stair
w. d.
broom cl.
LAUND.
41'-10"
lin.
KITCHEN
ref
SERVICE
c.   c.
up
ENTRY
balc. abv.
FOYER
steps
range
s
balc. above
d.w.
fireplace
BAR
LIVING-DINING
23'-8" x 20'
lamp
fence
drive-way
sliding glass doors
stone planter
TERRACE

second floor plan

roof line
BEDROOM 3 OR STUDIO
11' x 12'-4"
stor.
BATH
spiral stair
c.
stor.
lin.
down
BALCONY
wood railing
cross beams
HIGH LIVING RM. | CEILING BELOW

TWO-STORY CONTEMPORARY

A two-story foyer with an adjacent coat closet leads to the living room which has a dramatical high ceiling and a unique front facing window. A central feature of the living room is the recessed fireplace flanked by two windows. The formal dining space leads to a rear terrace through sliding glass doors. An efficient "U" shaped kitchen serves both the formal and informal dining areas conveniently. Three bedrooms are located upstairs. The master suite has a large walk-in closet and another linear one. The master bath includes a whirlpool tub, a separate shower and a compartmentalized toilet. The other two bedrooms share a full bath.

First floor — 810 sq. ft.
Second floor —
781 sq. ft.
Garage — 513 sq. ft.
Basement — 746 sq. ft.

Total living area:
1,591 sq. ft.

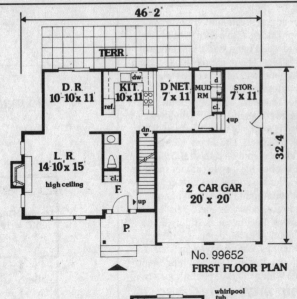

No. 99652
FIRST FLOOR PLAN

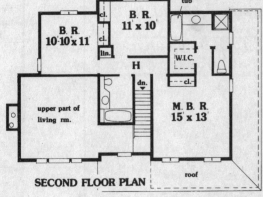

SECOND FLOOR PLAN

Refer to **Pricing Schedule B** on the order form for pricing information

PERFECT FIRST HOME

A front porch with turned posts and railing, along with a corner-box window add interest to the exterior of this home. The living room has sliding glass doors and an 11' ceiling that slopes toward the fireplace. The secluded master bedroom features a 9' sloped ceiling and corner windows. There is a private master bath with a walk-in closet. The dining area and the kitchen enjoy a cathedral ceiling. The kitchen has ample cabinet space and a double corner sink that enjoys the natural light of the corner-box window. Bedrooms 2 and 3 have closets with convenient sliding doors. Economical to build, this is a perfect first home. With a private master bedroom, it is also an ideal retirement home with plenty of room for guests.

Main area — 1,078 sq. ft.
Garage — 431 sq. ft.

Total living area:
1,078 sq. ft.

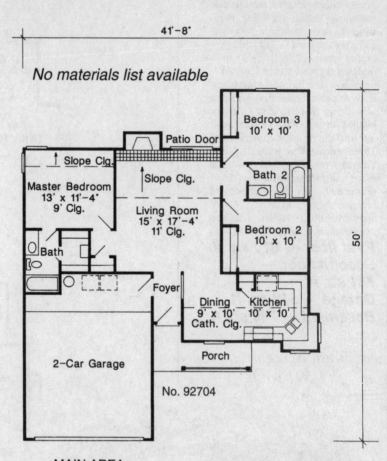

No materials list available

41'-8"

50'

Bedroom 3
10' x 10'

Patio Door

Slope Clg.

Slope Clg.

Master Bedroom
13' x 11'-4"
9' Clg.

Bath 2

Living Room
15' x 17'-4"
11' Clg.

Bedroom 2
10' x 10'

Bath

Foyer

Dining
9' x 10'
Cath. Clg.

Kitchen
10' x 10'

Porch

2-Car Garage

No. 92704

MAIN AREA

Refer to **Pricing Schedule A** on the order form for pricing information

COMPACT WITH A SPACIOUS FEEL

This compact plan features a roomy breakfast room and kitchen combination. The use of 10' ceilings in the Great room gives the home a spacious feel. Twin arches off the entry add architectural interest to this efficient layout. A bay window in the master bedroom provides a cozy sitting area for the owner. The master bath is highlighted by a double vanity and huge walk-in closet. Bedrooms two and three are located on one side the house away from the master bedroom to provide more privacy for the owner. No materials list available for this plan.

Main area — 1,087 sq. ft.
Porch — 20 sq. ft.

Total living area:
1,087 sq. ft.

Refer to **Pricing Schedule A** on the order form for pricing information

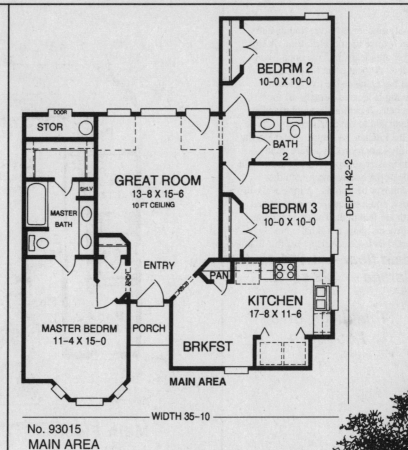

STOR

DOOR

BEDRM 2
10-0 X 10-0

BATH
2

GREAT ROOM
13-8 X 15-6
10 FT CEILING

SHLV

MASTER
BATH

BEDRM 3
10-0 X 10-0

ENTRY

PAN

KITCHEN
17-8 X 11-6

MASTER BEDRM
11-4 X 15-0

PORCH

BRKFST

MAIN AREA

DEPTH 42-2

WIDTH 35-10

No. 93015
MAIN AREA

An
EXCLUSIVE DESIGN
By Belk Home Designs

STYLE AND CONVENIENCE

Roof ornamented eaves and an entry porch spice up this elevation. A small foyer area leads into the open living space. A focal point fireplace and a wet bar enhance the living room. Dining is located directly off the kitchen. A peninsula counter and an island add to the ample counter space in the kitchen. A built-in pantry in the utility/laundry room is very handy. The master suite is located on the right side of the home, away from the secondary bedrooms. A long walk-in closet and a private, compartmented bath are featured. The two secondary bedrooms share a full hall. No materials list is available for this plan.

Main floor — 1,664 sq. ft.
Garage — 399 sq. ft.

Total living area:
1,664 sq. ft.

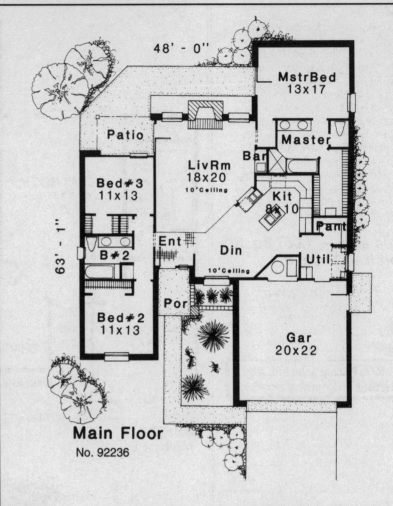

Main Floor
No. 92236

Refer to **Pricing Schedule B** on the order form for pricing information

EXTRA LARGE FAMILY ROOM

Attractive bay windows add to the curb appeal of this home. A split entry foyer gives rise to a lovely formal living room highlighted by a bay window and a fireplace. The dining room flows from the living room and directly accesses the kitchen. A rear deck is accessed from the dining room adding living space in the warmer weather. The bedrooms reside in there own private wing. The master suite includes a walk-in closet and a three quarter private bath. The additional bedrooms share the full hall bath. On the lower level, the spacious family room unfolds. The bay window offers natural illumination while a fireplace give warmth and atmosphere. A terrific and relaxing family living area. This plan is available with a slab foundation only. No materials list is available for this plan.

Main floor — 1,196 sq. ft.
Lower level —
1,682 sq. ft.
Garage — 715 sq. ft.

Total living area:
1,682 sq. ft.

Refer to **Pricing Schedule B** on the order form for pricing information

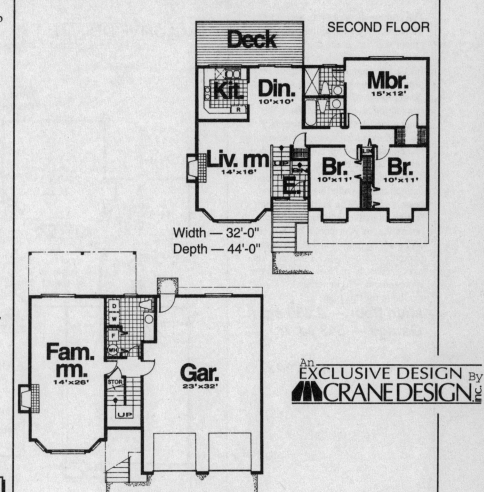

SECOND FLOOR

Deck

KiL

Din. 10'x10'

Mbr. 15'x12'

Liv. rm 14'x16'

Br. 10'x11'

Br. 10'x11'

Width — 32'-0"
Depth — 44'-0"

Fam. rm. 14'x26'

Gar. 23'x32'

STOR

UP

FIRST FLOOR

No. 94035

An EXCLUSIVE DESIGN By
CRANE DESIGN inc.

WELCOMING GRACEFUL ARCHES

The combination of brick and siding finishes, and a welcoming pair of graceful arches at the entry create this all-time favorite curb elevation. Inside, the angled foyer design provides views to the Great room and dining room. Columns with connecting arches add drama at the front door. A see-through fireplace between the Great room and the dining room is an elegant detail. The kitchen features a large cooktop work island and eating bar. Loads of cabinet and counter space make this layout a cook's dream. The master bedroom features a bath complete with all the amenities. A whirlpool tub, shower and double vanity with knee space make this a true owner's retreat. An oversized walk-in closet complete the arrangement. No materials list available for this plan.

Main floor — 2,250 sq. ft.
Garage — 543 sq. ft.

Total living area:
2,250 sq. ft.

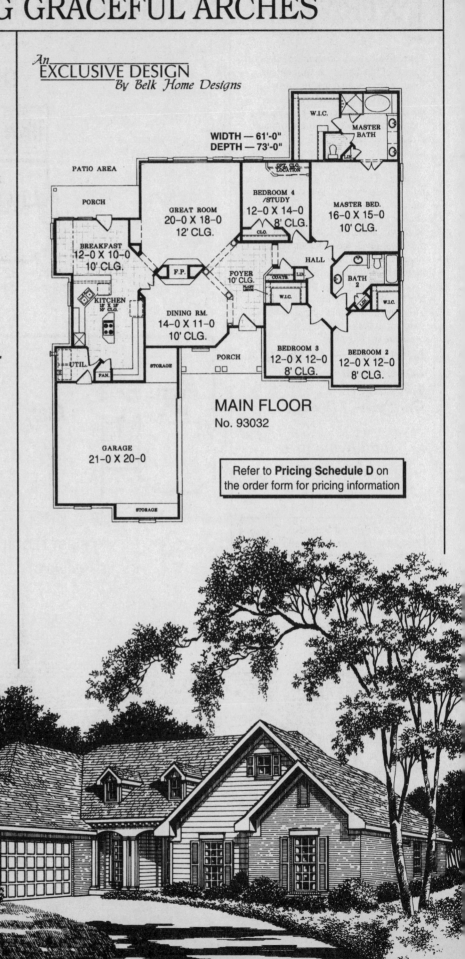

An
EXCLUSIVE DESIGN
By Belk Home Designs

WIDTH — 61'-0"
DEPTH — 73'-0"

MAIN FLOOR
No. 93032

Refer to **Pricing Schedule D** on the order form for pricing information

PRIVATE MASTER SUITE

A welcoming porch shelters the entrance of this home. The spacious Great room is enhanced by vaulted ceilings, a large fireplace, and built-in shelves and cabinets. The well-equipped kitchen has a double sink with a window over it, adding natural light and a view of the rear yard. The master bedroom has a decorative ceiling and a private master bath with a walk-in closet. Its location gives this room a secluded feeling. The laundry area is conveniently located in the hall outside of the master bedroom. Two additional bedrooms are located at the other end of the house and share a full bath.

**Main living area —
1,293 sq. ft.
Garage — 433 sq. ft.
Porch — 76 sq. ft.**

*Total living area:
1,293 sq. ft.*

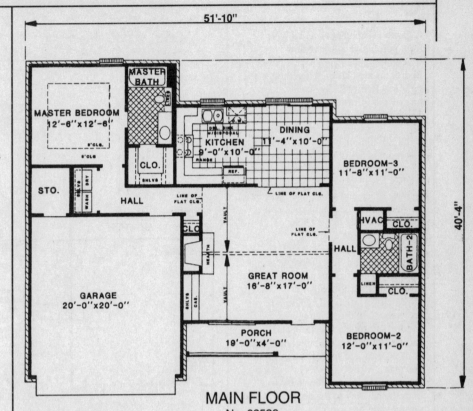

MAIN FLOOR
No. 92523

Refer to **Pricing Schedule A** on the order form for pricing information

Design 98742

UNIQUE GAZEBO SHAPED NOOK

A gazebo shaped nook and a wide front porch give a festive and welcoming appearance to this home. Bedrooms are clustered together, to the right and family living spaces, both formal and informal, are to the left. The nook, with its eight sided vaulted ceiling, is equally striking inside. Naturally illuminated by bay windows, this room is filled with light. Potted plants bloom in this sunny spot. The kitchen has plenty of cupboard and counter space and a sink that faces into the nook. A large pantry adds still more storage capacity. Other amenities include a built-in dishwasher, range and oven. The dining room and living room flow together. These rooms could be furnished either formally or informally, as dictated by family preference. In the living room, windows flank the fireplace, and sliding glass doors open onto the patio or deck. Storage space is plentiful in this plan. A coat closet is just inside the entry and a long storage closet lines the hallway to the bedrooms. The master suite has a large walk-in closet and a wide linen closet. The secondary bedrooms are equal in size and share a dual compartment bathroom with a slender window over the mirror. No materials list available for this plan.

Main floor — 1,664 sq. ft.

Total living area: 1,664 sq. ft.

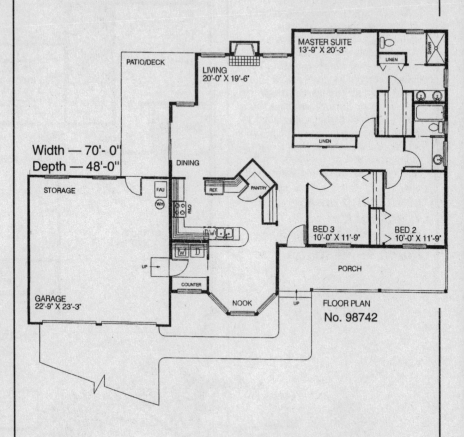

Width — 70'- 0"
Depth — 48'-0"

FLOOR PLAN
No. 98742

Refer to **Pricing Schedule B** on the order form for pricing information

BRICK STABILITY

This home offers one floor convenience. The large den has a stepped ceiling and a fabulous fireplace. Shelves and cabinets have been built-in to the side of the fireplace, resulting in even more convenience. The formal dining room and the informal breakfast bay sandwich the kitchen. The efficient kitchen includes a cooktop island, double ovens, built-in pantry and more than ample cabinet and counter space. The master bedroom includes a master bath and a large walk-in closet. Two additional bedrooms share a full hall bath. There is added storage behind the garage.

**Main area —
1,869 sq. ft.
Garage and storage —
561 sq. ft.**

*Total living area:
1,869 sq. ft.*

Refer to **Pricing Schedule C** on the order form for pricing information

74'-10"

40'-4"

CLO.

MASTER BEDROOM
13'-0"x16'-8"

10' CLG.

9' CLG.

MASTER BATH

BATH#2

LINEN

CLO.

CLO.

HALL

BEDROOM#2
13'-0"x11'-6"

CLO.

BEDROOM#3
13'-0"x11'-6"

HEARTH

DEN
16'-2"x20'-0"

11' CLG.

9' CLG.

FOYER
6'-0"x8'-0"

PORCH

BREAKFAST
13'-0"x10'-0"

COOKTOP

DBL.
OVENS

KITCHEN
13'-0"x12'-0"

REF.

PAN.

DINING
13'-0"x12'-0"

W   D

UTILITY
7'-0"x7'-0"

STORAGE
11'-0"x7'-0"

GARAGE
22'-0"x22'-0"

MAIN AREA
No. 92536

COMPACT THREE BEDROOM

Sloping and cathedral ceilings and style to this compact three bedroom home. The spacious living room is the heart of the home. A fireplace in the middle of the rear wall gives warmth and atmosphere to the room. An elegant dining room flows from the living room and into the kitchen. Conveniently the kitchen accesses the garage for easy grocery unloading. A sloped ceiling tops the master suite which includes a walk-in closet and a private double vanity bath. A second full bath is located between the two secondary bedrooms. This home can be built on a slab foundation only. No materials list is available for this plan.

First floor — 1,398 sq. ft.
Garage — 390 sq. ft.

Total living area:
1,398 sq. ft.

Refer to **Pricing Schedule A** on the order form for pricing information

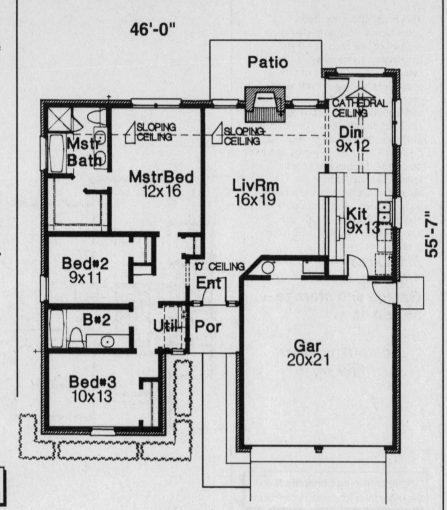

Main Floor
No. 92270

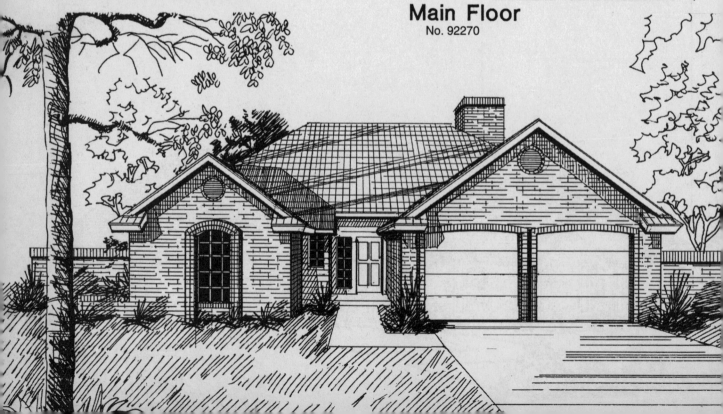

AMENITY PACKED AFFORDABILITY

Don't let this brick beauty's square footage of only 1,484 square feet fool you. The amenities found in larger homes can be found here. Take the den for an example. Look at the decorative ceiling and the fireplace, not to mention that feeling of spaciousness. The master bedroom, also with decorative ceiling, is spacious and has ample storage space between two closets. The private master bath will spoil you. The efficient kitchen has equal access to the sunny breakfast area or the formal dining area. Add two additional bedrooms, another full bath, utility room, more storage space, garage and patio and you can see this is affordability without scrimping.

**Main living area —
1,484 sq. ft.
Garage & Storage —
544 sq. ft.
Porch — 110 sq. ft.**

*Total living area:
1,484 sq. ft.*

Refer to **Pricing Schedule A** on the order form for pricing information

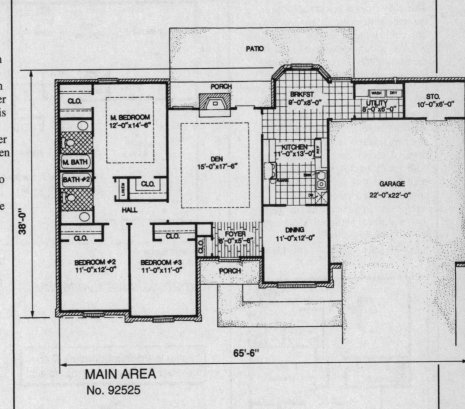

MAIN AREA
No. 92525

COUNTRY-STYLED DETAILING

This cozy front porch shelters the entrance with a country style welcome. The circle window and the double front window add illumination and detail to the front of the home. Directly from the foyer, to the right, are the formal living room and adjoining dining room. The informal areas are laid out in an open format, giving the rear of the home a spacious, airy feeling. The sleeping quarters are on the second floor. A roomy master suite equipped with a walk-in closet, double vanity, spa tub, separate shower and a compartmented toilet; will be a welcomed retreat at the end of the day. Two additional bedrooms share use of the full bath in the hallway. No materials list available for this plan.

FIRST FLOOR
No. 94100

No materials list available

FAM RM 16'2 x 17' cath cl'g
DIN 9' x 12'2
KIT 10' x 14'2
DIN RM 11'2 x 15'
Lav
Entry
Laun
LIV RM 12'4 x 15'3
GARAGE 21'8 x 21'8
FOYER
Covered Entry
40'
48'

MBR 16' x 13'8
MBATH
WI Closet
BATH
BR3 12'4 x 10'
Balcony
Foyer Below
BR2 12'4 x 12'6
36'
31'4

SECOND FLOOR

Refer to **Pricing Schedule C** on the order form for pricing information

First floor — 1,228 sq. ft.
Second floor — 952 sq. ft.
Garage — 479 sq. ft.
Basement — 1,228 sq. ft.

Total living area: 2,180 sq. ft.

PRIVATE MASTER BEDROOM

The classic covered porch welcomes you to this well-designed home. The vaulted family room opens to the dining room and onto the back patio. The efficient kitchen provides ample storage and counter space. The master suite has a large walk-in closet, and is conveniently located at the opposite end of the home from the other two bedrooms. The master bath, with a double vanity and a separate linen closet completes this suite. The two additional bedrooms are generously sized with large closets and a nice window detail. A second full bath and a laundry room complete this great layout. No materials list is available for this plan.

Main floor — 1,328 sq. ft.
Garage — 472 sq. ft.
Width — 49'-0"
Depth — 50'-0"

Total living area:
1,328 sq. ft.

Refer to **Pricing Schedule A** on the order form for pricing information

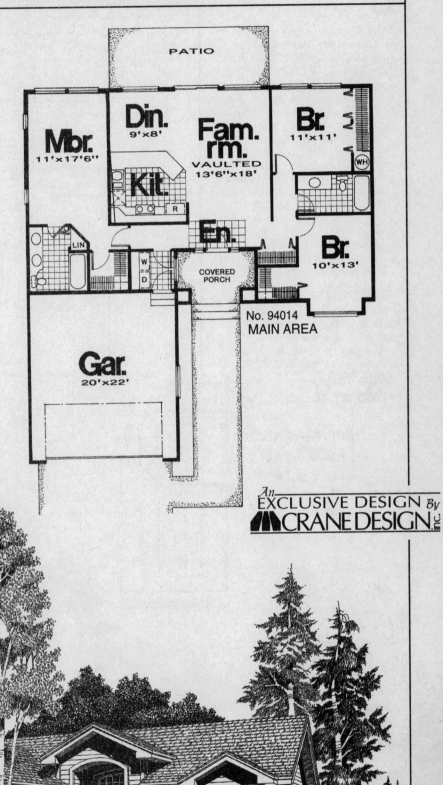

No. 94014
MAIN AREA

An
EXCLUSIVE DESIGN *By*
CRANE DESIGN inc.

Design 93031

ELEGANT ENTRY TO A GRAND ROOM

This traditional southern elevation features an entry flanked by large square columns and dominated by a gable finished with dentil molding and a graceful archway. Upon entering, an angled foyer opens the home to a large Great room with a fireplace. A formal dining room is defined with a series of columns that give the home an elegant, gracious feel. The master suite is entered through double doors and is privately located away from the other bedrooms. The master bath features all the luxuries with an angled whirlpool tub, separate shower and double vanities. An enormous walk-in closet completes the arrangement. The kitchen features a pantry and plenty of cabinet and counter space. A coffered ceiling treatment adds character to the breakfast room located on the rear of the home. Bedrooms two and three are arranged nearby with convenient access to the second bath. No materials list available for this plan.

**Main floor —
1,955 sq. ft.**

*Total living area:
1,955 sq. ft.*

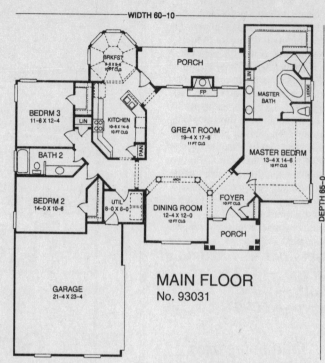

MAIN FLOOR
No. 93031

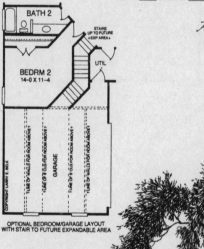

OPTIONAL BEDROOM/GARAGE LAYOUT
WITH STAIR TO FUTURE EXPANDABLE AREA

An
EXCLUSIVE DESIGN
By Belk Home Designs

Refer to **Pricing Schedule C** on the order form for pricing information

LUXURY AND CONVENIENCE

This charming design offers a great deal of luxurious features, unexpected in this size home. The raised entry with double doors and high glass opens up to the foyer area. Large sliding glass doors in the formal provide natural light and outdoor views. The dining room is separated from the foyer and living area by a half wall and column. The large kitchen, nook and leisure room complete the informal gathering areas. Large sliding glass doors giving the leisure room a feeling of outdoor openness. The secondary bedrooms are split from the master wing. The master bath has a large walk-in closet, walk-in shower, private water closet room and a whirlpool tub. The master suite opens to the lanai through sliding glass doors. The large lanai features plenty of room perfect for outdoor entertaining.

Main level — 1,784 sq. ft.
Garage — 491 sq. ft.

Total living area:
1,784 sq. ft.

Refer to **Pricing Schedule B** on the order form for pricing information

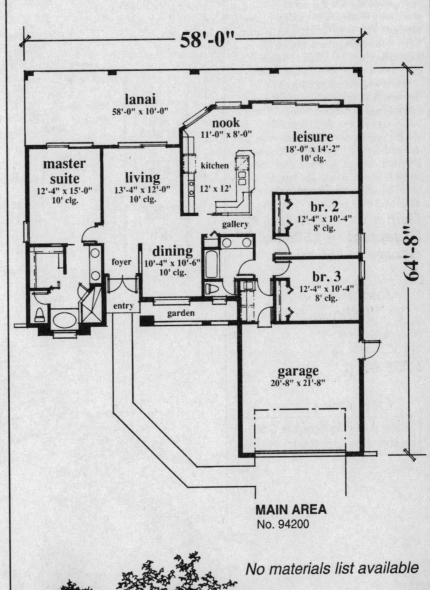

MAIN AREA
No. 94200

No materials list available

ONE LEVEL LIVING

An open plan gives this home spaciousness despite its modest square footage. The large Great room opens fully to the dining room, both with high ceilings of 11-1/2 feet. These rooms then open up to a stunning and efficient kitchen equipped with a dinette. A skylight enhances the natural light in the Great room. The luxurious master suite is privately located and separated from the other two bedrooms. It includes a dressing area, with a huge walk-in closet, and a sizeable linear closet. The laundry is conveniently located between the two additional bedrooms in a wide hallway.

Main area — 1,506 sq. ft.
Basement — 1,506 sq. ft.
Garage — 455 sq. ft.

Total living area:
1,506 sq. ft.

Refer to **Pricing Schedule B** on the order form for pricing information

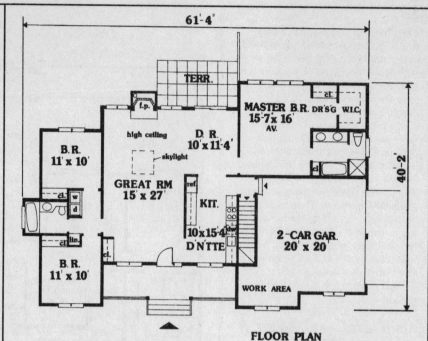

FLOOR PLAN
No. 99651

INVITING COVERED PORCH

The charming covered porch invites you into this home. The bayed living room welcomes you to the rest of the main floor. The large family room, with a fireplace and access to the back deck, opens to the breakfast nook and the open kitchen. A laundry room, with a toilet, is tucked out of the way at the end of the family room. The upper level has three ample bedrooms. A master bedroom, with a squared bay window and a large closet, includes a private bath. The second and third bedrooms share a full bath and a linen closet. You can't miss with this well laid out country style home! This plan is available with a crawlspace foundation only. No materials list is available for this plan.

First floor — 778 sq. ft.
Second floor — 699 sq. ft.

Total living area: 1,477 sq. ft.

Refer to **Pricing Schedule A** on the order form for pricing information

An EXCLUSIVE DESIGN By CRANE DESIGN inc.

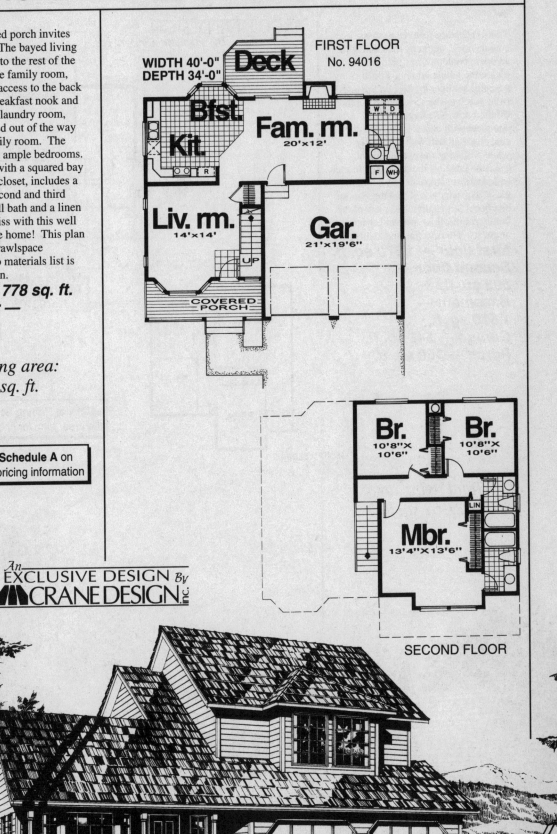

FIRST FLOOR
No. 94016

WIDTH 40'-0"
DEPTH 34'-0"

Deck

Bfst.

Kit.

Fam. rm.
20'x12'

Liv. rm.
14'x14'

Gar.
21'x19'6"

UP

COVERED PORCH

SECOND FLOOR

Br.
10'8"X 10'6"

Br.
10'8"X 10'6"

Mbr.
13'4"X13'6"

LIN

Design 93106

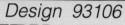

CONTEMPORARY CLASSIC COUNTRY

An
EXCLUSIVE DESIGN
By Ahmann Design Inc.

This 1-1/2 story features a classic country look, perfectly matched with an open, contemporary plan sure to please the whole family. You'll enjoy peaceful summer breezes on the large front porch or the screened-in porch off the back. The large kitchen, complete with center island, lets the chef stay in touch with the family while preparing the evening meal. Take the edge off the day in the master suite jacuzzi surrounded by a wall of glass. Upstairs you'll find three more bedrooms with a dramatic view of the family room below, perfect for family or guests. No materials list available.

First floor — 1,570 sq. ft.
Second floor —
592 sq. ft.
Basement —
1,570 sq. ft.
Garage — 548 sq. ft.
Porch — 160 sq. ft.

Total living area:
2,162 sq. ft.

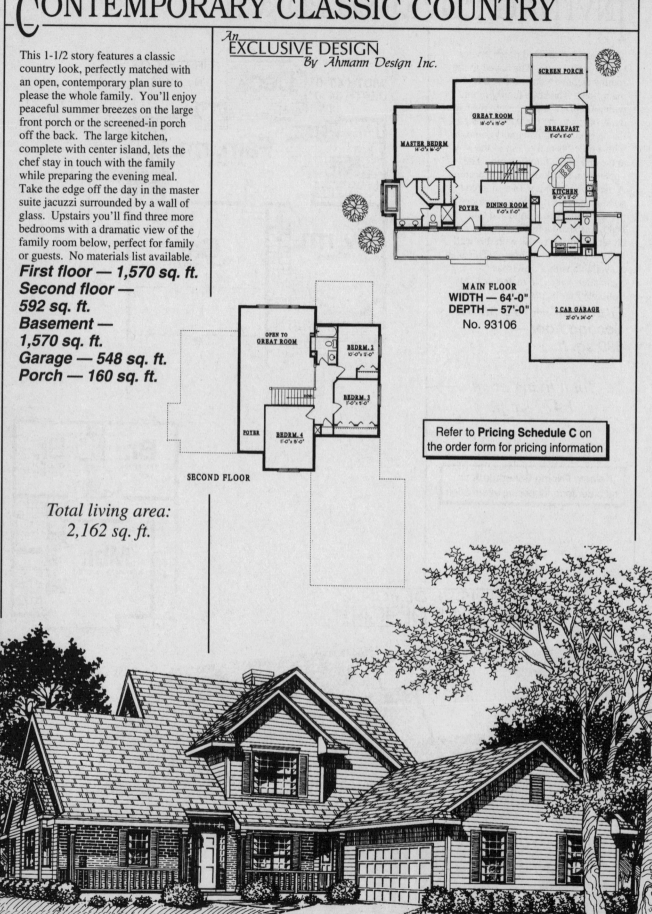

SECOND FLOOR

MAIN FLOOR
WIDTH — 64'-0"
DEPTH — 57'-0"
No. 93106

Refer to **Pricing Schedule C** on the order form for pricing information

Design 92634

ELEGANT ELEVATION

As you enter the foyer of this transitional two-story home, you will immediately be impressed with the high ceiling, the elegantly styled staircase and the arched opening to the formal living room. These features, combined with the open dining room, create a stunning effect. The kitchen is conveniently located in the center of the home and is visually open to the family room and the breakfast area, allowing light from the multiple rear windows to permeate through the combined areas. The dramatic balcony overlooks the foyer and the plant shelf, and leads to the master bedroom suite with a sloped ceiling, a walk-in closet and an ultra bath. Three bedrooms and a bath with a skylight and a double vanity complete this family size home. No materials list available.

**First floor — 1,309 sq. ft.
Second floor — 1,119 sq. ft.
Basement — 1,277 sq. ft.
Garage — 452 sq. ft.**

Total living area: 2,428 sq. ft.

Refer to **Pricing Schedule D** on the order form for pricing information

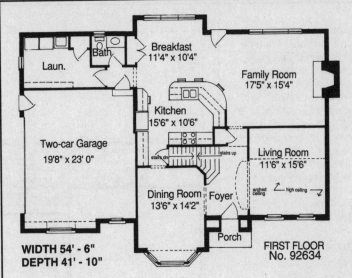

WIDTH 54' - 6"
DEPTH 41' - 10"

FIRST FLOOR
No. 92634

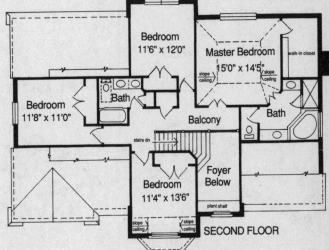

SECOND FLOOR

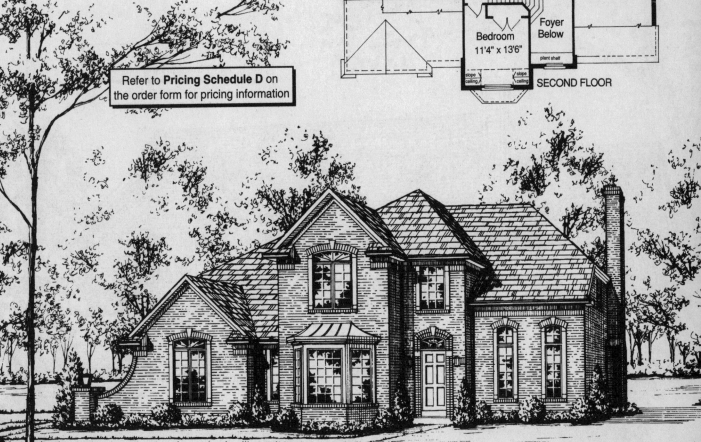

WARM AND INVITING

If this house could talk, it would be extending a warm welcome. From the porch to the cozy fire in the fireplace of the vaulted ceiling den, this house offers your guests comfort. It offers you the luxury of a master suite including private, compartmented master bath with walk-in closet. Two additional bedrooms are a nice size and have ample closet space. There is a full hall bath. The well-equipped kitchen has a built-in pantry and a double sink with a window above, providing a view of the rear yard. This house may be just what you're looking for.

**Main living area —
1,363 sq. ft.
Garage & storage —
434 sq. ft.
Porch — 85 sq. ft.**

*Total living area:
1,363 sq. ft.*

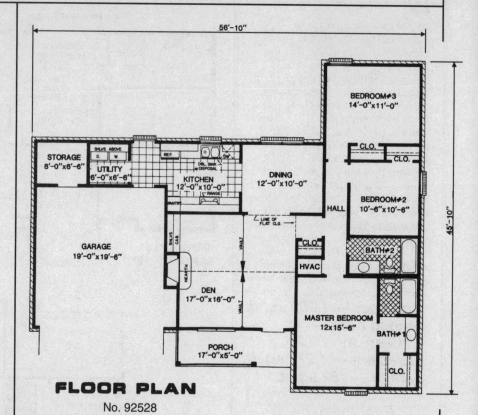

FLOOR PLAN
No. 92528

Refer to **Pricing Schedule A** on the order form for pricing information

EXPANDABLE HOME

An efficient kitchen adjoins the dining room that has sliders to the patio. The extra-large living room gives a wide-open feeling to all who enter. Two bedrooms and a full bath complete the first floor. On the second floor, you'll find the spacious master suite with a room-sized walk-in closet and master bath. The other bedroom and full bath can be used to accommodate visiting guests. This plan is available with a slab, crawl or basement foundation option. Please specify when ordering.

First floor — 957 sq. ft.
Second floor — 800 sq. ft.

Total living area: 1,757 sq. ft.

Refer to **Pricing Schedule B** on the order form for pricing information

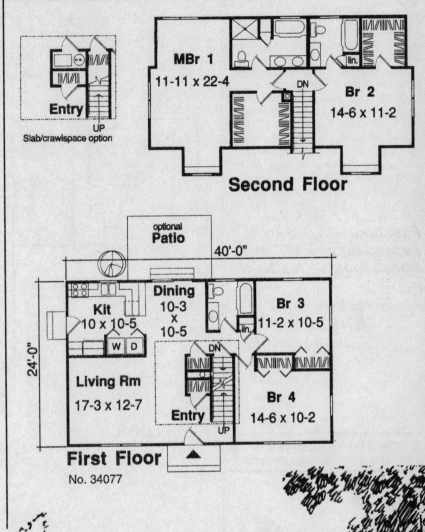

Entry
UP
Slab/crawlspace option

MBr 1
11-11 x 22-4

DN

Br 2
14-6 x 11-2

Second Floor

optional **Patio**

40'-0"

Dining
10-3 x 10-5

Kit
10 x 10-5

W D

Br 3
11-2 x 10-5

24'-0"

Living Rm
17-3 x 12-7

DN

lin.

Br 4
14-6 x 10-2

Entry
UP

First Floor
No. 34077

STREAMING WITH NATURAL LIGHT

Design 91514

This beautiful three bedroom home offers a two-story Great room with an attractive front window that almost wraps around the front of the home. An exquisite fireplace provides a warm focal point for the room. There is formal as well as informal eating space. The formal dining room flows easily from the large kitchen which provides an eating nook. A vaulted ceiling adds interest to the master suite which includes a spa tub, double vanity, separate shower and large wardrobe space. The two bedrooms upstairs have ample closet space and share a full hall bath. There is even a bonus option for a fourth bedroom.

First floor — 1,230 sq. ft.
Second floor — 477 sq. ft.
Bonus room — 195 sq. ft.

Total living area:
1,707 sq. ft.

Refer to **Pricing Schedule B** on the order form for pricing information

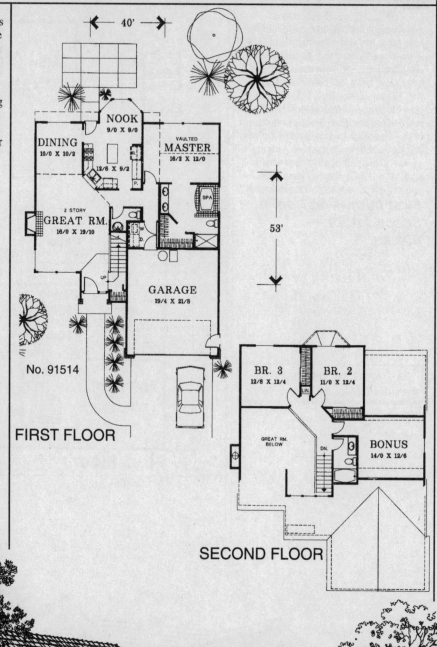

No. 91514

FIRST FLOOR

SECOND FLOOR

ENHANCED EXTERIOR

A gabled roofline and arched front windows enhance the exterior of this modest sized home. Vaulted ceilings and an open interior design create a spacious feeling that this home is larger than its 1,207 sq. ft. The efficient floor plan offers a master bedroom with a generous closet and bath, while providing privacy from the other two bedrooms that share the second bath. The home is completed by a dining room and kitchen with much storage, many counter tops and a built-in pantry. This compact design is ideal for first time home buyers or the empty-nester. No materials list is available for this plan.

**Main living area —
1,207 sq. ft.
Garage — 440 sq. ft.**

*Total living area:
1,207 sq. ft.*

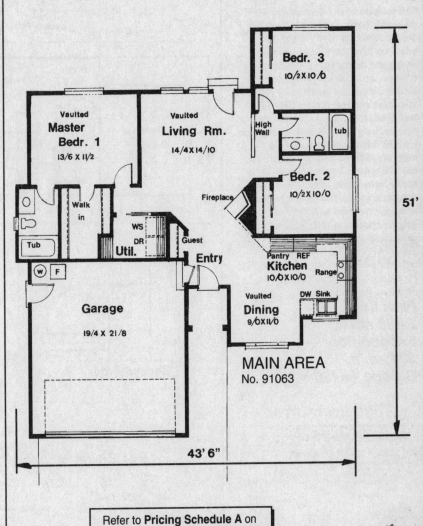

MAIN AREA
No. 91063

Refer to **Pricing Schedule A** on
the order form for pricing information

SEPARATE STUDIO WITH VIEW

The mixture of stone, glass and wood gives this home a special flavor. Vaulted ceilings to the left of the spacious foyer enclose the exciting living and dining rooms. Family living areas include a center, bar-style kitchen, breakfast area, family room and entertainment center. Special features include: easy access to the washer/dryer area, an optional deck or patio at the rear of the house, an impressive stone fireplace situated in the living room, a private studio above, open to downstairs areas and a two-car garage. The private bedroom wing features two large bedrooms and a master bedroom suite with dressing area, closets and a spacious bathroom. This plan is available with a slab, crawl or basement foundation option. Please specify when ordering. No materials list available.

**First floor —
2,238 sq. ft.
Second floor —
284 sq. ft.
Garage — 480 sq. ft.**

*Total living area:
2,522 sq. ft.*

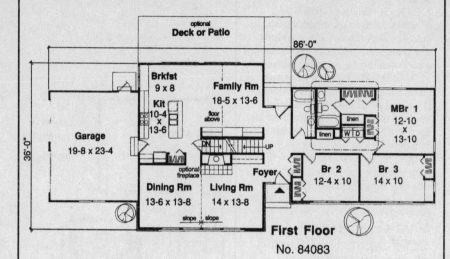

86'-0"

36'-0"

optional
Deck or Patio

Brkfst
9 x 8

Family Rm
18-5 x 13-6

Kit
10-4
x
13-6

floor
above

MBr 1
12-10
x
13-10

linen

linen W D

Garage
19-8 x 23-4

DN   UP

Br 2
12-4 x 10

Br 3
14 x 10

optional
fireplace

Foyer

Dining Rm
13-6 x 13-8

Living Rm
14 x 13-8

slope   slope

First Floor

No. 84083

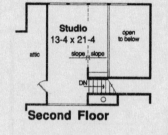

Studio
13-4 x 21-4

open
to below

attic   slope   slope

DN

Second Floor

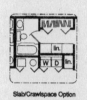

lin.

W D lin.

Slab/Crawlspace Option

Refer to **Pricing Schedule D** on
the order form for pricing information

AN AFFORDABLE RANCH

For the family just starting out, this plan is ideal. There is a living room that leads to a kitchen and adjacent dining area. There are two bedrooms and a larger master bedroom. Each bedroom has its own spacious closet, but shares a full bath. A garage is located on the left side of the home and there is also a patio. This plan is completed with a basement or slab/crawl space option.

***Main living area —
1,092 sq. ft.
Garage — 473 sq. ft.***

*Total living area:
1,092 sq. ft.*

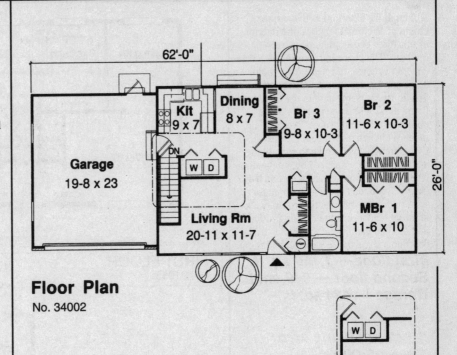

Floor Plan

No. 34002

Slab/crawlspace option

Refer to **Pricing Schedule A** on the order form for pricing information

UPDATED VICTORIAN

Design 91053

Although the exterior has the antique charm of Victorian features, the interior of this three bedroom home is truly modern. The charming features include a covered veranda, turreted sitting room, and a private deck for the master suite. Spaciousness is apparent in the family living areas with no separation of the nook and the family room. An efficient, modern kitchen serves both the casual living areas as well as the formal dining and living room enhanced by a patio door leading to the front veranda. A touch of elegance is added upstairs in the master suite with its turreted sitting room, walk-in closet, and a separate dressing room with double vanities. Two ample sized bedrooms share the second full bathroom.

First floor — 1,150 sq. ft.
Second floor — 949 sq. ft.
Garage — 484 sq. ft.

Total living area:
2,099 sq. ft.

Refer to **Pricing Schedule C** on the order form for pricing information

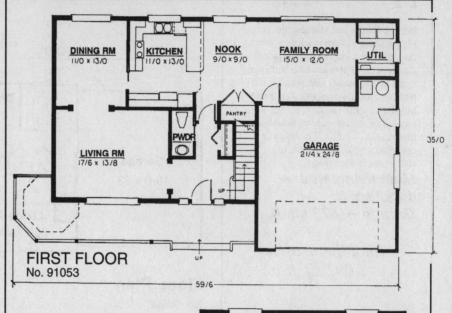

FIRST FLOOR
No. 91053

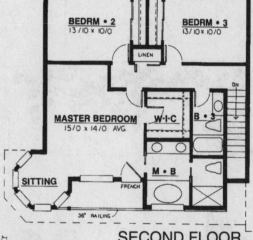

SECOND FLOOR

OPULENT LUXURY

A magnificent columned entry leads to a tiled entrance foyer graced by a staircase. The formal living and dining rooms are located in the traditional positions, to either side of the foyer. Built-in shelves and a stone hearth fireplace further enhance the living room. A spacious island kitchen and a breakfast area access the covered veranda which is accented by skylights. The family room flows from the breakfast room. A cathedral ceiling crowns this room while a fireplace adds warmth. Full oak paneling enhances the study. The lavish master suite includes decorative ceiling treatments, two walk-in closets, a huge bath and a sitting area. Three additional bedrooms, each with private access to a full bath and a walk-in closet, are located on the second floor. No materials list is available for this plan.

First floor — 2,804 sq. ft.
Second floor —
979 sq. ft.
Basement — 2,804 sq. ft.
Garage — 802 sq. ft.

Total living area:
3,783 sq. ft.

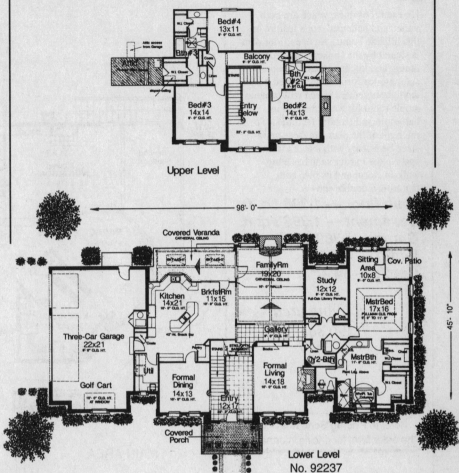

Upper Level

Lower Level
No. 92237

Refer to **Pricing Schedule F** on the order form for pricing information

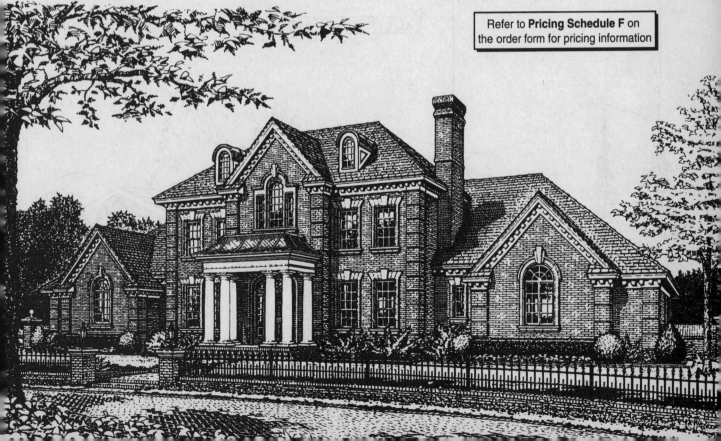

ATTRACTIVE ROOF LINES

Design 90983

Unusual roof lines, which are both varied and balanced, are a feature of this hillside home. An open floor plan is shared by the sunken living room, dining and kitchen areas. An open staircase leads to the unfinished daylight basement which will provide ample room for future bedrooms, bathroom and laundry facilities. To the right of the plan, are three good-sized bedrooms with lots of closet space....the master suite has a big walk-in closet and its own bath featuring a double shower.

Main floor — 1,396 sq. ft.
Basement — 1,396 sq. ft.
Garage — 389 sq. ft.
Width — 48'-0"
Depth — 54'-0"

Total living area:
1,396 sq. ft.

Refer to **Pricing Schedule A** on the order form for pricing information

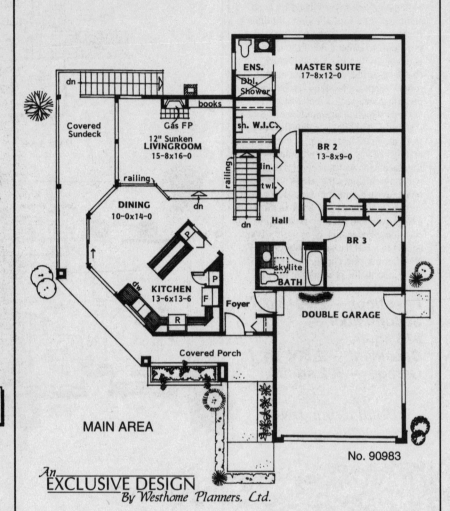

MASTER SUITE
17-8x12-0

ENS.
Dbl. Shower

books

sh. W.I.C.

BR 2
13-8x9-0

dn

Covered Sundeck

Gas FP

12" Sunken
LIVINGROOM
15-8x16-0

railing

railing

lin.

twl

dn

Hall

dn

BR 3

DINING
10-0x14-0

skylite

BATH

KITCHEN
13-6x13-6

dw

P

F

R

Foyer

DOUBLE GARAGE

Covered Porch

MAIN AREA

No. 90983

An
EXCLUSIVE DESIGN
By Westhome Planners. Ltd.

TRADITIONAL SPLENDOR

A gourmet kitchen with an elegant eating bar that will comfortably seat seven people and open to the family room is a popular feature of this home. A large deck, conveniently located off the kitchen/family room is ideally suited for those summer barbecues. Note, also, the close proximity of the formal dining room to the kitchen. With 6 bedrooms and 4 1/2 bathrooms this home accommodates easily a large or extended family. The bayed sitting area in the master bedroom is an ideal quiet spot for the avid reader. The lower level (daylight basement to the rear) was designed for two guest rooms, a party room and a multipurpose area and full bath. No materials list available.

Main level — 2,498 sq. ft.
Upper level — 1,190 sq. ft.

Total living area:
3,688 sq. ft.

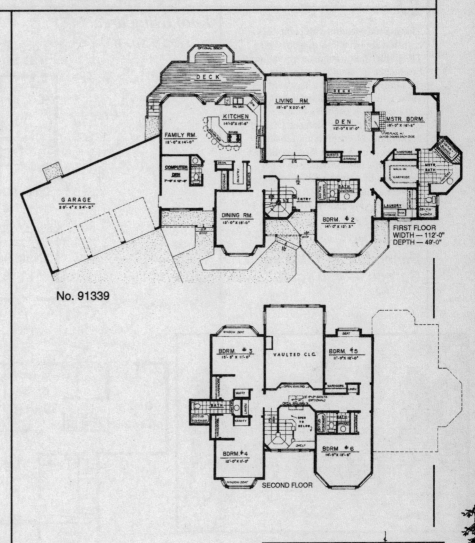

No. 91339

Design 34851

BAY WINDOWS ADD PLENTY OF LIGHT

This classic exterior with plenty of curbside appeal encloses a cozy plan. The living/dining room combination is brightened by abundant windows and the family areas share a backyard view, patio access, a fireplace and an entrance to the kitchen which is equipped with a built-in pantry. This family home features a master suite complete with a room-sized walk-in closet and a private bath, two other bedrooms that share a hall bath and a two-car garage.

First floor — 1,056 sq. ft.
Second floor — 874 sq. ft.
Basement — 1,023 sq. ft.
Garage — 430 sq. ft.

Total living area: 1,930 sq. ft.

No. 34851
First Floor

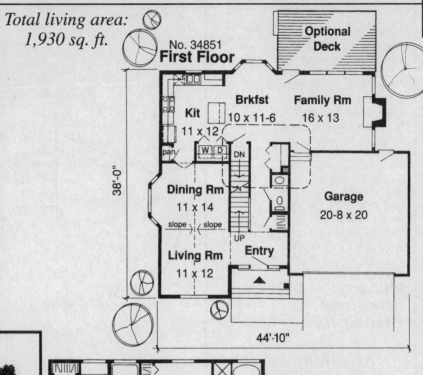

Kit 11 x 12
Brkfst 10 x 11-6
Family Rm 16 x 13
pan
W D
DN
Dining Rm 11 x 14
slope | slope
UP
Living Rm 11 x 12
Entry
Garage 20-8 x 20
38'-0"
44'-10"
Optional Deck

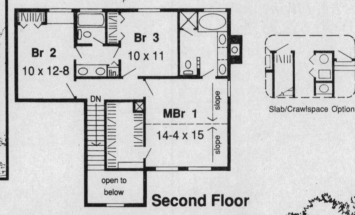

Second Floor

Br 2 10 x 12-8
Br 3 10 x 11
lin.
DN
MBr 1 14-4 x 15
slope
slope
open to below

Slab/Crawlspace Option

Refer to **Pricing Schedule C** on the order form for pricing information

STATELY AND DIGNIFIED

This plan gives a stately and dignified elevation yet, the plan encompasses all the conveniences a modern family requires today. The exterior is enhanced by multi-paned windows and a two-story arched entrance. The large master suite includes a private master bath with an oval tub, separate shower, compartmented toilet and double vanity. An expansive den is located to the rear with a ornate fireplace that includes built-in shelves on either side. The efficient kitchen has a large pantry, peninsula counter with double sink and eating bar, and a sunny breakfast area. An elegant evenings entertaining is sure to transpire in the formal dining room with the lovely bay window. On the second floor there are three additional bedrooms, each with a walk-in closet, that share the full double vanity bath.

First floor — 1,250 sq. ft.
Second floor — 783 sq. ft.
Garage — 555 sq. ft.

Refer to **Pricing Schedule C** on the order form for pricing information

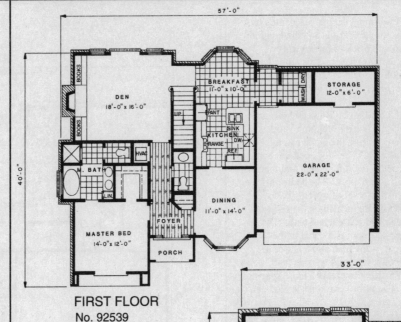

FIRST FLOOR
No. 92539

Total living area: 2,033 sq. ft.

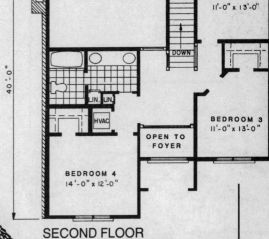

SECOND FLOOR

SPECTACULAR TRADITIONAL

This traditional design is accented by the use of gable roofs and the blend of stucco and brick to form a truly spectacular exterior. This home has the look and feel of a much larger home. Entering the den from the covered front porch, we find a high vaulted ceiling, built-in cabinets, and fireplace. The dining room is open to the den creating the Great room feel for this area. The U-shaped kitchen is adjacent to the dining area and features built-in appliances. The bedrooms are designed in a split fashion. Two bedrooms are located on the right of the plan and share a hall bath. The master bedroom is located to the left and rear of the plan and features a large walk-in closet, private bath, and a raised ceiling to create a more spacious feel. The utility closet is also located in this area.

Main area — 1,237 sq. ft.
Garage — 436 sq. ft.

Total living area:
1,237 sq. ft.

Refer to **Pricing Schedule A** on the order form for pricing information

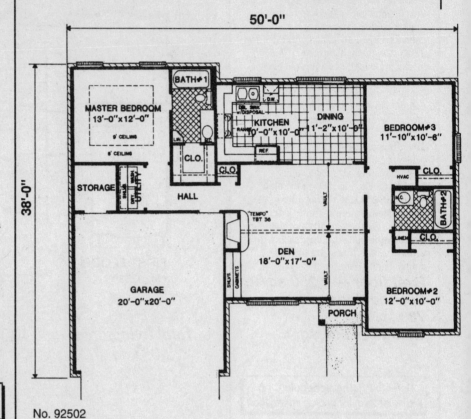

No. 92502
MAIN AREA

DAYLIGHT BASEMENT LOT

An attractive two-story double door entry leads to a gallery area. A private den is directly to the right, and a half-bath and coat closet are to the left. The first floor master suite gives the owner privacy as well as luxury. The living room and dining room are to the rear of the home and flow conveniently into each other. A cozy fireplace enhances the family room, which is located next to the efficient kitchen and nook area. Three additional bedrooms, a game room with an optional wetbar and a full bath are located on the lower level.

First floor — 2,196 sq. ft.
Lower floor —
1,542 sq. ft.

Total living area:
3,738 sq. ft.

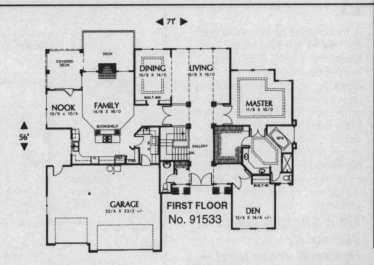

FIRST FLOOR
No. 91533

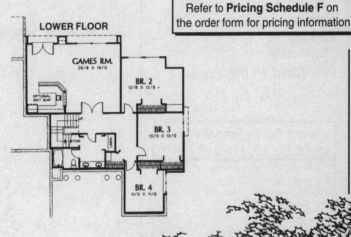

LOWER FLOOR

Refer to **Pricing Schedule F** on the order form for pricing information

ROOM TO GROW

Affordability is the key in this split level for the first-time buyer. The lower level is ready to finish when more space is needed for that expanding family. Having all living areas on one level makes life more convenient. The dining room is open to the living room and has beautiful arched openings. The lower level will always be there for future expansion of two bedrooms, bath and recreation room. A great house for the family starting out. No materials list available.

Main & upper levels — 992 sq. ft.

Optional lower level — 532 sq. ft

Optional garage — 226 sq. ft.

Total living area: 992 sq. ft.

Refer to **Pricing Schedule A** on the order form for pricing information

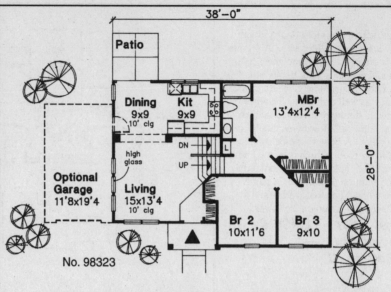

No. 98323

Main & Upper Levels *No materials list available*

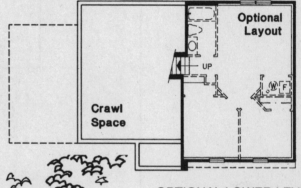

OPTIONAL LOWER LEVEL

EXECUTIVE TRIMMINGS

The use of quoins and segmented arches around the windows and entryway add distinguished executive embellishment to this home. The entry leads to the foyer and gallery area. The front study includes a fireplace flanked by windows. Across from the study is the master suite, topped by a vaulted ceiling and equipped with a lavish bath and a walk-in closet. The living room includes a second fireplace, also flanked by windows. A wetbar and a third fireplace with wood storage accent the family room, which is open to the breakfast nook and the kitchen. A convenient work island is situated in the center of the country kitchen. Two additional bedrooms are on the second floor, each equipped with a walk-in closet and access to the full bath. A materials list is not available for this plan.

First floor — 2,273 sq. ft.
Second floor —
562 sq. ft.

Total living area:
2,835 sq. ft.

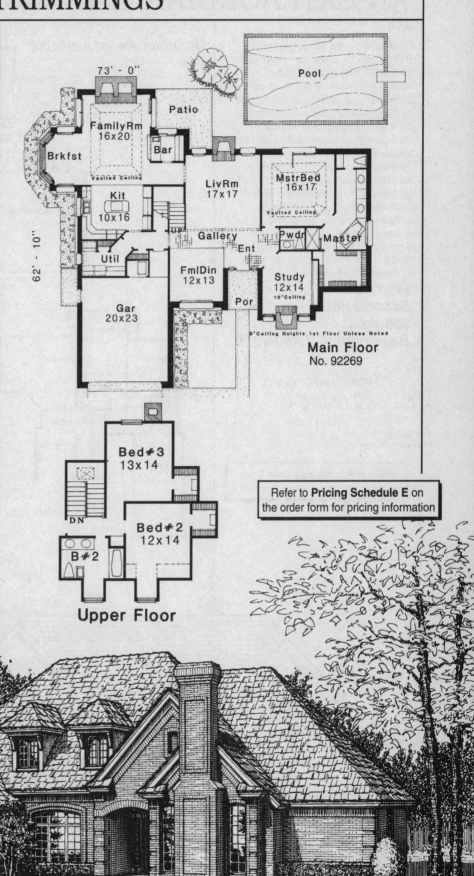

Pool

73' - 0"

Patio

FamilyRm
16x20

Brkfst

Bar

Vaulted Ceiling

LivRm
17x17

MstrBed
16x17

Kit
10x16

Vaulted Ceiling

62' - 10"

up

Gallery

Pwdr

Master

Util

Ent

FmlDin
12x13

Study
12x14
10'Ceiling

Gar
20x23

Por

9" Ceiling Heights 1st Floor Unless Noted

Main Floor
No. 92269

Bed#3
13x14

DN

Bed#2
12x14

B#2

Upper Floor

Refer to **Pricing Schedule E** on the order form for pricing information

ODELL
87

AN EXTRAORDINARY HOME

Upon entering the foyer, your view will go directly to the cozy fireplace and stylish French doors of the Great room. A grand entry into the formal dining room, coupled with the volume ceiling, pulls these two rooms together for a spacious feeling. From the roomy, well-equipped kitchen, there is a pass-through to the Great room. Natural light will flood the breakfast area through large windows. Located between the first floor master bedroom suite and the garage is the laundry, adding convenience and protecting the living areas from noise and disorder. Split stairs, graced with wood railings, lead to the versatile second floor with two additional bedrooms.

First floor — 1,524 sq. ft.
Second floor —
558 sq. ft.
Basement — 1,460 sq. ft.

Total living area:
2,082 sq. ft.

Refer to **Pricing Schedule C** on the order form for pricing information

No materials list available

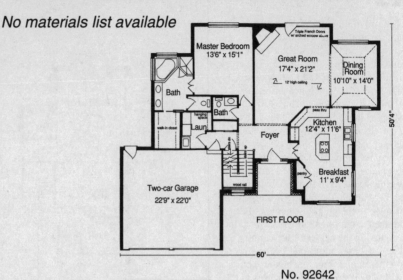

No. 92642

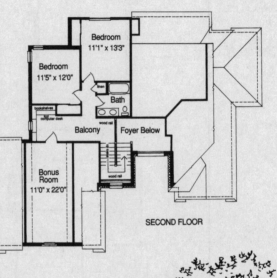

ATTRACTIVE VACATION RETREAT

Soaring windows and a wrap-around deck create an attractive exterior for this vacation retreat. The interior shows off vaulted ceilings and a spacious Great room concept. A captivating view, through the tower bay windows, is featured in this home's efficient kitchen. The Great room combines the living and dining rooms; each with French doors exiting to the deck. The entire upper floor contains a vaulted master bedroom and adjoining bath. No materials list available for this plan.

First floor — 1,329 sq. ft.
Second floor — 342 sq. ft.
Garage — 885 sq. ft.
Deck — 461 sq. ft.

Total living area: 1,671 sq. ft.

Refer to **Pricing Schedule B** on the order form for pricing information

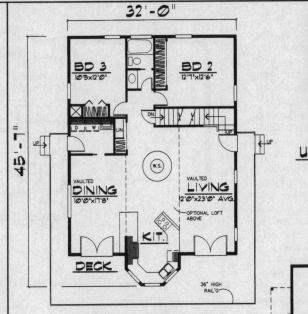

MAIN FLOOR PLAN

No. 91071

No materials list available

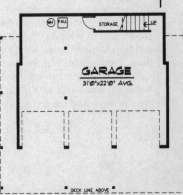

UPPER FLOOR

LOWER FLOOR

CHARMING TWO-STORY

A full basement is included with this plan providing the option of creating an expanded play area in the lower level. This charming two-story home is designed with everything your family will need to enjoy a comfortable and relaxed environment. The boxed window and deluxe entry enhance the exterior; while an easy flow traffic pattern creates step saving convenience in the interior. The open stairway, spacious Great room and breakfast area form an area large enough for real family enjoyment. A favorable indoor-outdoor special relationship is created with the use of French doors and an oversized window in the breakfast area. The U-shaped kitchen is highlighted by a corner sink and provides a pleasant work area for the cook and cook's helper. A half bath and laundry room round out the first floor. The master bedroom suite, with walk-in closet plus two additional bedrooms and a bath with skylight area, is located on the second floor.

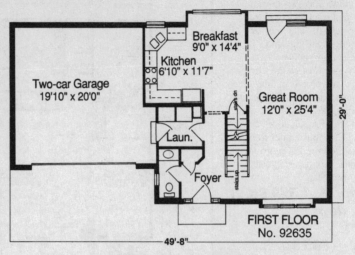

FIRST FLOOR
No. 92635

No materials list available

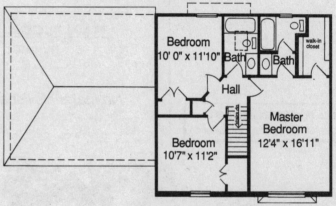

SECOND FLOOR

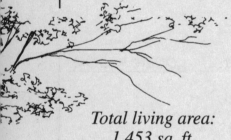

Total living area:
1,453 sq. ft.

Refer to **Pricing Schedule A** on the order form for pricing information

First floor — 748 sq. ft.
Second floor — 705 sq. ft.
Basement — 744 sq. ft.
Garage — 396 sq. ft.

COMFORT AND STYLE

This three-bedroom, two-bath home offers comfort and style. The master suite is complete with its own bath with a skylight. In the center of this design the kitchen includes an eating nook that takes full advantage of the view, and is just the right size for family gatherings. The large sundeck is easily accessible from the master suite, nook and living/dining area. A gas fireplace adds a cozy touch to the living room and the open staircase to the basement level ties both floors together very nicely. The unfinished daylight basement will provide plenty of space for family recreation, extra bedrooms and storage space. The front porch is a very practical feature and leads you into an attractive foyer complete with vaulted ceiling.

Main area — 1,423 sq. ft.
Basement — 1,423 sq. ft.
Garage — 399 sq. ft.
Width — 46' 0"
Depth — 52'- 0"

Total living area:
1,423 sq. ft.

Refer to **Pricing Schedule A** on the order form for pricing information

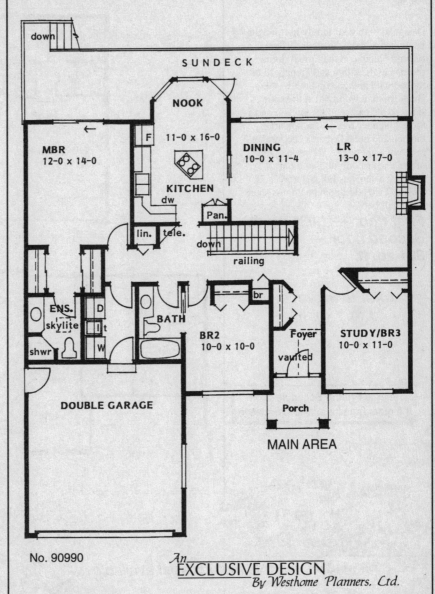

No. 90990

An
EXCLUSIVE DESIGN
By Westhome Planners, Ltd.

REFINED AND DISTINCTIVE

Designed with your family in mind this home boasts many features. There is a furniture alcove in the formal dining room, a high ceiling and French doors topped with arched windows in the Great room, a wood rail at the split stairs, large pantry in the kitchen and a roomy laundry room. The spacious kitchen and breakfast area encourages relaxing gatherings. The master suite offers a whirlpool tub, his-n-her vanities, a shower stall and a walk-in closet. Two additional bedrooms share a full hall bath.

First floor — 1,036 sq. ft.
Second floor —
861 sq. ft.

Total living area:
1,897 sq. ft.

Refer to **Pricing Schedule C** on
the order form for pricing information

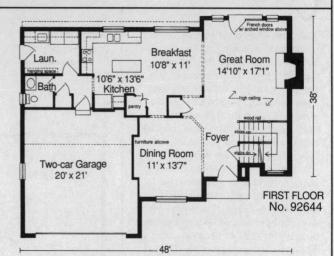

FIRST FLOOR
No. 92644

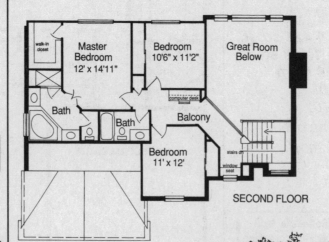

SECOND FLOOR

No materials list available

COZY COUNTRY TRIMMINGS

A wrap-around porch and dormer windows lend an old-fashioned country feeling to this home. Yet inside, a floor plan designed for today's lifestyle unfolds. A great room enhanced by a large hearth fireplace and a vaulted ceiling gives a cozy welcome to guests. It is separated by the breakfast bar from the kitchen/dining area. An island extends the work space in this efficiently laid out area. The dining area has direct access to the rear yard. The first floor master suite also includes a vaulted ceiling and is highlighted by a private, double vanity bath. Two additional bedrooms on the second floor share a full double vanity bath in the hall. No materials list is available for this plan.

First floor — 1,061 sq. ft.
Second floor — 499 sq. ft.

Total living area: 1,560 sq. ft.

Refer to **Pricing Schedule B** on the order form for pricing information

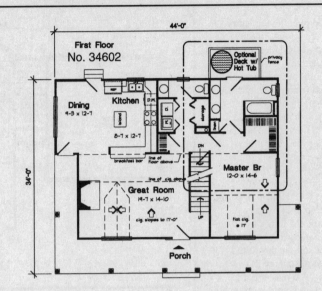

First Floor No. 34602

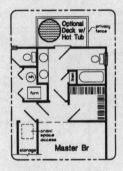

Alternate Foundation Plan

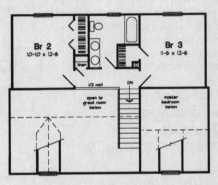

Second Floor Plan

EUROPEAN INSPIRED

The copper hood over the two story bay and the stucco quoins on the corners accent the arched top windows and porch to create this European-styled home. Enter the grand foyer from the covered front porch and you will find the large dining room to the left and the very spacious den with a brick fireplace to the right. The stairs lead to the upstairs balcony that overlooks the foyer and the large arch top window over the front door. To the rear of the dining room is the gourmet kitchen with built-in desk and the breakfast room with its bay windows. Passing the utility room and pantry is the two-car garage at the far left. The master suite with vaulted ceiling is located upstairs with two other bedrooms. The master bath features an oversized corner tub with a large vanity area, separate shower stall and private toilet compartment. This area is complemented by a large walk-in closet. Across the balcony are two additional bedrooms with a bath between.

Main floor — 1,065 sq. ft.
Second floor —
974 sq. ft.
Garage — 626 sq. ft.

Total living area:
2,039 sq. ft.

Refer to **Pricing Schedule C** on
the order form for pricing information

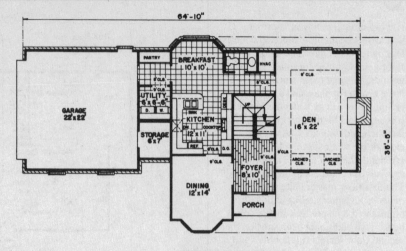

FIRST FLOOR PLAN

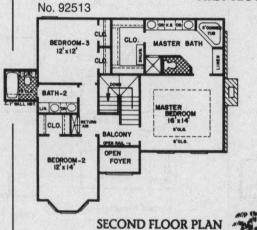

SECOND FLOOR PLAN

STATELY, YET ELEGANT LUXURY

This unique living room adds interest from the outside as well as on the inside. Three narrow, angled, two-story multi-paned windows give a look of distinction to the elevation and the room itself. The formal dining room is located across the foyer and next to the kitchen. The well-appointed kitchen serves both the formal dining room and the informal breakfast room with equal ease. A peninsula counter doubles as an informal eating bar for those meals on the go or after school snacks. An expansive den is provided for informal gatherings. Its large hearth fireplace and built-in wetbar add to the festivities. A large luxurious master suite gives privacy and convenience to the home owner. Three additional bedrooms, each large and with a walk-in closet, have easy access to a full bath. A second floor children's den with built-in cabinets and shelves keeps children's noise and play things in a fun and organized manner.

First floor — 2,380 sq. ft.
**Second floor —
1,504 sq. ft.**
Garage — 806 sq. ft.

*Total living area:
3,884 sq. ft.*

Refer to **Pricing Schedule F** on the order form for pricing information

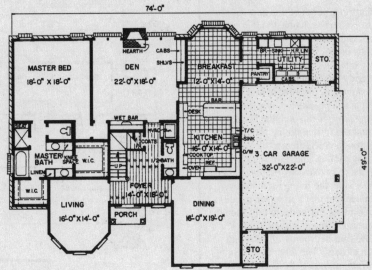

No. 92534

FIRST FLOOR PLAN

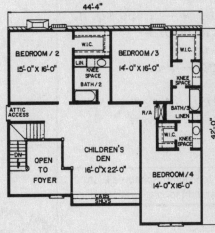

SECOND FLOOR PLAN

CHARMING PORCH SHELTERS ENTRY

The charming porch of this home gives a warm country welcome to all your guests. Start your day in the sunny breakfast nook. From that large country kitchen comes the aroma of bacon and eggs being cooked on the island stove top. More than ample work space is provided in this kitchen, just steps away from both the breakfast nook and the formal dining room. The family room, convenient to the breakfast nook is a nice size and features a cozy two-way fireplace. On the other side, the living room enjoys the atmosphere that a fireplace creates. With a built-in bar in the family room, entertaining is made easy. Upstairs there are four bedrooms, all boasting walk-in closets. The large master suite has its own private bath. This plan is available with a basement, slab or crawlspace foundation. Please specify when ordering.

First floor — 1,450 sq. ft.
Second floor — 1,341 sq. ft.
Garage — 2-car

Total living area: 2,791 sq. ft.

Refer to **Pricing Schedule E** on the order form for pricing information

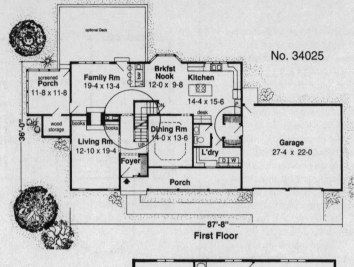

No. 34025

First Floor

optional Deck

screened Porch 11-8 x 11-8

Family Rm 19-4 x 13-4

Brkfst Nook 12-0 x 9-8

Kitchen 14-4 x 15-6

wood storage

books

Living Rm 12-10 x 19-4

Dining Rm 14-0 x 13-6

Garage 27-4 x 22-0

L'dry

Foyer

Porch

36'-0"

87'-8"

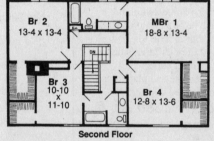

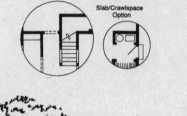

Second Floor

Br 2 13-4 x 13-4

MBr 1 18-8 x 13-4

Br 3 10-10 x 11-10

Br 4 12-8 x 13-6

Slab/Crawlspace Option

A LOT OF LIVING SPACE

There's a lot of living space in this four bedroom home with brick trim. Expansive windows in the vaulted living room allow for plenty of light, and the corner is the perfect place for a wood stove. The kitchen is generously sized and close to the garage for ease in unloading groceries. Two secondary bedrooms, one with a walk-in closet, share the main bath. There is a plant shelf above the staircase, which leads to the master suite and loft or optional bedrooms. The master suite bath features a skylight and walk-in closet. No materials list available for this plan.

**First floor — 1,076 sq. ft.
Second floor —
449 sq. ft.**

*Total living area:
1,525 sq. ft.*

Refer to **Pricing Schedule B** on the order form for pricing information

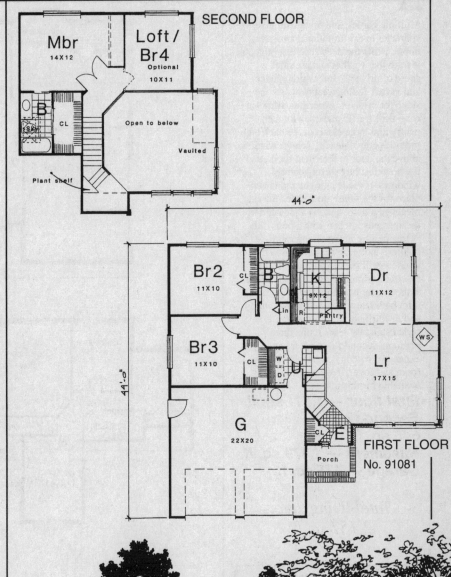

SECOND FLOOR

Mbr
14X12

Loft /
Br 4
Optional
10X11

B

CL

Open to below

Vaulted

Plant shelf

44'-0"

44'-0"

Br 2
11X10

CL

B

K
9X12

Dr
11X12

Lin

R

Pantry

WS

Br 3
11X10

CL

W
D

Lr
17X15

G
22X20

CL

E

Porch

FIRST FLOOR
No. 91081

Design 92631

A TRADITIONAL TWO-STORY

Multiple gables, and brick trim give character to this traditional two-story home, while the deep set entry protects it from the weather and provides a sense of privacy. Interesting angles and varied ceiling treatments set the stage for pride of ownership, while an easy-flow traffic pattern, a kitchen pantry and large closet in the back hall, provides convenience. A high window above the door in the Great room, and the breakfast bay surrounded by windows, provide a bright and cheery place for the family to gather. Serving meals on a daily basis is a pleasure in the spacious kitchen with a peninsula. A tray ceiling in the dining room, columns at the corner and a box window will make you eager to entertain. Rounding out the first floor is the master bedroom suite with an ultra bath featuring a dual bowl vanity and a whirlpool tub. An elegantly styled staircase leads to the three bedroom second floor, where an expansive balcony overlooks the Great room and foyer. No materials list is available for this plan.

First floor — 1,511 sq. ft.
Second floor —
646 sq. ft.
Basement — 1,479 sq. ft.
Garage — 475 sq. ft.

Total living area:
2,157 sq. ft.

Refer to **Pricing Schedule C** on the order form for pricing information

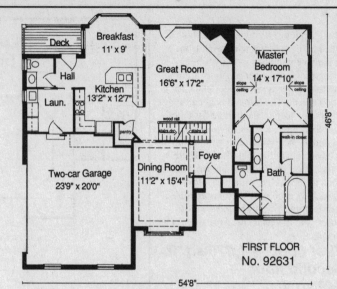

FIRST FLOOR
No. 92631

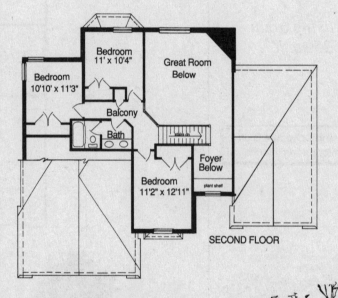

SECOND FLOOR

LAVISH ACCOMMODATIONS

From its stately exterior, to its great attention to detail, this home personifies luxury. The central den has a large fireplace and built-in cabinets and shelves. A decorative ceiling adds just the right touch to the room. Columns define the entrance to the formal dining room, adding a feeling of elegance. The island kitchen is well thought out and includes a walk-in pantry. The informal breakfast room is directly accessible from either the kitchen or the den. The master bedroom includes a decorative ceiling, huge walk-in closet and a luxurious master bath. Each of the additional bedrooms have private access to a full bath. Two of the bedrooms have a walk-in closet, the other enjoys a private bath, making it the perfect guest room.

Main living area—2,733 sq. ft.

Garage and storage — 569 sq. ft.

Total living area: 2,733 sq. ft.

Refer to **Pricing Schedule E** on the order form for pricing information

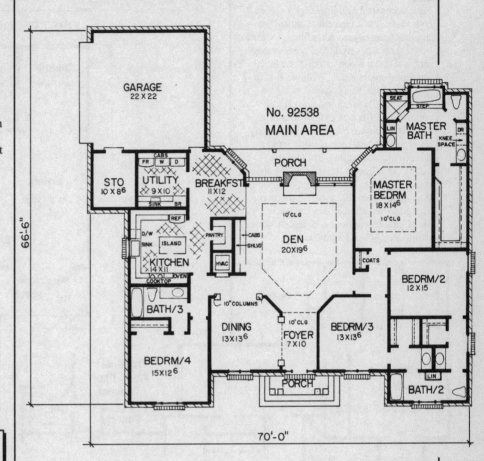

Design 91055

EXCELLENT FOR FIRST-TIME BUYERS

Simple construction lines and a gabled roof make this an excellent choice for the first time buyer. A traditional styled home with a covered front porch, a bay window and a wood exterior create an attractive appearance. With walls kept to a minimum, this home feels larger than it actually is. A spacious living room with a front bay window adjoins the formal dining room. The efficiently designed kitchen conveniently serves both the formal dining area and the eating bar adjacent to the large family room. Upstairs contain three bedrooms plus a playroom that separate the two secondary bedrooms. A generously sized master bedroom is complete with a walk-in-closet and a private bath.

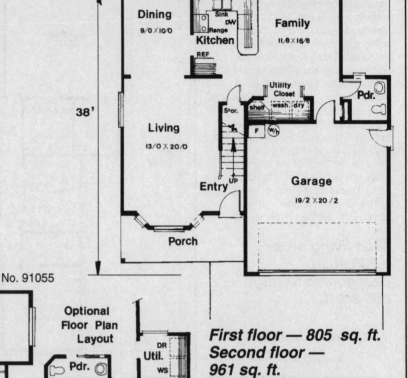

FIRST FLOOR

37'

38'

Dining 9/0 X 10/0

Kitchen — Sink, DW, Range, REF

Family 11/8 X 16/6

Living 13/0 X 20/0

Utility Closet — shelf, wash, dry, Stor.

Pdr.

Entry — UP

Garage 19/2 X 20/2

Porch

No. 91055

SECOND FLOOR

walk in

TUB   TUB

Bedr. 2 10/0 X 10/3

Master Bedr. 1 13/0 X 20/0

D.N

UP

Playroom 16/2 X 9/0

Bedr. 3 13/0 X 12/0

Optional Floor Plan Layout

Pdr.

DR, Util., WS

Refer to **Pricing Schedule B** on the order form for pricing information

First floor — 805 sq. ft.
Second floor — 961 sq. ft.
Garage — 540 sq. ft.

Total living area: 1,766 sq. ft.

Design 34037

CLAPBOARD FACADE GRACES PLAN

The tiled two-story foyer opens to the fireplaced family room with a 10-foot ceiling. An open kitchen/breakfast room arrangement adjoins the formal dining room and outdoor deck. Featured on the first floor for privacy, the master suite boasts a private bath and huge, walk-in closet. The two bedrooms upstairs share a skylit bath. A two-car garage gains entrance through a convenient utility. A materials list is not available for this plan.

**First floor — 1,880 sq. ft.
Second floor — 575 sq. ft.
Garage — 594 sq. ft.**

Total living area: 2,455 sq. ft.

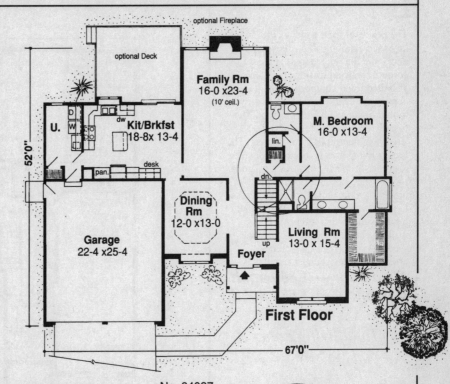

optional Fireplace

optional Deck

Family Rm
16-0 x23-4
(10' ceil.)

M. Bedroom
16-0 x13-4

Kit/Brkfst
18-8x 13-4

52'0"

pan.   desk

Garage
22-4 x25-4

Dining Rm
12-0 x13-0

lin.

dn.

up

Living Rm
13-0 x 15-4

Foyer

First Floor

67'0"

No. 34037

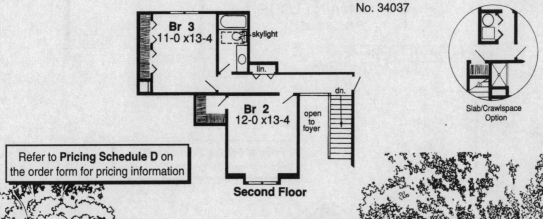

Br 3
11-0 x13-4

skylight

lin.

Br 2
12-0 x13-4

dn.

open to foyer

Second Floor

Slab/Crawlspace Option

Refer to **Pricing Schedule D** on the order form for pricing information

PALLADIAN WINDOW HIGHLIGHTS HOME

The beautiful front window, the keystone detailing above the garage doors and the brick quoins at the corners create a pleasing elevation. The tiled foyer equipped with a convenient coat closet accesses the living/dining room combination. The front window adds elegance and streaming natural light to the area. The family living area is located to the rear. A corner fireplace enhances the family room. The kitchen is open to the breakfast room and gives direct access to the formal dining area. A spacious master suite with a full bath and a walk-in closet is located close to the secondary bedrooms, a preferred arrangement for younger families.

Main floor — 1,685 sq. ft.
Basement — 1,685 sq. ft.

Total living area:
1,685 sq. ft.

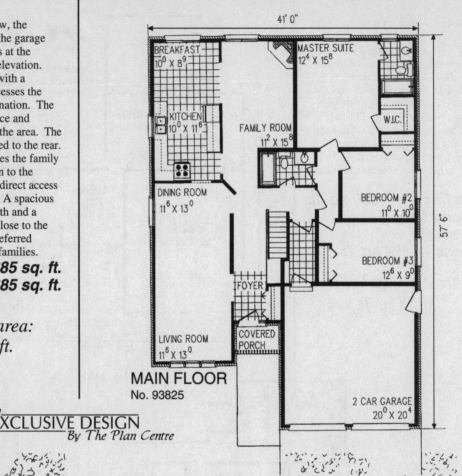

MAIN FLOOR
No. 93825

An
EXCLUSIVE DESIGN
By The Plan Centre

Refer to **Pricing Schedule B** on the order form for pricing information

ECONOMICALLY DESIGNED PLAN

An economically designed plan, where cost is a major consideration without affecting esthetics and quality of planning, is a feature of this home. This is accomplished with a first floor of slightly over 1,000 sq. ft., forming the main living spaces and two bedrooms. As the family grows, expansion takes place within the second floor shell where windows, roof and walls already exist to easily gain an additional two bedrooms and bath. Although the house is small in area, the rooms are comfortable and the flowing space of the living room, dining room and kitchen gives the effect of a larger space. The entry foyer is an imposing two stories. The living and dining rooms run from the front to the rear. The rear dining room wall consists of a large glazed sliding door giving access to a covered porch. The front living room wall is mostly glazed. Off the dining room is a fully equipped U-shaped kitchen with snack bar. The bedroom wing includes two comfortable sized bedrooms each with walk-in closets. The master bedroom has its own bath with a whirlpool tub. The second bedroom uses the other bath which has access from the rest of the house.

First floor — 1,078 sq. ft.
Second floor —
559 sq. ft. (expansion)
Basement — 1,078 sq. ft.
Garage — 409 sq. ft.

Total living area:
1,078 sq. ft.

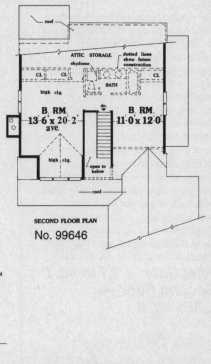

SECOND FLOOR PLAN

No. 99646

ATTIC STORAGE — dotted lines show future construction
skydome
CL   CL   BATH   CL
high clg.
B. RM. 13'-6 x 20'-2 ave.
B. RM. 11'-0 x 12'-0
high clg.
dn.
open to below
roof

FIRST FLOOR PLAN

40'-0"

57'-0"

P.
K. 9'-3 x 14'-4
dw
M. B. RM. 11 x 15
W.t.c.
D. RM. 10'-7 x 10'-4
ref.
CL
w.
d.
whirlpool tub
f.P.
L. RM. 16'-6 x 12'-7
dn.
B. RM. 11 x 11
W.t.c.
F. up
CL
P.
TWO CAR GAR. 19' x 20'

Refer to **Pricing Schedule A** on the order form for pricing information

Design 92210

GRANDEUR AND ELEGANCE

The distinctive covered entry to this stunning manor immediately give you the feel for the elegance that is to follow throughout the entire house. A grand double staircase is the highlight of the two story entry that opens to a large family room with a walk-in wet bar, fireplace and entertainment center. The wonderful, efficient island kitchen opens to the covered patio. The library has a cozy fireplace to curl up next to on cold winter evenings. Upstairs the master bedroom features a fireplace, its own study, and spacious master bath with walk-in closet. Two other bedrooms share an adjoining bath and also feature walk-in closets. This home is a dream that came true. No materials list available for this plan..

First floor — 2,745 sq. ft.
Second floor —
2,355 sq. ft.

Total living:
5,100 sq. ft.

Refer to **Pricing Schedule F** on
the order form for pricing information

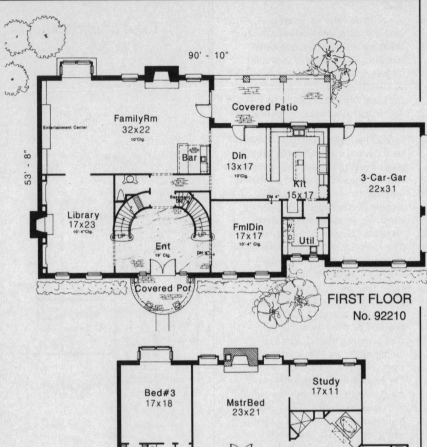

FIRST FLOOR
No. 92210

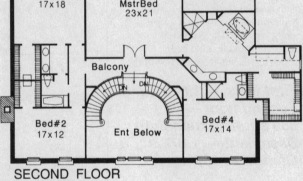

SECOND FLOOR

COUNTRY-CONTEMPORARY HOME

The long porch on this country-contemporary home sweeps across most of the front facade. A skylight brightens the recessed entry, which is offset to the right. The spacious master suite is more than just a place to sleep. Light streams into a sitting area from four sides. It has two sets of glass doors. One set opens on the front porch and the other set leads out onto a private covered porch with access to the rear yard. Skylights bathe the dual compartment bathroom in natural light. The window in front of the sink overlooks the front porch. A long eating bar provides ample counter space. The dining room and the living room are open to each other with a cozy fireplace providing partial separation.

Main floor — 2,424 sq. ft.
Garage — 962 sq. ft.

Total living area:
2,424 sq. ft.

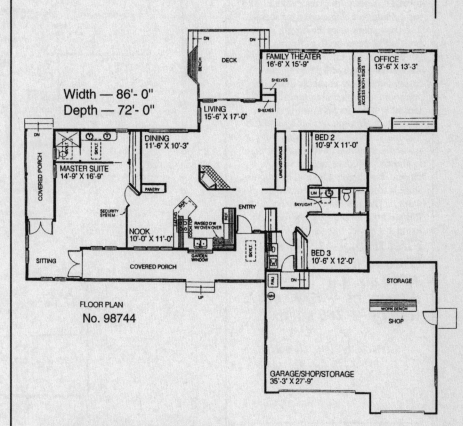

Width — 86'- 0"
Depth — 72'- 0"

FLOOR PLAN
No. 98744

Refer to **Pricing Schedule D** on the order form for pricing information

Design 93309

ROOM FOR EVERYONE

If your family needs to spread out into their own spaces, this is the house for you. The beautiful bay window in the formal dining room gives distinction to the outside and elegance to the inside. The living room and the dining room both enjoy the warmth of fireplaces. An expansive gourmet kitchen features a cooktop island with room for an eating bar. There is access to the deck, sun room and the dining room. Upstairs will impress you with spacious bedrooms — four to be exact. The master bedroom has a private master bath with a double vanity, step-in shower, separate tub and walk-in closet. The three additional bedrooms share a full hall bath with a double vanity. The attic may be finished as a loft/studio, if you desire. No materials list available for this plan.

First floor — 1,799 sq. ft.
Second floor — 1,318 sq. ft.
Basement — 1,799 sq. ft.
Garage — 768 sq. ft.

Total living area:
3,117 sq. ft.

Refer to **Pricing Schedule E** on the order form for pricing information

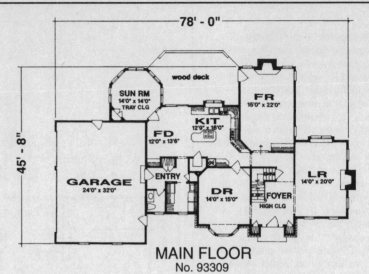

MAIN FLOOR
No. 93309

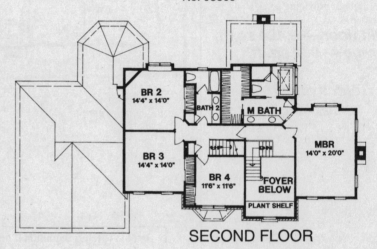

SECOND FLOOR

An
EXCLUSIVE DESIGN
By Patrick Morabito, A.I.A. Architect

Design 93704

REMINISCENT OF THE 1920'S

Reminiscent of the 1920's on the exterior, this bungalow reproduction has the floor plan and amenities on the interior, which are tailored to today's lifestyles. The ten foot high ceilings on the main level add to the spaciousness of the floor plan. The French doors in the foyer lead to a study, which has built-in bookcases and is also accessible from the master bedroom. The large kitchen and breakfast area are perfect for family mealtimes, and the study alcove upstairs can serve as a computer and homework center for the children. As with the original bungalows, the extensive use of porches extends the living area outside No materials list available..

First floor — 1,748 sq. ft.
Second floor — 558 sq. ft.

Total living area: 2,306 sq. ft.

An EXCLUSIVE DESIGN
By Building Science Associates

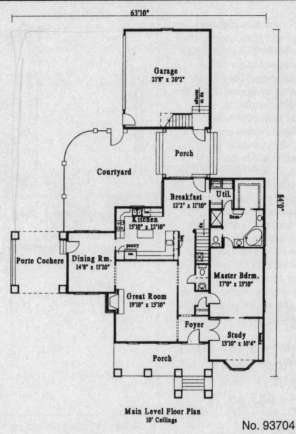

Main Level Floor Plan
10' Ceilings

No. 93704

Upper Level Floor Plan
8' Ceilings

Refer to **Pricing Schedule D** on the order form for pricing information

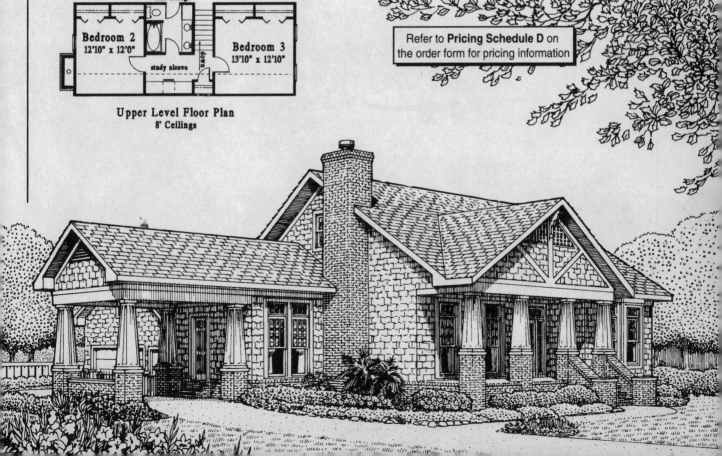

EXECUTIVE DWELLING

A grand first impression continues into the two-story foyer graced by a curved staircase. A comfortable study with a fireplace is accessed to the right through double doors. The formal living room and dining room are to the left and flow into each other. A butler's pantry adds convenience between the large kitchen and formal dining room. An island and a peninsula counter add to the work space in the wide open room that flows into the breakfast room. The family room is expansive and includes a second fireplace and built-in bookshelves and entertainment center. The first floor master suite is crowned by a cathedral ceiling and includes a extensive private bath and two walk-in closets. Three additional bedrooms, each with a walk-in closet and private access to a full bath, are on the second floor. No materials list is available for this plan.

First floor — 2,807 sq. ft.
Second floor — 1,063 sq. ft.
Garage — 633 sq. ft.

Total living area:
3,870 sq. ft.

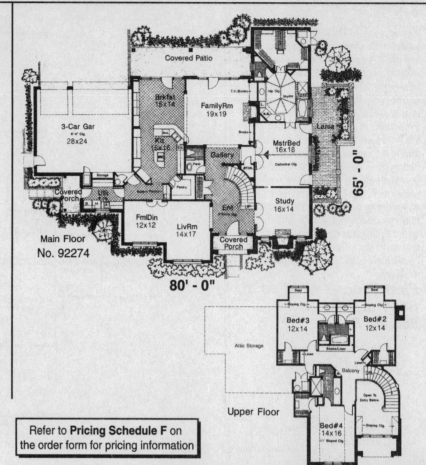

Main Floor
No. 92274

65' - 0"

80' - 0"

Upper Floor

Refer to **Pricing Schedule F** on the order form for pricing information

ATTRACTIVE BUNGALOW-STYLED RANCH

This attractive Ranch, in a bungalow style, is sure to please both family and friends. The exterior stone detail mixed with shaker siding gives this home a traditional air all its own. Inside, you will find three bedrooms perfect for the family that is just starting out. Or, convert the third bedroom into a den for the home worker, or a formal dining room for the entertainer of the family. In the garage, you will be pleasantly surprised when you discover all of the extra storage space. The open stairway to the lower level is inviting to everyone. The lower level offers additional space for future finish when the family grows. No materials list available.

**Main living area —
1,670 sq. ft.
Basement — 729 sq. ft.
Garage — 678 sq. ft.**

*Total living area:
1,670 sq. ft.*

An
EXCLUSIVE DESIGN
By Ahmann Design

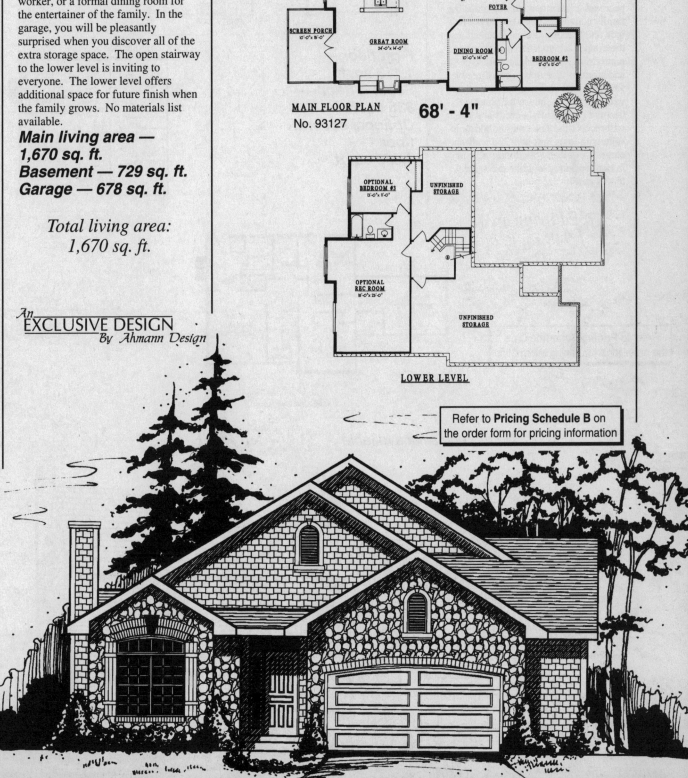

MAIN FLOOR PLAN
No. 93127

LOWER LEVEL

Refer to **Pricing Schedule B** on the order form for pricing information

Design 92636

FAMILY SIZED

The covered porch on this charming two-story home provides a place to relax and enjoy peaceful summer evenings. A window high above the foyer brings light to this area; while the living room, dining room and open stairway work together to create an impressive entry. Warmed by the fireplace and lighted by a bay window and glass door, the rear of this home becomes a favorite gathering place for family activities. Conveniently, a half bath and laundry room are located near the kitchen where a serving island and pantry provide a pleasant work area and storage. The option of a three or four bedroom second floor is available with this plan. Choose the plan that best fits your family's needs and you will receive the same master bedroom suite with luxurious bath and walk-in closet. A balcony overlooks the entry in both options providing excitement to this family size home.

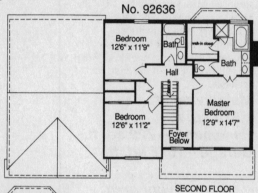

First floor — 1,113 sq. ft.
Second floor — 835 sq. ft.
Optional second floor — 1,080 sq. ft.

Total living area: 1,948 sq. ft. or 2,193 sq. ft.

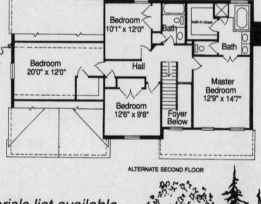

Refer to **Pricing Schedule C** on the order form for pricing information

No materials list available

ATTENTION TO DETAILS

The beautiful detailing around the windows and door of this home add to its curb appeal. Once inside, the attention to detailing adds to the feeling of luxury and elegance. The large living room has a focal point fireplace in the center of the outside wall. There is also access to the rear yard through this room. The master suite is located at the opposite end of the house from the two additional bedrooms. This arrangement insures the privacy of the homeowner. The decorative ceiling and lavish master bath provide convenience and elegance to the suite. The two additional bedrooms are a nice size and share a full hall bath. There is an informal breakfast room and a formal dining room both located next to the efficient kitchen. A laundry room and double garage complete this well thought-out floor plan. This plan is available with either a basement, slab, or crawl space foundation. Please specify when ordering. No materials list available for this plan.

**Main living area —
1,708 sq. ft.
Garage — 400 sq. ft.**

*Total living area:
1,708 sq. ft.*

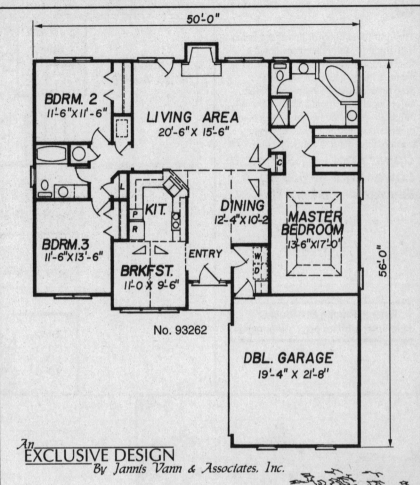

An
EXCLUSIVE DESIGN
By Jannis Vann & Associates, Inc.

No. 93262

Refer to **Pricing Schedule B** on the order form for pricing information

Design 34681

ENTRY CROWNED BY CLERESTORY

The split foyer entry of this charmer has a half-flight of stairs that leads down to a family room, a utility room, a powder room, a study, and a two-car garage. Step up to a large living room, and an adjoining dining room and kitchen. A hall bath serves the two front bedrooms tucked down the hall while the rear master suite features a private bath.

Upper floor — 1,331 sq. ft.
Lower floor — 663 sq. ft.
Garage — 584 sq. ft.

Total living area:
1,994 sq. ft.

Refer to **Pricing Schedule C** on the order form for pricing information

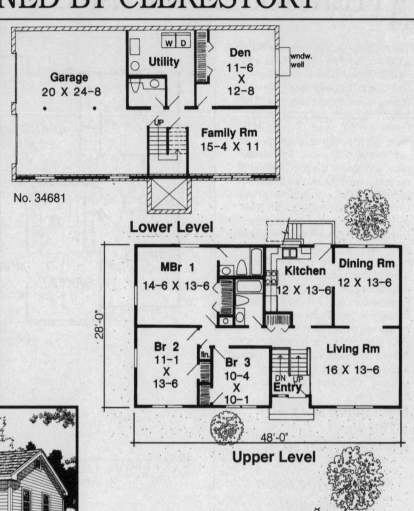

No. 34681

Lower Level

Garage 20 X 24-8
Utility
Den 11-6 X 12-8
wndw. well
W D
UP
Family Rm 15-4 X 11

Upper Level

MBr 1 14-6 X 13-6
Kitchen 12 X 13-6
Dining Rm 12 X 13-6
Br 2 11-1 X 13-6
Br 3 10-4 X 10-1
Living Rm 16 X 13-6
DN Entry UP
28'-0"
48'-0"

TRADITIONAL ELEGANCE

Stateliness and elegance are the two words which best describe this fine two-story Traditional brick home. Entering the home through the intricately detailed entrance, we find the living room on the left and the large dining room on the right of the magnificent two story foyer. To the rear of the foyer, beyond the guest bath, is the spacious den with it's fireplace and built-in cabinets. The master bedroom is located to the left of the den with its vaulted ceilings and the master bath. His-n-her closets, separate vanities, toilet compartment and the large shower stall surround the whirlpool tub. This separation of the master bedroom from the other rooms provides maximum privacy. The very large kitchen and breakfast room is located to the right of the den. Upstairs we find three oversized bedrooms and a children's den.

Main floor — 2,553 sq. ft.
Second floor —
1,260 sq. ft.
Garage — 714 sq. ft.

Total living area:
3,813 sq. ft.

Refer to **Pricing Schedule F** on the order form for pricing information

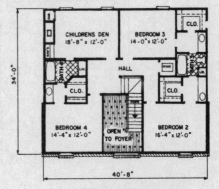

SECOND FLOOR PLAN   No. 92504

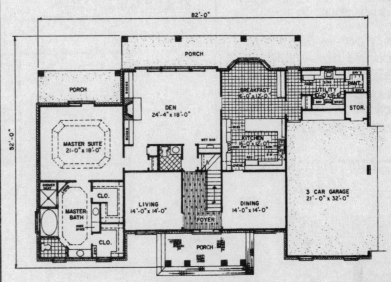

FIRST FLOOR PLAN

A TOUCH OF VICTORIAN STYLING

Design 93230

The covered porch and pointed roof on the sitting alcove of the master suite give this home a touch of victorian styling. Yet, the layout in the interior is certainly modern. The formal areas occupy the front of the home. The high traffic areas are in the rear of the home. The kitchen/breakfast area has a half-bath sandwiched between them and the family room, which enjoys a corner fireplace. On the second floor, the master suite occupies the depth of the house. The sitting alcove has the natural light from the windows surrounding it. The master bath and walk-in closet make life very convenient. Two additional bedrooms share a full hall bath. No materials list available for this plan.

First floor — 887 sq. ft.
Second floor — 877 sq. ft.
Basement — 859 sq. ft.
Garage — 484 sq. ft.
Deck — 261 sq. ft.
Porch — 252 sq. ft.

Total living area:
1,764 sq. ft.

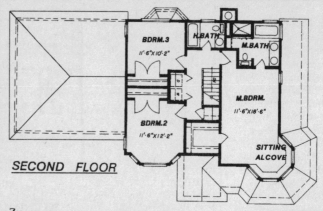

SECOND FLOOR

An EXCLUSIVE DESIGN
By Jannis Vann & Associates, Inc.

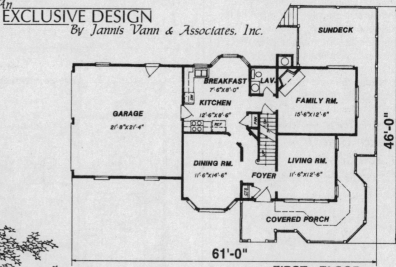

FIRST FLOOR
No. 93230

Refer to **Pricing Schedule B** on the order form for pricing information

SPACIOUS FAMILY AREAS

The attractive exterior of this home is just the icing on the cake. The layout of this plan is just perfect for the young family. The kitchen, breakfast room and family room are in an open layout, giving a feeling of spaciousness and making family interaction simple. The efficient kitchen includes a cooktop peninsula and a corner sink. The sunny breakfast area will start the day on a bright note. A cozy family room with focal point fireplace will add to a relaxing evening. The formal living and dining rooms are located at the front of the house. The second floor includes three bedrooms, two full baths and a bonus room to be decided on in the future. One of the bedrooms, the master bedroom, has a private master bath with a walk-in closet and a decorative ceiling. The two additional bedrooms are spacious with ample closet space.

First floor — 902 sq. ft.
Second floor — 819 sq. ft.
Finished staircase — 28 sq. ft.
Bonus room — 210 sq. ft.
Basement — 874 sq. ft.
Garage — 400 sq. ft.

Total living area:
1,749 sq. ft.

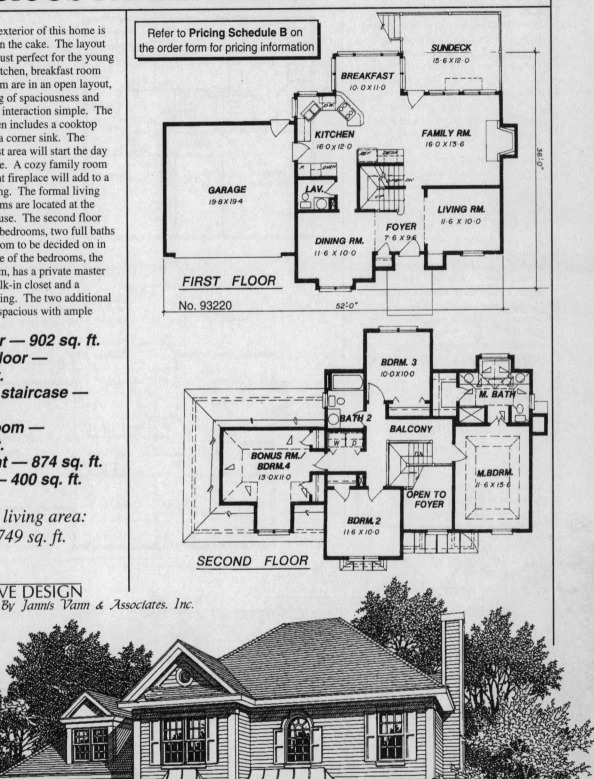

Refer to **Pricing Schedule B** on the order form for pricing information

FIRST FLOOR
No. 93220

SECOND FLOOR

An
EXCLUSIVE DESIGN
By Jannis Vann & Associates, Inc.

LUXURY PERSONIFIED

Design 92623

The classic good looks of this Colonial two-story are accentuated by an arch topped window over the entrance and the use of brick trim and dental molding across the front. The tray ceiling and the corner columns in the formal living room and dining room pull these two rooms into a unit to create a large and charming area for entertaining. For family convenience the stairs are located with access directly into the kitchen. Windows located on either side of the corner sink flood the counter with natural light. The sunken family room with fireplace brings a warm feeling to this private area of the house. A luxurious bedroom suite with double walk-in closets and a sloped ceiling is the highlight of this four bedroom second floor. A balcony overlooking the foyer, a plant shelf, arched window, skylight, and a laundry chute are extra features that help to make this a home unsurpassed in style and value. No materials list available for this plan.

**First floor — 1,365 sq. ft.
Second floor — 1,288 sq. ft.**

Total living area: 2,653 sq. ft.

Refer to **Pricing Schedule E** on the order form for pricing information

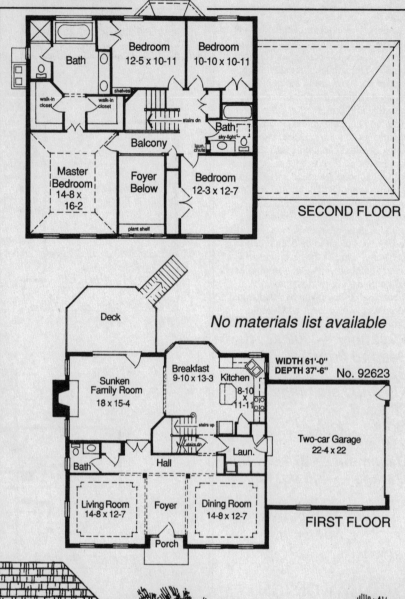

No materials list available

WIDTH 61'-0"
DEPTH 37'-6"   No. 92623

SECOND FLOOR

FIRST FLOOR

STUNNING, YET RESERVED

This attractive elevation demands attention. Once inside, the foyer with a high ceiling, allows you to enter either the formal areas or the family room. The formal living room has a view of the front yard and a large fireplace. The dining room includes a bumped out window and a pocket door dividing it from the dinette. A second fireplace enhances the family room, which flows easily into either the dinette or the sun room. A gourmet kitchen with a built-in pantry, desk and a terrific island/snack bar will delight the cook of the household. A super master suite is located on the second floor and includes a lavish master bath with a corner tub, step-in shower, compartmented toilet and a double vanity. The three additional bedrooms have ample closet space and are of a good size. Bedroom two has private access to a full bath. A bonus room has been included to take care of your future needs. No materials list available for this plan.

First floor — 2,228 sq. ft.
Second floor — 1,625 sq. ft.
Basement — 2,228 sq. ft.
Garage — 816 sq. ft.
Bonus — 347 sq. ft.

Total living area: 3,853 sq. ft.

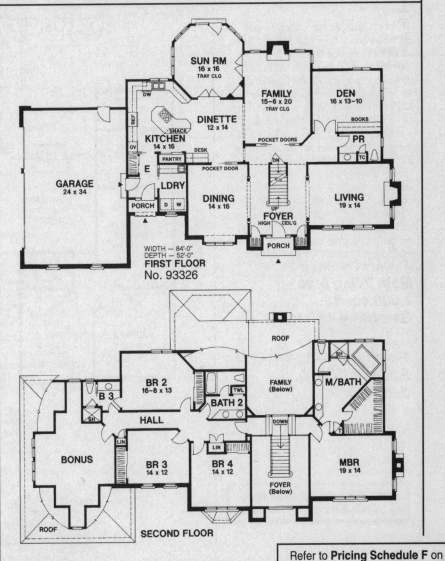

FIRST FLOOR
No. 93326
WIDTH — 84'-0"
DEPTH — 52'-0"

SECOND FLOOR

An EXCLUSIVE DESIGN
By Patrick Morabito, A.I.A. Architect

Refer to **Pricing Schedule F** on the order form for pricing information

FOR TODAY'S SOPHISTICATED OWNER

Design 93027

This best seller features a traditional elevation and a floor plan full of all the amenities required by today's sophisticated homeowner. A formal dining room opens off the foyer and features a classic bay window. The kitchen is notable for an angled eating bar opening the kitchen to the living room beyond, and providing a view of the cozy living room fireplace from the kitchen. The master bedroom includes a luxury master bath with his-n-her vanities and knee space. A whirlpool tub/shower combination and walk-in closet area. Ten foot ceilings in the major living areas including the master bedroom and one of the bedrooms give the impression of a much larger home. No materials list available for this plan.

**Main living area —
1,500 sq. ft.
Garage — 437 sq. ft.**

*Total living area:
1,500 sq. ft.*

Refer to **Pricing Schedule A** on the order form for pricing information

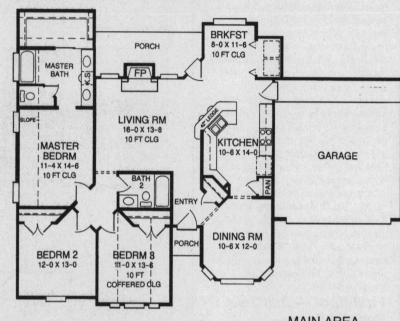

An
EXCLUSIVE DESIGN
By Belk Home Designs

WIDTH 59-10

DEPTH 44-4

MASTER BATH

MASTER BEDRM
11-4 X 14-6
10 FT CLG

BEDRM 2
12-0 X 13-0

BEDRM 8
11-0 X 13-6
10 FT COFFERED CLG

PORCH

FP

LIVING RM
16-0 X 13-8
10 FT CLG

BRKFST
8-0 X 11-6
10 FT CLG

KITCHEN
10-6 X 14-0

GARAGE

BATH 2

ENTRY

PORCH

DINING RM
10-6 X 12-0

MAIN AREA
No. 93027

AN APPEALING ELEVATION

No. 93263

The stone and siding combination of this elevation provides great curb appeal. The floor plan has been arranged for the lifestyle of today's modern family. The living area and the dining room flow into each other, creating a feeling of spaciousness. The living area includes a fireplace that can be seen from the entry. Both the formal dining area and the informal breakfast room are bathed with natural light from their abundance of windows. The efficient kitchen has a corner double sink and a built-in pantry. A peninsula counter separates the kitchen from the breakfast room. The laundry room is conveniently located next to the kitchen. Four bedrooms will comfortably accommodate your family. The master suite is sure to be the owner's private retreat. A decorative ceiling and a private bath add to its beauty and conveniences. The three additional bedrooms share a full hall bath. No materials list available for this plan.

Main floor — 1,609 sq. ft.
Basement — 1,579 sq. ft.
Garage — 406 sq. ft.

Total living area:
1,609 sq. ft.

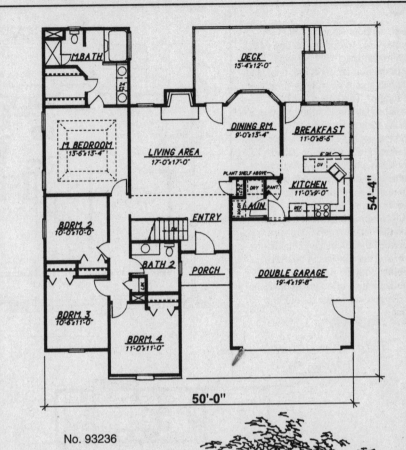

No. 93236

Refer to **Pricing Schedule B** on the order form for pricing information

An
EXCLUSIVE DESIGN
By Jannis Vann & Associates, Inc.

OPEN PLAN LIGHTS TRADITIONAL HOME

Here's a home that combines century-old traditional styling with a bright and spacious open plan. The combination family room, nook and kitchen area is over thirty-three feet in length. This offers lots of possibilities for decorating. At one end is the gas fireplace feature wall, and the opposite end has a very well-planned kitchen with an island. The nook has a bay window further enhancing the appearance of the room and increasing the space even more. We've added a very practical feature, something from a by-gone era, the butler or serving pantry between the kitchen and the dining room. This consists of an overhead cabinet with glass doors and a lower cabinet which often incorporates an under counter fridge for chilling wine.

An EXCLUSIVE DESIGN
By Westhome Planners, Ltd.

FIRST FLOOR
No. 90991

PATIO

NOOK
8-0x12-8

FAMILY ROOM
15-6x12-8

KITCHEN
10-0x12-8

dw

BATH

Gas FP

R

LIVINGROOM
13-0x16-0

Butler's Pan.

D W

DINING
13-0x12-0

DOUBLE GARAGE
21-6x26-0
(560 sq. ft.)

Covered Entry

open over

up

FOYER

dn

VERANDAH

Total living area:
2,170 sq. ft.

BR3
11-4x12-0

whirlpool

Bath

shlvs.

ENS.

twl

W.I.C.

Make-up Vanity

lin

dn

brm

BR2
13-0x12-0

railing

MASTER SUITE
13-0x20-4

Foyer below

plant shelf

SECOND FLOOR

Refer to **Pricing Schedule C** on
the order form for pricing information

First floor — 1,173 sq. ft.
Second floor — 997 sq. ft.
Basement — 1,164 sq. ft.
Garage — 574 sq. ft.
Width — 63'-0"
Depth — 36'-0"

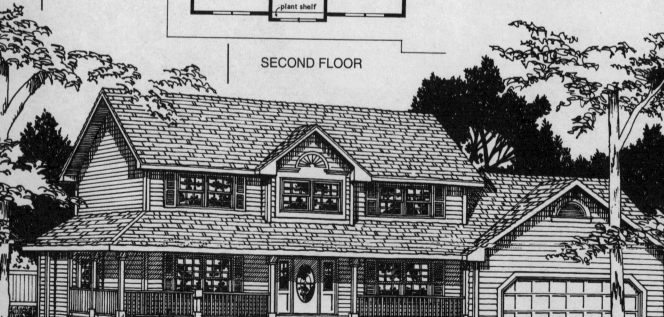

Design 92641

A UNIQUE FACADE

Multiple gables, a recessed entry and a front positioned chimney, combine to present a unique facade. Amenities include wood rails at the stairs, a rounded step, colonial columns and a vaulted ceiling gracing the living areas. The hallway from the garage provides a service entrance with easy access to the well-equipped kitchen. The master bedroom suite is enhanced by French doors leading to the deck. Two additional bedrooms, with private access to the bath, are located on the second floor, where a view of the foyer and the Great room are provided at the stairs.

**First floor —
1,516 sq. ft.
Second floor —
480 sq. ft.
Basement — 1,477 sq. ft.**

*Total living area:
1,996 sq. ft.*

Refer to **Pricing Schedule C** on the order form for pricing information

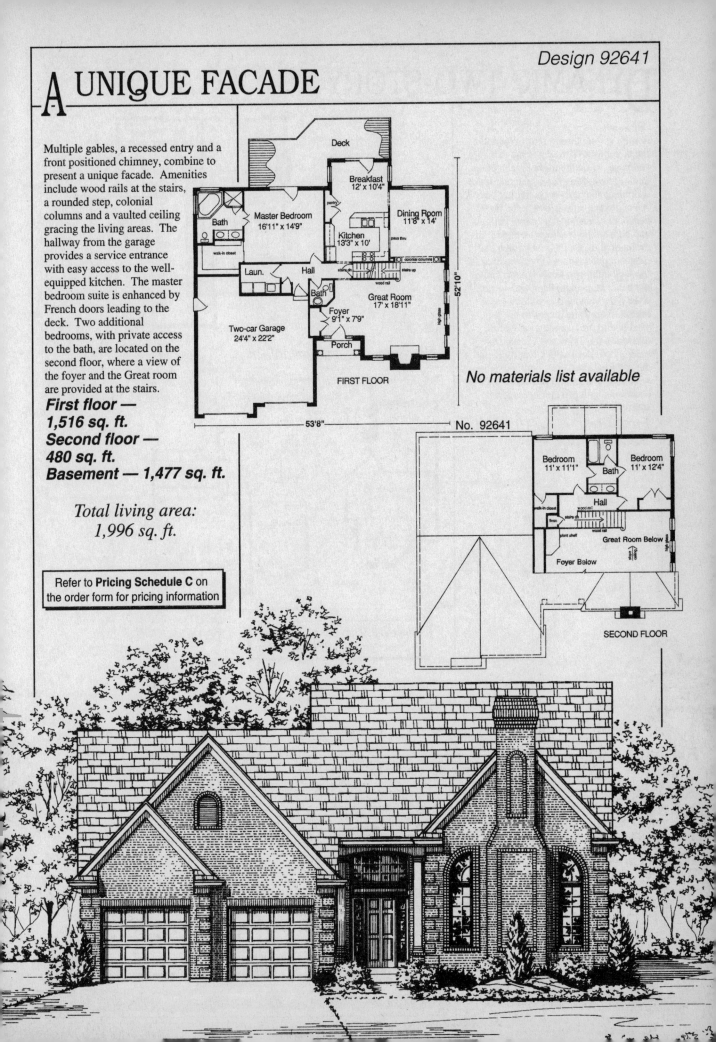

No materials list available

FIRST FLOOR

No. 92641

SECOND FLOOR

DYNAMIC TWO-STORY

A high ceiling through the foyer and the Great room showcases the deluxe staircase, while the triple French doors and high windows across the rear make this a bright and lively gathering place. An octagonal sitting area at the master bedroom offers an eleven foot ceiling and adds to the spacious feeling of this dramatic retreat. Ease of serving daily meals or quick snacks is emphasized in the well-equipped kitchen enhanced by the bar area, center island and an extra-wide pantry. Multiple windows at the breakfast area and access to the rear yard add to the overall good feeling offered in this home. A second floor balcony overlooks the Great room and the open hall leads to a bedroom suite with private bath and two additional bedrooms with private access to a shared bath.

First floor — 1,710 sq. ft.
Second floor — 693 sq. ft.

Total living area: 2,403 sq. ft.

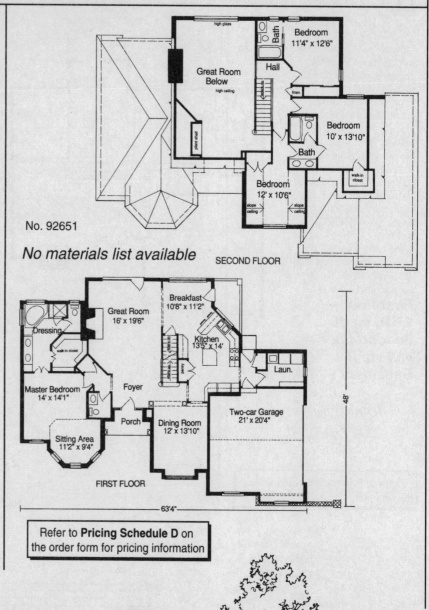

No. 92651

No materials list available

SECOND FLOOR

FIRST FLOOR

Refer to **Pricing Schedule D** on the order form for pricing information

BEAUTIFUL FAMILY HOME

Whatever the stage your growing family is in, this home can accommodate. If you have small children, you will appreciate all the bedrooms on the same floor and being close to the master suite. If the children are teenagers, the eating bar in the kitchen will be convenient for those endless snacks or meals on the run, and the family room will be a cozy place for all to relax. The mudroom entrance from the garage allows the dirt to be kept away from the living areas. A convenient half bath and laundry room flank the mudroom entry. The formal living room and dining room flow into each other making entertaining a snap. The wood deck expands your living space in the warmer weather. No materials list available for this plan.

First floor — 1,145 sq. ft.
Second Floor — 1,004 sq. ft.
Basement — 1,145 sq. ft.
Garage — 480 sq. ft.

Total living area: 2,149 sq. ft.

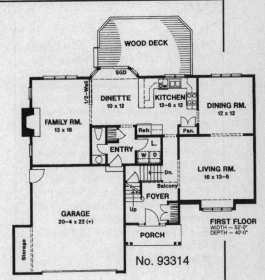

No. 93314

An
EXCLUSIVE DESIGN
By Patrick Morabito, A.I.A. Architect

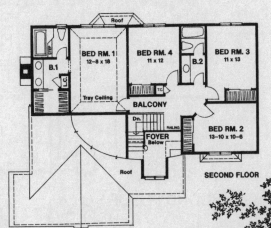

Refer to **Pricing Schedule C** on the order form for pricing information

Design 93816

COUNTRY ROMANCE

This plan features:

Three bedrooms, two full and one-half baths, an old-fashioned wrap-around porch, adding charm and romance to the elevation. An open layout adding a spacious feeling with a corner fireplace in the living room giving warmth and coziness to winter nights. You'll also find a formal dining room flowing from the living room, a cook top island kitchen with an eating bar and a breakfast nook for informal eating. The first floor master suite boasts a lovely double vanity bath with privacy. Two additional bedrooms on the second floor share use of a full bath in the hall.

**First floor —
1,546 sq. ft.
Second floor —
568 sq. ft.**

An
EXCLUSIVE DESIGN
By The Plan Centre

*Total living area:
2,114 sq. ft.*

Refer to **Pricing Schedule C** on
the order form for pricing information

56'-10"

58'-10"

2 CAR GARAGE
6.7 X 6.0
22⁶ X 19⁷

MUD/
LAUNDRY
3.2 X 4.0
10⁵ X 13⁷

BREAKFAST

KITCHEN
4.0 X 4.3
13⁴ X 14⁴

DINING ROOM
2.8 X 4.3
9' X 14³

ENSUITE

W.I.C.

CL.

MASTER SUITE
15⁶ X 11²
4.8 X 3.4

FOYER

LIVING ROOM
18⁴ X 18³
5.6 X 5.6

COVERED PORCH

FIRST FLOOR
No. 93816

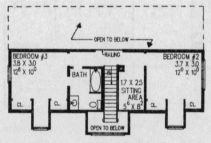

OPEN TO BELOW

RAILING

BEDROOM #3
3.8 X 3.0
12⁶ X 10⁰

BATH

1.7 X 2.5
SITTING
AREA
5⁶ X 8²

BEDROOM #2
3.7 X 3.0
12⁰ X 10⁰

CL.

CL.

CL.

CL.

OPEN TO BELOW

SECOND FLOOR

LUXURIOUS ONE LEVEL LIVING

From the attractive elevation, with a sheltered entrance, to the cozy family room, luxury and convenience abounds. The formal living room includes a focal point fireplace and access to the kitchen. The formal dining room is located across the hall from the living room and the kitchen. A breakfast bar, a work island, a double sink and an abundance of storage and counter space are featured in the kitchen. The dinette and the family room flow from the kitchen. A second fireplace and a built-in tv/stereo cabinet are included in the family room. Two secondary bedrooms are located to the far right of the home. One is equipped with a walk-in closet and they each have direct access to a three quarter bath. The master suite is privately located at the other end of the home. This plan is available with a slab foundation only. No materials list available.

Main floor — 3,254 sq. ft.
Garage — 588 sq. ft.

Total living area:
3,254 sq. ft.

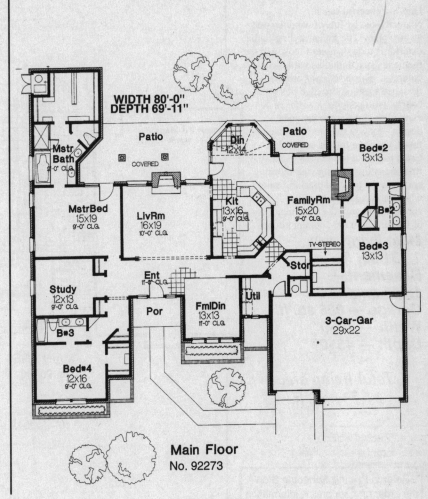

WIDTH 80'-0"
DEPTH 69'-11"

Patio
COVERED

Mstr Bath
8'-0" CLG.

Din
12x14

Patio
COVERED

Bed#2
13x13

MstrBed
15x19
9'-0" CLG.

LivRm
16x19
10'-0" CLG.

Kit
13x16
9'-0" CLG.

FamilyRm
15x20
9'-0" CLG.

B#2

TV-STEREO

Bed#3
13x13

Study
12x13
9'-0" CLG.

Ent
11'-0" CLG.

FmlDin
13x13
11'-0" CLG.

Stor

Util

B#3

Por

3-Car-Gar
29x22

Bed#4
12x16
9'-0" CLG.

Main Floor
No. 92273

Refer to **Pricing Schedule F** on
the order form for pricing information

SURROUNDED WITH SUNSHINE

Here's a cheerful rancher, characterized by lots of windows and an airy plan. The Italian styling of the exterior is today's hottest look, and the theme is carried indoors with tile and columns. This home was originally designed to sit on the edge of a golf course, with panoramic vistas in every direction, hence the open design. As you step into the spacious foyer, your eye travels across the Great room out to the view at the rear. Imagine sitting having your morning coffee in the turreted breakfast nook, while carrying on in happy conversation with the other members of the family in the adjacent kitchen.

Main living area — 1,731 sq. ft.
Basement — 1,715 sq. ft.
Garage — 888 sq. ft.
Width — 74'-0"
Depth — 45'-0"

Total living area: 1,731 sq. ft.

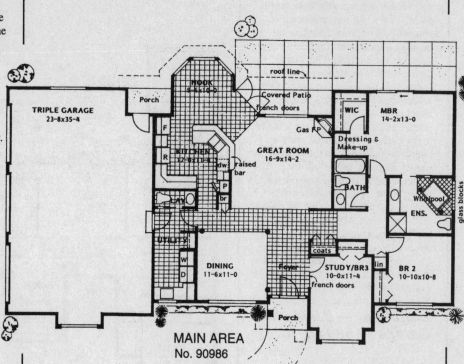

MAIN AREA
No. 90986

An
EXCLUSIVE DESIGN
By Westhome Planners, Ltd.

Refer to **Pricing Schedule B** on the order form for pricing information

A MAIN FLOOR MASTER RETREAT

Design 90992

A main floor master retreat makes this an ideal home for empty-nesters and families alike. From the most pleasant traditional styling to the great floor plan this versatile home will be hard to beat for livability and economy. A great family area at the rear, with an island kitchen and a gas fireplace for that cozy touch, creating a favorite gathering point for family and friends. Nearby is a handy utility room complete with a half bath. Both of these areas open onto a backyard patio. Upstairs there are two large bedrooms with closets and a spacious family bath, all accented with dormer windows.

First floor — 1,306 sq. ft.
Second floor —
647 sq. ft.
Garage — 504 sq. ft.
Width — 62'-0"
Depth — 35'-6"

Total living area:
1,953 sq. ft.

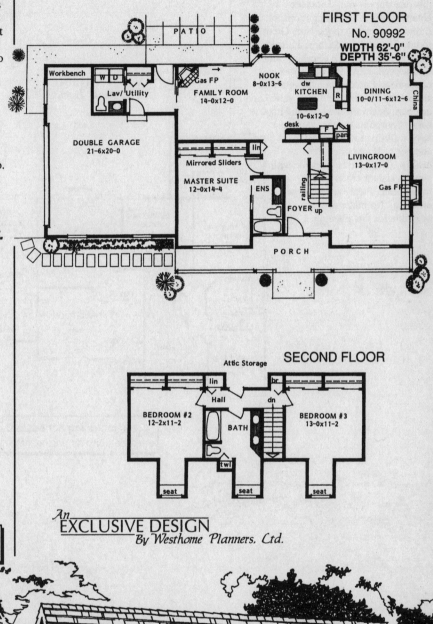

FIRST FLOOR
No. 90992
WIDTH 62'-0"
DEPTH 35'-6"

PATIO

Workbench

W D

Lav/ Utility

Gas FP

FAMILY ROOM
14-0x12-0

NOOK
8-0x13-6

dw KITCHEN

R

DINING
10-0/11-6x12-6

China

DOUBLE GARAGE
21-6x20-0

10-6x12-0

desk

F pan

LIVINGROOM
13-0x17-0

Mirrored Sliders

lin

MASTER SUITE
12-0x14-4

ENS

railing

FOYER up

Gas FP

PORCH

SECOND FLOOR

Attic Storage

lin

Hall

br

dn

BEDROOM #2
12-2x11-2

BATH

BEDROOM #3
13-0x11-2

twl

seat

seat

seat

An **EXCLUSIVE DESIGN**
By Westhome Planners, Ltd.

DIGNIFIED TRADITIONAL

Design 93049

Traditional composition distinguishes this one story home. Dramatic columns define the dining room and frame the entrance to the large Great room. The kitchen features a breakfast bar and an abundance of cabinet and counter space. All bedrooms are conveniently grouped on the opposite side of the home. The master suite has an enormous walk-in closet and luxury bath. Bedrooms two and three also have walk-in closets. A bath and another bedroom or study is nearby. This plan is available with either a slab or crawl space foundation. Please specify when ordering. No materials list available for this plan.

Main floor — 2,292 sq. ft.
Garage — 526 sq. ft.

Total living area:
2,292 sq. ft.

An EXCLUSIVE DESIGN
By Belk Home Designs

WIDTH 80-7

DEPTH 50-6

MSTR BATH

MASTER BEDROOM
14-0 X 15-0
10 FT CLG

BEDROOM 4 /STUDY
11-4 X 10-0
8 FT CLG

GREAT ROOM
16-10 X 16-10
12 FT CLG

BRKFST RM
12-6 X 10-6
10 FT CLG

FP

UTILITY
11-8 X 5-6

BATH 2

PWDR

FOYER
10 FT CLG

KITCHEN
12-6 X 16-10
10 FT CLG

GARAGE

BEDROOM 2
11-2 X 12-2
8 FT CLG

BEDROOM 3
12-4 X 11-8
8 FT CLG

PORCH

DINING ROOM
14-8 X 13-4
12 FT CLG

STORAGE

MAIN AREA
No. 93049

Refer to **Pricing Schedule D** on
the order form for pricing information

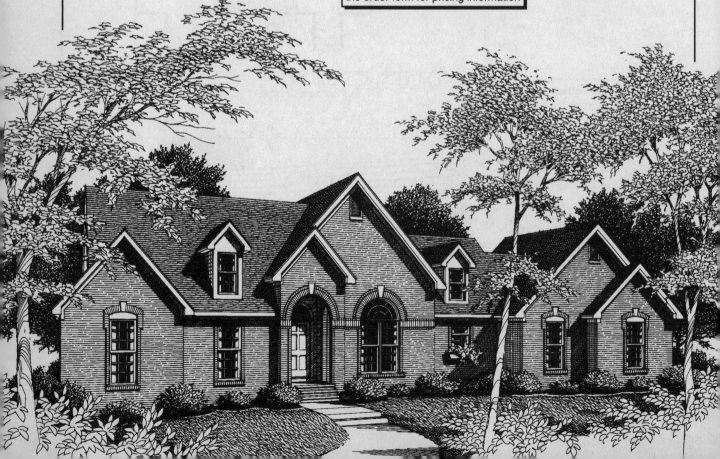

EXQUISITE ARCHITECTUAL DETAILS

The details of brick around the windows on the outside, the octagon ceiling in the dining room, the 10' foot ceilings, the vaulted ceilings, all these touches give an exquisite look to this home. The formal entry and gallery look through the impressive, vaulted, and fireplaced, living room to the back yard. The efficient, island kitchen/dinette opens to the vaulted family room that features a fireplace and wet bar. All the bedrooms have walk-in closets for ample storage space. The master suite has a vaulted ceiling and a sitting area. The master bath is spacious having all the amenities and two walk-in closets. A home designed for today's active family. No materials list available for this plan.

Main area — 3,292 sq. ft.

Total living area:
3,292 sq. ft.

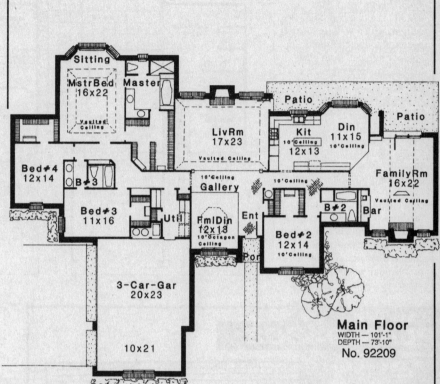

Main Floor
WIDTH — 101'-1"
DEPTH — 73'-10"

No. 92209

Refer to **Pricing Schedule F** on the order form for pricing information

IDEAL COURTYARD HOMES

These homes offer plenty of options for your living needs. If you need a three bedroom charmer, complete with two full baths, then plan #94302 is for you! Plan #94303 is a two bedroom, delight, with a walk-out master bedroom to the enormous outdoor terrace. Both plans feature a roomy fireplaced living room, with plenty of windows and access to the large outdoor terrace. The kitchen areas flow into the main living areas/dining rooms via a roomy four stool snackbar counter. Each plan offers a two-car garage, with access to the kitchen, and conveniently located laundry facilities in the bedroom wing. If outdoor living is a big part of your lifestyle, notice the enclosed service court which makes outdoor entertaining even more enjoyable.

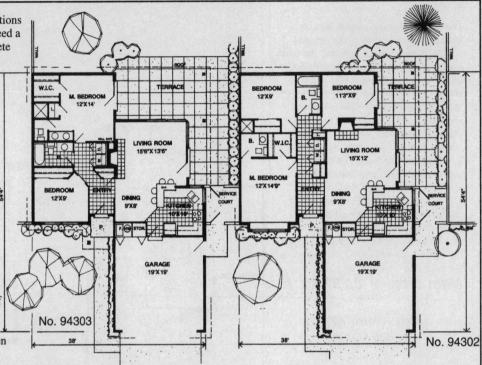

No. 94303   No. 94302

Refer to **Pricing Schedule A** on the order form for pricing information

PLAN 94302

Main floor — 1,137 sq. ft.
Garage — 390 sq. ft.

Total living area:
1,137 sq. ft.

No materials list available

PLAN 94303

Main floor — 1,013 sq. ft.
Garage — 390 sq. ft.

Total living area:
1,013 sq. ft.

GRACIOUS RANCH

Elegance surrounds you in this three bedroom ranch. The immense great room complete with fireplace, has high cathedral ceilings with large windows opening to the rear. Lovely arches open into the formal dining room. An open kitchen is a gourmet's dream with plenty of counter and cupboard space, including a large pantry and built-in desk. The luxurious master bedroom is highlighted by cathedral ceilings, two walk-in closets, tilted shower, whirlpool tub and double vanity. There is plenty of storage space in the large two stall garage. No materials list available.

**Main living area —
1,387 sq. ft.
Basement — 1,387 sq. ft.**

*Total living area:
1,387 sq. ft.*

Refer to **Pricing Schedule A** on the order form for pricing information

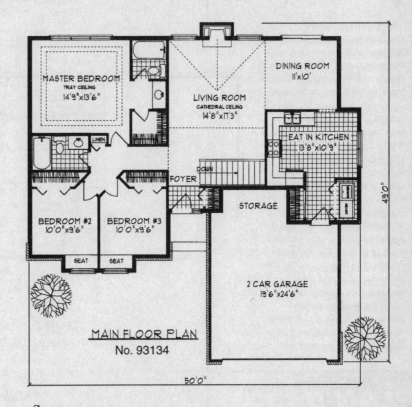

MASTER BEDROOM
TRAY CEILING
14'9"x13'6"

LIVING ROOM
CATHEDRAL CEILING
14'8"x17'3"

DINING ROOM
11'x10'

LINEN

EAT IN KITCHEN
13'8"x10'9"

BEDROOM #2
10'0"x9'6"

BEDROOM #3
10'0"x9'6"

SEAT

SEAT

FOYER

DOWN

STORAGE

2 CAR GARAGE
19'6"x24'6"

49'0"

50'0"

MAIN FLOOR PLAN
No. 93134

An
EXCLUSIVE DESIGN
By Ahmann Design

CHARMING SOUTHERN TRADITIONAL

This charming southern traditional styled home has all the features and looks of a much larger home. The covered front porch with its striking columns, brick quoins, and dentil moulding add a rich elegance to this stately design. Entering the foyer we find the spacious Great Room with its vaulted ceilings and fireplace as well as built in cabinets. The dining room is open to the Great Room which opens up to the whole middle of the plan. The utility room is adjacent to the kitchen and this leads to the two - car garage with its storage rooms. To the right of the foyer is the bedroom wing with bedrooms two and three having their own walk-in closets and a hall bath to serve them. The master bedroom is located to the rear of the hall and features a large walk-in closet and compartmentalized bath.

Total living area: 1,271 sq. ft.

63'-10"

38'-10"

GARAGE
21'-0"x21'-0"

KITCHEN
12'-0"x9'-0"

DINING
11'-0"x11'-0"

MASTER BEDROOM
14'-0"x12'-0"

CLO

BATH#1

UTILITY
6'-6"x7'-7"

CLO

BATH#2

GREAT ROOM
15'-6"x16'-0"

STORAGE
6'-6"x10'-5"

CLO

HALL

BEDROOM#2
11'-0"x11'-0"

PORCH
20'-10"x5'-0"

BEDROOM#3
11'-0"x11'-0"

CLO

MAIN FLOOR
No. 92503

**Main living area — 1,271 sq. ft.
Garage — 506 sq. ft.**

Refer to **Pricing Schedule A** on the order form for pricing information

TODAY'S LIFESTYLE

Design 93253

A modern family needs a floor plan that takes today's lifestyle into consideration. The formal areas of this home are located in the front. The family room includes a fireplace and access to the patio. A breakfast area flows directly into the family room. The well-appointed kitchen includes an eating bar, double sinks, built-in pantry and an abundance of counter and cabinet space. The master suite is situated to make it a private area. A decorative ceiling and private bath add to the room's elegance and conveniences. Three additional bedrooms are located at the far end of the house and share a full bath. No materials list available for this plan.

Main floor — 2,542 sq. ft.
Garage — 510 sq. ft.

Total living area:
2,542 sq. ft.

Refer to **Pricing Schedule D** on the order form for pricing information

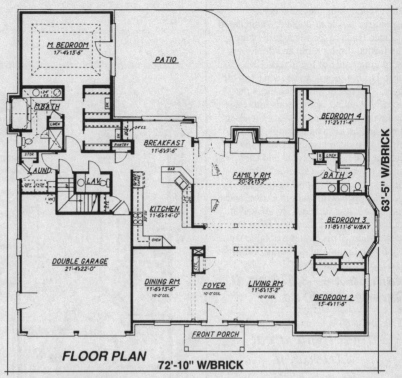

FLOOR PLAN

No. 93253

72'-10" W/BRICK

63'-5" W/BRICK

M. BEDROOM
17'-4x13'-6"

PATIO

BEDROOM 4
11'-2x11'-4"

M BATH

BREAKFAST
11'-6x9'-6"

BATH 2

LINEN

PANTRY

FAMILY RM.
20'-2x15'2"

BEDROOM 3
11'-8x11'-6" W/BAY

LAUND

LAV

KITCHEN
11'-6x14'-0"

BAR

OVEN

DOUBLE GARAGE
21'-4x22'-0"

DINING RM.
11'-6x13'-6"
10'-0 CEIL.

FOYER
10'-0 CEIL.

LIVING RM.
11'-6x13'-2"
10'-0 CEIL.

BEDROOM 2
15'-4x11'-6"

FRONT PORCH

An
EXCLUSIVE DESIGN
By Jannis Vann & Associates, Inc.

A DISTINCTIVELY UNIQUE HOME

Design 92279

This eye-catching elevation is as impressive inside as outside. A sheltered entrance leads to the foyer/gallery area. The formal dining room and the library are to either side of the foyer. The formal living room can be seen from the foyer. A large fireplace enhances the room. A vaulted ceiling adds interest to the lavish master suite. A large walk-in closet and an ultra bath complete this retreat. An open layout between the kitchen, the breakfast room and the family room create a spacious, airy feeling. Three additional bedrooms, each equipped with walk-in closets and easy access to a full bath are located at the opposite end of the home from the master suite. This plan is available with a slab foundation only. No materials list is available for this plan.

Main floor — 3,079 sq. ft.
Garage — 630 sq. ft.

Total living area:
3,079 sq. ft.

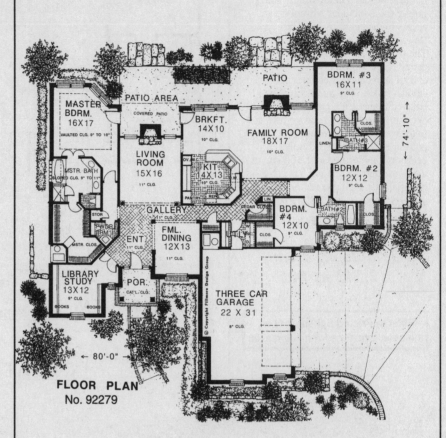

FLOOR PLAN
No. 92279

Refer to **Pricing Schedule E** on the order form for pricing information

WINDOWS ADD DISTINCTION

The windows of this home give it character and distinction. The formal areas are located at the front of the home. The living room and the dining room enjoy the natural light from the bayed windows. The expansive family room is enhanced by a fireplace and view of the rear yard. A U-shaped kitchen efficiently serves the dining room and the breakfast bay. Both the breakfast bay the the family room have access to the patio. The master suite is elegantly crowned by a decorative ceiling. The private master bath offers a garden tub and a step-in shower. Two large additional bedrooms share a full hall bath. There is a convenient second floor laundry center. No materials list available for this plan.

First floor — 1,126 sq. ft.
Second floor — 959 sq. ft.
Basement — 458 sq. ft.
Garage — 627 sq. ft.

Total living area: 2,085 sq. ft.

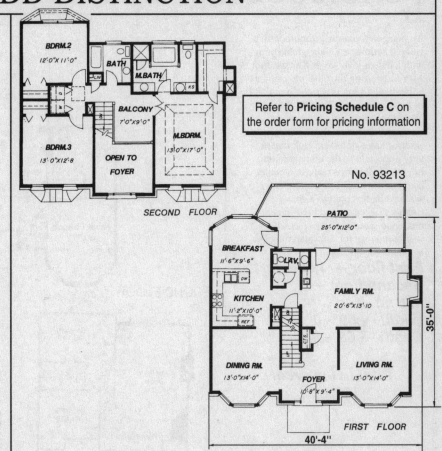

Refer to **Pricing Schedule C** on the order form for pricing information

SECOND FLOOR

BDRM.2 12'0"X11'0"
BATH
M.BATH
BALCONY 7'0"X9'0"
M.BDRM. 13'0"X17'0"
BDRM.3 13'0"X12'8
OPEN TO FOYER
LIN

No. 93213

FIRST FLOOR

PATIO 25'0"X12'0"
BREAKFAST 11'6"X9'6"
LAV.
KITCHEN 11'2"X10'0"
DW
REF.
FAMILY RM. 20'6"X13'10
DINING RM. 13'0"X14'0"
FOYER 10'8"X9'4"
LIVING RM. 13'0"X14'0"
40'-4"
35'-0"

An
EXCLUSIVE DESIGN
By Jannis Vann & Associates, Inc.

LUXURIOUS IN A MODERATE SIZE

Design 92610

An octagonal master bedroom with a vaulted ceiling, a sunken great room with a balcony above, and an exterior with an exciting roof line provide this home with all the luxurious amenities in a moderate size. The first floor master bedroom targets this home to the empty nester market. The elegant exterior has a rich solid look that is very important to the discriminating buyer. The kitchen features a center island and a breakfast nook. The sunken Great room has a cozy fireplace. Elegant and luxurious in a moderate size, this home has what you're looking for. No materials list available for this plan.

First floor — 1,626 sq. ft.
Second floor — 475 sq. ft.
Width — 59' - 0"
Depth — 60' - 8"

Total living area: 2,101 sq. ft.

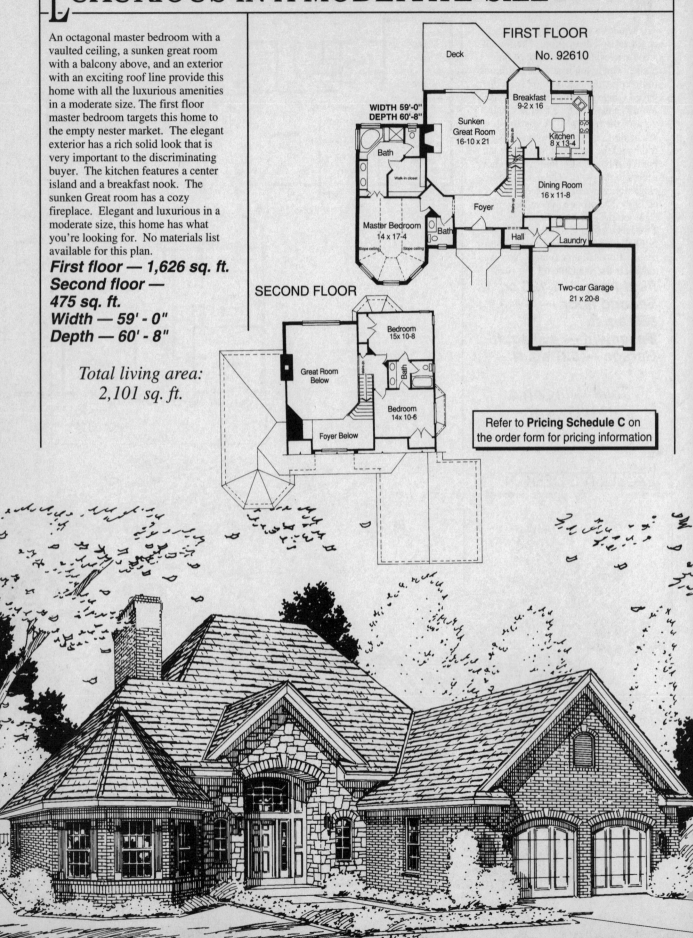

FIRST FLOOR
No. 92610

Deck

WIDTH 59'-0"
DEPTH 60'-8"

Breakfast
9-2 x 16

Sunken
Great Room
16-10 x 21

Kitchen
8 x 13-4

Bath

Walk-in closet

Dining Room
16 x 11-8

Foyer

Master Bedroom
14 x 17-4

Bath

Slope ceiling   Slope ceiling

Hall

Laundry

Two-car Garage
21 x 20-8

SECOND FLOOR

Great Room
Below

Bedroom
15 x 10-8

Bath

Bedroom
14 x 10-6

Foyer Below

Refer to **Pricing Schedule C** on the order form for pricing information

ENHANCED BY A COLUMNED PORCH

The porch on this home is reminiscent of times gone by. Yet, this home is anything but old-fashioned. The Great room uses a modern decorative ceiling along with the fireplace. The amenities in the efficient kitchen/breakfast area will please the cook of your household. A dining room is available for formal entertaining. A private retreat, the master bedroom, has a master bath and walk-in closet. Walk-in closets are included in both bedrooms located at the other side of the house. A full bath is located in close proximity to both bedrooms. A garage, an additional storage area and a utility room complete this plan.

Main living area — 1,754 sq. ft.
Garage & storage — 552 sq. ft.
Porch — 236 sq. ft.

Total living area: 1,754 sq. ft.

Refer to **Pricing Schedule B** on the order form for pricing information

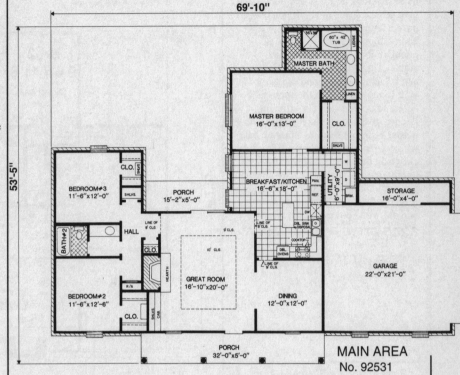

69'-10"

53'-5"

MASTER BATH

MASTER BEDROOM
16'-0"x13'-0"

CLO.

BEDROOM #3
11'-6"x12'-0"

CLO.

PORCH
15'-2"x5'-0"

BREAKFAST/KITCHEN
16'-6"x18'-0"

UTILITY

STORAGE
16'-0"x4'-0"

BATH #2

HALL

CLO.

GREAT ROOM
16'-10"x20'-0"

GARAGE
22'-0"x21'-0"

BEDROOM #2
11'-6"x12'-6"

DINING
12'-0"x12'-0"

PORCH
32'-0"x5'-0"

MAIN AREA
No. 92531

ROOM FOR MORE

Family vacations are memories in the making. This home will help to make those precious times. Three bedrooms give private space to all. If you don't have a large family, make one bedroom into a study or maybe a hobby room; the possibilities are yours. The living room has a fireplace and is large and open and can extend your living area out of the home with access to two decks. The efficient kitchen opens to the dining area. The master bedroom features a private bath with corner tub. There are also two closets in this room. Looking forward to retirement? This home may be what you are looking for. All the living area is on one floor, yet it is spacious and laid out with convenience in mind.

Main area — 1,127 sq. ft.

Total living area:
1,127 sq. ft.

Refer to **Pricing Schedule A** on the order form for pricing information

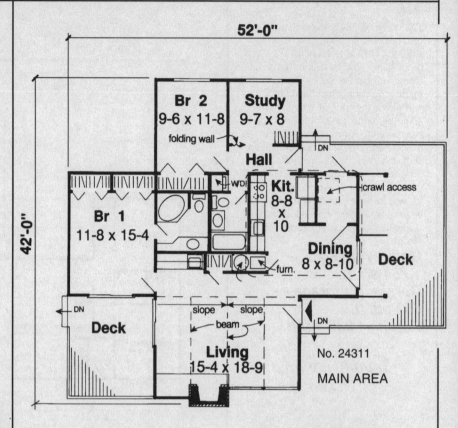

An EXCLUSIVE DESIGN
By Marshall Associates

Basement Option

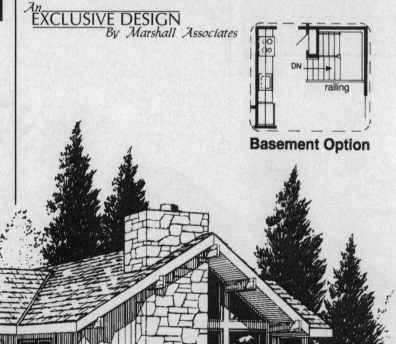

SLIGHT WESTERN TOUCH

Enter this home through a covered porch. The use of a vaulted ceiling in the den area gives this home a spacious feel at the onset. The well-equipped kitchen has ample counter and storage space and flows easily into the eating area. The master bedroom is enhanced by the decorative ceiling and private master bath. The two additional bedrooms are of good size and have use of a full hall bath. A carport, additional storage space and a handy utility room with laundry area complete this plan.

**Main living area —
1,203 sq. ft.
Garage — 400 sq. ft.
Porch — 170 sq. ft.**

*Total living area:
1,203 sq. ft.*

Refer to **Pricing Schedule A** on the order form for pricing information

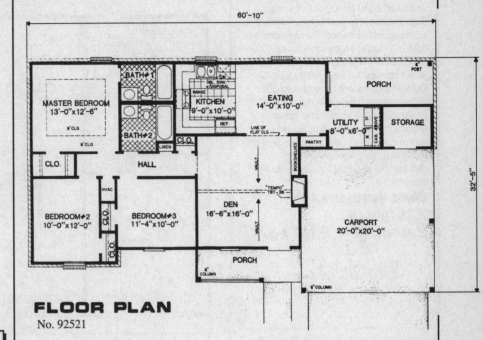

FLOOR PLAN
No. 92521

ASTONISHING THREE BEDROOM

This home features the convenience of one-floor living with the elegance you usually find in houses of larger square footage. The living room is highlighted by a cozy gas log fireplace and a cathedral ceiling. The formal dining room is accented by an arched entrance and crowned in a cathedral ceiling. You'll enjoy an evening retreat to the spacious master suite with cathedral ceiling, walk-in closet, and an open vanity. The two smaller bedrooms each have a large wall length closet. The efficient eat-in kitchen has ample counter space and lots of cupboards; and is convenient to main floor laundry and two stall garage. No material list available for this plan.

**Main living area —
2,161 sq. ft.
Basement — 2,161 sq. ft.**

*Total living area:
2,161 sq. ft.*

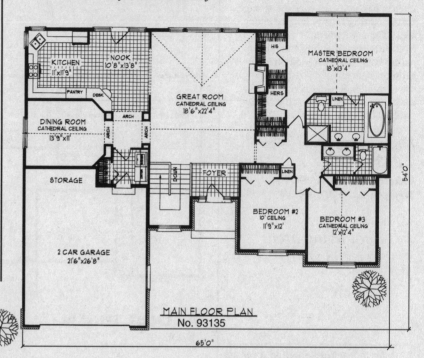

An
EXCLUSIVE DESIGN
By Ahmann Design

KITCHEN
11'x11'9"

NOOK
10'8"x13'8"

PANTRY DESK

DINING ROOM
CATHEDRAL CEILING
13'9"x11'

STORAGE

2 CAR GARAGE
21'6"x26'8"

GREAT ROOM
CATHEDRAL CEILING
18'6"x22'4"

HIS

HERS

ARCH

ARCH ARCH

DN

FOYER

LINEN

MASTER BEDROOM
CATHEDRAL CEILING
18'x13'4"

LINEN

BEDROOM #2
10' CEILING
11'9"x12'

BEDROOM #3
CATHEDRAL CEILING
12'x12'4"

54'0"

65'0"

MAIN FLOOR PLAN
No. 93135

Refer to **Pricing Schedule C** on the order form for pricing information

ELEGANT LUXURY

Design 92288

A two-story entrance hall, dominated by a cascading staircase give an immediate first impression of luxury. The sunken living room gives formal entertaining a cozy atmosphere. The formal dining room is across the entry hall from the living room. A fireplace, built-in shelves and a cathedral ceiling accent the study. A vaulted ceiling crowns the lavish master suite. A skylight, double vanity, whirlpool tub and a separate shower are featured in the master bath. A double walk-in closet provides extensive storage space. A second fireplace enhances the two-story family room which is open to the kitchen and breakfast room. Three additional bedrooms, all with private access to a full bath and walk-in closets, are located on the second floor.

First floor — 2,736 sq. ft.
Second floor — 1,276 sq. ft.

Total living area:
4,012 sq. ft.

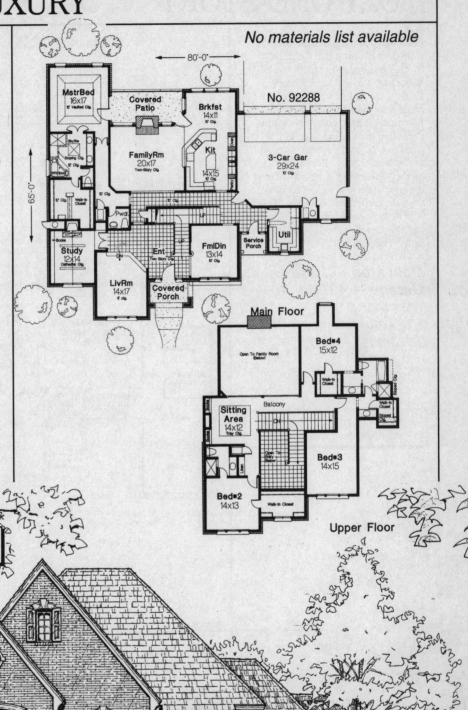

Refer to **Pricing Schedule F** on the order form for pricing information

COZY ONE-STORY

Design 92705

Enter this home through the covered front door entrance into the raised foyer. The large living room has built-in bookshelves and French doors flanking the fireplace. The dining room, conveniently placed off the foyer and kitchen, enjoys the natural light from the decorative front windows. There is a breakfast nook for informal eating. For added privacy, the master suite is located at the opposite end of the house away from the secondary bedrooms. Take note of the interesting ceiling details and private master bath in the master suite. The secondary bedrooms share a full bath located between them.

Main area — 1,849 sq. ft.
Garage — 437 sq. ft.

Total living area:
1,849 sq. ft.

Refer to **Pricing Schedule C** on the order form for pricing information

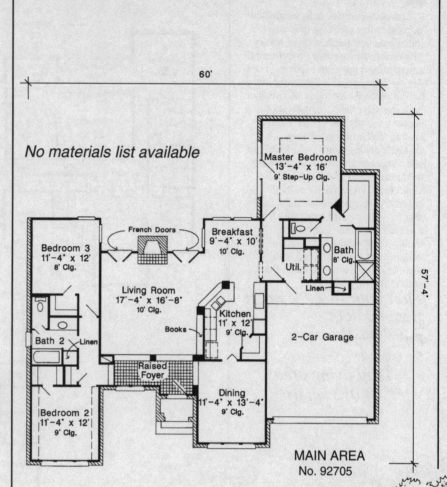

No materials list available

MAIN AREA
No. 92705

DISTINGUISHED STYLING

A home designed for today's lifestyle. Formal areas are located to either side of the foyer. A decor ceiling accents the elegant dining room. Bay windows allow for natural illumination and further enhance the living and dining rooms. An open layout between the kitchen and the breakfast area provides an open, airy atmosphere to this spacious family living area. Amenities abound in the kitchen. A center work island/snack bar, a walk-in pantry and ample storage and workspace have been included. The family room includes a cozy fireplace and flows easily from the breakfast room. The sleeping quarters are located on the second floor. The grand master suite is crowned by a vaulted ceiling and includes a compartmented, luxurious bath. Two additional bedrooms and an office share the full, double vanity bath in the hall. No materials list available for this plan.

First floor — 1,377 sq. ft.
Second floor — 1,264 sq. ft.
Basement — 1,316 sq. ft.

Total living area: 2,641 sq. ft.

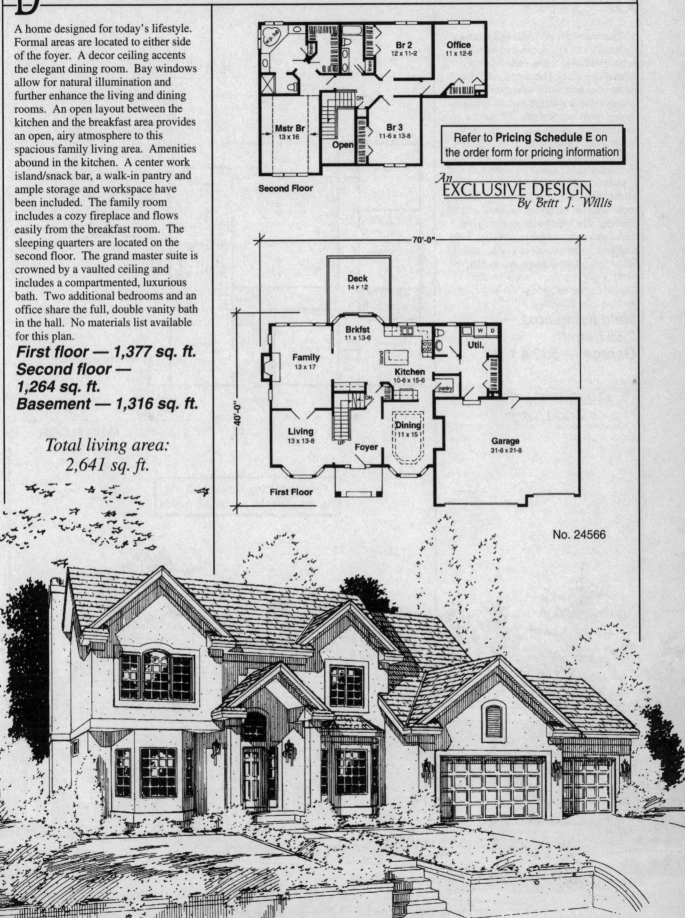

Second Floor

Br 2
12 x 11-2

Office
11 x 12-6

Mstr Br
13 x 16

Open

Br 3
11-6 x 13-8

Refer to **Pricing Schedule E** on the order form for pricing information

An EXCLUSIVE DESIGN
By Britt J. Willis

70'-0"

40'-0"

Deck
14 x 12

Brkfst
11 x 13-6

Family
13 x 17

Kitchen
10-6 x 15-6

island

pantry

W D

Util.

Living
13 x 13-8

UP

DN.

Foyer

Dining
11 x 15

Garage
31-8 x 21-8

First Floor

No. 24566

CLASSIC LOUISIANA COTTAGE

Design 92509

The combination of stucco and brick on the exterior of this home lend an air of sophistication to the already fine lined formal elegance. The oversized living room is located to the left of the entrance foyer with the equally spacious dining room on the right. To the rear of the dining room you will find the very large country kitchen with it's breakfast bar and adjoining breakfast room. This huge kitchen is packed with cabinets and appliances. To the left of the kitchen/breakfast area is the large Great room with its' brick fireplace and ample cabinets. The split bedroom plan gives the master suite complete privacy. This master suite has a vaulted ceiling, doors to the rear covered porch and an alcoved bath. The other three bedrooms are located on the left side of the house, two with walk-in closets.

Main living area — 2,551 sq. ft.
Garage — 532 sq. ft.

Total living area: 2,551 sq. ft.

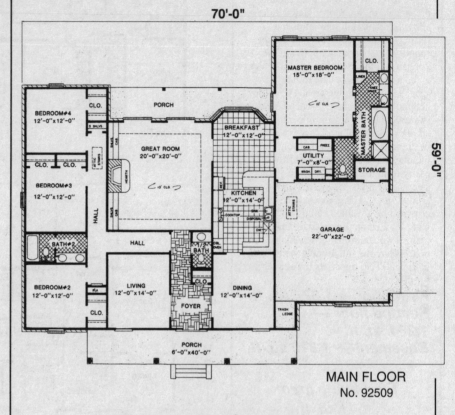

MAIN FLOOR
No. 92509

Refer to **Pricing Schedule D** on the order form for pricing information

TRADITIONAL BRICK ELEVATION

This lovely home features a traditional brick elevation and an inside design packed with all the luxuries normally seen in a larger home. The foyer, with angled stair, opens to a gallery leading to both the living room and the nearby formal dining room. Spacious, two-story ceilings are used in the living, dining, and family rooms. A corner fireplace serves the kitchen, breakfast room and family room, and gives the area a cozy feel. A see-through fireplace between the master bedroom and bath adds a dramatic touch to the master suite. Three bedrooms and a bath complete the upstairs. No materials list available for this plan.

First floor — 1,910 sq. ft.
Second floor — 834 sq. ft.
Garage — 489 sq. ft.

Total living area: 2,744 sq. ft.

Refer to **Pricing Schedule E** on the order form for pricing information

An
EXCLUSIVE DESIGN
By Belk Home Designs

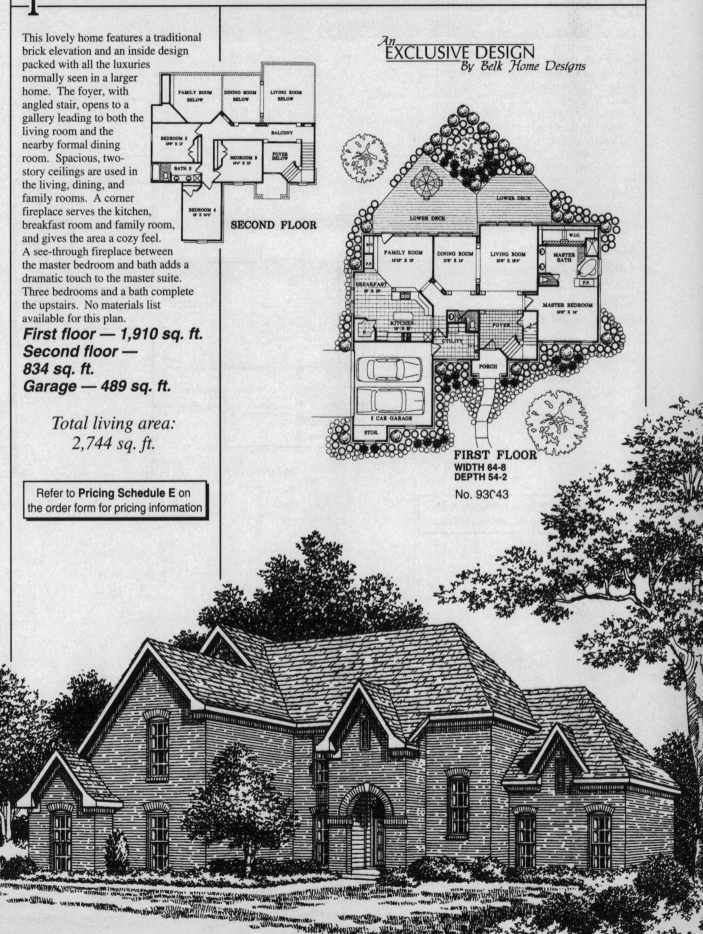

SECOND FLOOR

FIRST FLOOR
WIDTH 64-8
DEPTH 54-2

No. 93043

SECLUDED MASTER SUITE

This convenient one-level design offers a secluded master suite with a luxurious master bath. Notice that the additional bedrooms are located on the other side of the house. This makes a nice sound barrier for parents of teenagers. The kitchen is well-equipped and makes use of a peninsula counter for an eating bar and additional work space. The open layout between the kitchen, breakfast area and Great room gives a feeling of space. There is a dining room for formal entertaining. Two additional bedrooms have access to a full hall bath. With ample storage space and a garage, this plan is sure to please.

**Main living area —
1,680 sq. ft.
Garage & Storage —
538 sq. ft.
Porch — 24 sq. ft.**

*Total living area:
1,680 sq. ft.*

66'-10"

44'-10"

CLO.

MASTER BEDROOM
13'-0"x16'-0"

KNEE SPACE

MASTER BATH

60"x42" TUB

BEDROOM #3
11'-0"x12'-0"

CLO.

LINEN

SHLVS
CABINETS

HEARTH

BREAKFAST
11'-0"x9'-6"

VAULT

UTILITY
6'-0"x6'-0"

WASH
DRYER

SHLVS

STORAGE
12'-0"x4'-0"

BATH #2

LINEN

HALL

SHLVS
CABINETS

R/A

GREAT ROOM
17'-0"x16'-0"

VAULT

DBL OVEN

COOKTOP

KITCHEN
11'-0"x12'-6"

DBL SINK w/DISPOSAL

DW

BEDROOM #2
11'-0"x12'-6"

CLO.

CLO.

FOYER
6'-0"x8'-0"

DINING
12'-0"x12'-0"

REF

GARAGE
22'-0"x22'-0"

PORCH

MAIN AREA
No. 92527

Refer to **Pricing Schedule B** on the order form for pricing information

FOR THE FIRST TIME BUYER

This compact plan is perfect for the first time home buyer. Inside, the family room features a corner fireplace. The efficiently designed kitchen has a corner sink with windows. The master suite includes a large walk-in closet. Two additional bedrooms, each with a walk-in closet, and a bath complete the home. This plan is available with either a slab or crawl space foundation. Please specify when ordering. No materials list available for this plan.

Main living area — 1,310 sq. ft.
Garage — 449 sq. ft.

Total living area: 1,310 sq. ft.

Refer to **Pricing Schedule A** on the order form for pricing information

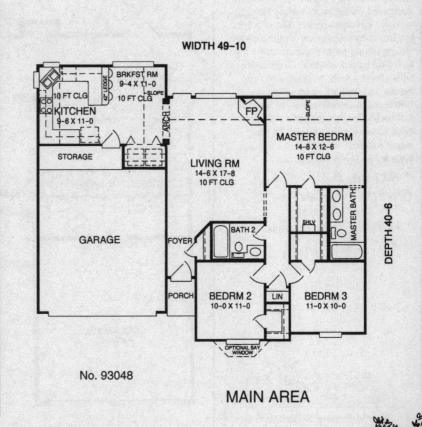

WIDTH 49-10

BRKFST RM
9-4 X 11-0
10 FT CLG

42" LEDGE

10 FT CLG

KITCHEN
9-6 X 11-0

STORAGE

ARCH

FP

SLOPE

MASTER BEDRM
14-8 X 12-6
10 FT CLG

LIVING RM
14-6 X 17-8
10 FT CLG

GARAGE

FOYER

BATH 2

SHLV

MASTER BATH

DEPTH 40-6

PORCH

BEDRM 2
10-0 X 11-0

LIN

BEDRM 3
11-0 X 10-0

OPTIONAL BAY WINDOW

No. 93048

MAIN AREA

An EXCLUSIVE DESIGN
By Belk Home Designs

VARIED ROOFLINE ADDS INTEREST

Come in out of the rain through the sheltered entrance of this stylish three bedroom. Once in the foyer, your eyes are drawn to the glowing fire of the fireplaced living room, adding not only warmth, but atmosphere. The efficient kitchen conveniently serves the elegant formal dining room accentuated by a beautiful bayed window. The master suite sports a walk-in closet and private master bath. The secondary bedrooms have easy access to the hall full bath. The screen porch and wood deck add to the living space in the warm weather.

Main living area — 1,642 sq. ft.
Garage — 2-car

Total living area: 1,642 sq. ft.

WIDTH 57'-0"
DEPTH 66'-0"

SCREEN PORCH
15'-0" x 17'-0"

WOOD DECK

DINING ROOM
17'-0" x 14'-0"

LIVING ROOM
16'-0" x 19'-0"

MASTER BEDROOM
14'-0" x 15'-0"

KITCHEN
11'-0" x 13'-0"

FOYER

BEDROOM #3
11'-0" x 10'-0"

BEDROOM #2
17'-0" x 13'-0"

2 CAR GARAGE
23'-0" x 24'-0"

MAIN FLOOR
No. 93100

Refer to **Pricing Schedule B** on the order form for pricing information

An
EXCLUSIVE DESIGN
By Ahmann Design Inc.

ATTRACTIVE GABLED DESIGN

This attractive gable has boxed front windows and uses a mixture of brick and siding giving it great curb appeal. The large spacious floor plan gives a good feeling upon entering the home. Standing in the entry you can look into the cathedral ceiling living room at the cozy fire in the fireplace. Or, maybe, your guests would like to enjoy the outdoors on your large covered patio. The island kitchen has cornerwindows surrounding the sink area. The master bedroom features its own master bath. The two additional bedrooms share a bath. No materials list is available for this plan..

Main living area — 1,830 sq. ft.
Garage — 440 sq. ft.

Total living area: 1,830 sq. ft.

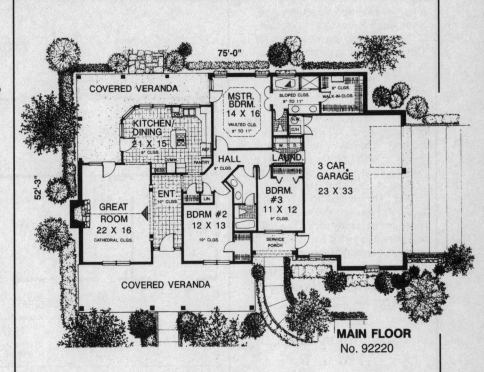

MAIN FLOOR
No. 92220

Refer to **Pricing Schedule C** on the order form for pricing information

TERRIFIC FRONT PORCH

If you are looking for a country type home with a few extra touches, this may be the house you are looking for. The country feeling comes from the front porch. Those extra touches abound in the expansive living area with a fireplace, the two front bedrooms that enjoy bay windows and the sunny breakfast area that includes a built-in pantry and access to the rear sun deck. The master suite provides the owner with a private retreat. The master bath includes a walk-in closet, oval tub, double vanity and separate shower. The two additional bedrooms are located on the opposite side of the house and have easy access to a full hall bath. The added convenience of a main floor laundry is included.

Main floor — 1,778 sq. ft.
Basement — 1,008 sq. ft.
Garage — 728 sq. ft.

Total living area:
1,778 sq. ft.

Refer to **Pricing Schedule B** on the order form for pricing information

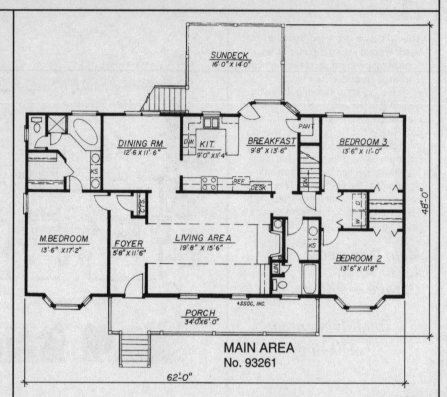

MAIN AREA
No. 93261

An EXCLUSIVE DESIGN
By Jannis Vann & Associates, Inc.

EMPTY-NESTERS OR THOSE WITH TEENS

The 2-story foyer is naturally lighted by an arched dormer window within the ceiling. To the left of the foyer is a sunken Great room with a cathedral ceiling and stone fireplace. The octagonal dining room features dramatic angular views. The first floor master bedroom, with walk-in closet and master bath, is perfect for empty-nesters or families with teenagers. The house can be constructed as a 3 bedroom plan comprising 2,069 sq. ft. of living space or additional living space can be provided in the bonus room. No materials list available.

First floor — 1,557 sq. ft.
Second floor — 512 sq. ft.
Optional bonus — 280 sq. ft.

Total living area: 2,069 sq. ft.

Refer to **Pricing Schedule C** on the order form for pricing information

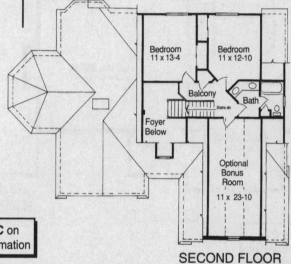

FIRST FLOOR

No. 92608

SECOND FLOOR

Design 93107

AN AFFORDABLE BRICK HOME

This affordable brick home will greet your family with coziness and charm. The family will love gathering around the fireplace in the living room and the open plan lets everyone stay in touch no matter which room they are in.

You will enjoy the coziness of the bedroom wing to the left, which offers a large master suite, complete with a walk-in closet and double vanity. No materials list available for this plan.

**Main living area —
1,868 sq. ft.
Basement — 1,868 sq. ft.
Garage — 782 sq. ft.**

*Total living area:
1,868 sq. ft.*

**WIDTH 72'-0"
DEPTH 42'-4"**

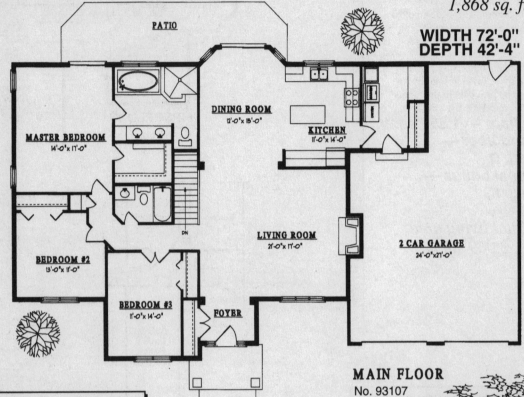

PATIO

DINING ROOM
12'-0" x 13'-0"

KITCHEN
11'-0" x 14'-0"

MASTER BEDROOM
14'-0" x 17'-0"

LIVING ROOM
21'-0" x 17'-0"

2 CAR GARAGE
24'-0" x 27'-0"

BEDROOM #2
13'-0" x 11'-0"

BEDROOM #3
11'-0" x 14'-0"

FOYER

DN

MAIN FLOOR
No. 93107

Refer to **Pricing Schedule C** on the order form for pricing information

An
EXCLUSIVE DESIGN
By Ahmann Design Inc.

COMFORTABLE WITH STYLE

An attractive front elevation with a covered porch entrance leads into a formal living room/dining room combination, crowned by a vaulted ceiling and enhanced by a fireplace. A well-appointed kitchen, including an angled peninsula counter, is open to both the nook and the family room. An optional fireplace in the family room would add coziness to this informal living area. The second floor master suite is topped by a vaulted ceiling and equipped with a spa tub, double sink and a compartmented shower and water closet. Two additional bedrooms share a full bath in the hallway.

First floor — 913 sq. ft.
Second floor — 813 sq. ft.

Total living area: 1,726 sq. ft.

Refer to **Pricing Schedule B** on the order form for pricing information

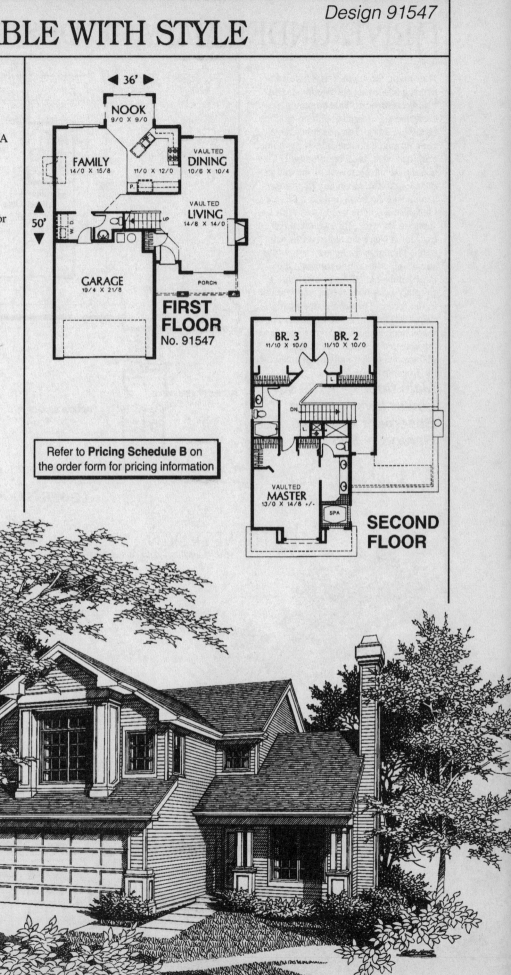

DRIVE-UNDER GARAGE DESIGN

A growing family in today's world needs a home that can accommodate future expansion. This home will easily be able to grow with your family's needs. The bedrooms have been arranged on one side of the home. Families with small children will appreciate the closeness of the master bedroom to the secondary bedrooms. The master bedroom enjoys a private bath with a double vanity, oval tub and separate shower. The two secondary bedrooms share the use of a full hall bath. The large living area enjoys the streaming natural light through the large, multi-paned, front window. A fireplace adds atmosphere and warmth to the room. The dining area flows from the kitchen and living area. A wood deck adds to the living space in the warmer weather. A future playroom and full bath are planned for the lower level.

Main floor — 1,269 sq. ft.
Lower level — 56 sq. ft.
Basement — 382 sq. ft.
Garage — 598 sq. ft.

Total living area:
1,325 sq. ft.

FLOOR PLAN
No. 93265

Refer to **Pricing Schedule A** on the order form for pricing information

No materials list available

DECK
14.0 x 10.0

KITCHEN
8.0 x 9.6

DINING
10.0 x 9.6

M.BATH

M. BEDROOM
14.0 x 14.0

PLANT SHELF

LIVING AREA
14.8 x 15.6

BDRM-3
9.4 x 11.6

BDRM-2
10.4 x 9.6

ENTRY

45'-0"

30'-0"

FUTURE PLAYROOM
15.0 x 22.8

DOUBLE GARAGE
22.0 x 26.0

LOWER FLOOR

An
EXCLUSIVE DESIGN
By Jannis Vann & Associates, Inc.

PERFECT FOR A WALK-OUT LOT

This two-story will be perfect for your walk-out lot. The covered entry leads into the open living room featuring a three-way gas fireplace separating the dining area. The private master bedroom has a large walk-in closet and a large master bath with a corner whirlpool and a separate shower. Upstairs there are two more bedrooms, each having direct access to the full bath. A third half bath is found near the first floor laundry. The lower level can easily be made into a fitness/recreation area or a theater room. No materials list available

First floor — 1,168 sq. ft.
Second floor — 494 sq. ft.
Basement — 1,168 sq. ft.

An
EXCLUSIVE DESIGN
By Ahmann Design

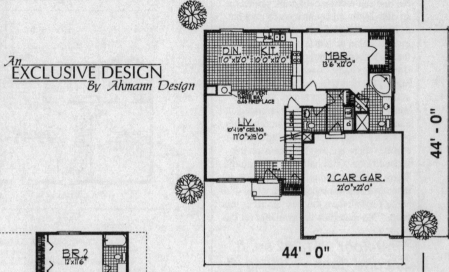

MAIN FLOOR PLAN
No. 93138

Total living area:
1,662 sq. ft.

Refer to **Pricing Schedule B** on the order form for pricing information

Design 93212

OLD-FASHIONED MODERN TOUCHES

No one can resist a cool drink served on an old-fashioned country porch on a hot day. A country-style porch and dormers give this plan an old-fashioned country feel. The large living room has a cozy fireplace to gather around on a winter's night. There is a formal dining room and an informal breakfast room. The U-shaped kitchen is efficiently arranged and has ample work space. The master suite offers a private master bath and a walk-in closet. There are two bedrooms on the second floor, a full hall bath and a study. There is even a bonus room to decide on later. An old-fashioned country feel with some very modern touches describes this home. No materials list available for this plan.

First floor — 1,362 sq. ft.
Second floor — 729 sq. ft.
Bonus room — 384 sq. ft.
Basement — 988 sq. ft.
Garage — 559 sq. ft.
Porch — 396 sq. ft.

Total living are:
2,091 sq. ft.

Refer to **Pricing Schedule C** on the order form for pricing information

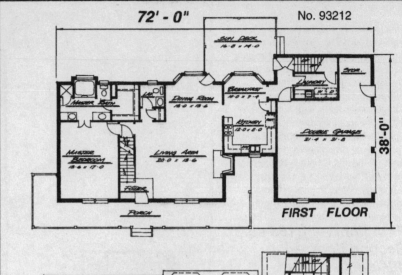

72' - 0"   No. 93212

38' - 0"

FIRST FLOOR

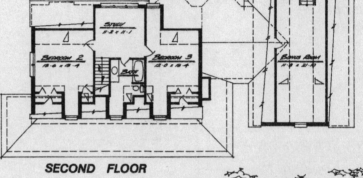

SECOND FLOOR

No materials list available

An EXCLUSIVE DESIGN
By Jannis Vann & Associates, Inc.

INFLUENCED BY YESTERYEAR

Design 24404

A country wrap-around porch gives the visitor an impression of times gone by, yet on the inside, the conveniences of today's lifestyle are apparent. The foyer area includes a coat closet. A tray ceiling adds elegance to the formal dining room. Double doors lead the way from the dining room into the huge kitchen. A center island/snack bar and built-in planning desk are just two of the many conveniences in the efficient kitchen. A large fireplace at the far end of the expansive family room serves as a warm focal point. A vaulted ceiling and a lavish bath enhance the master suite. Two additional bedrooms, with walk-in closets, share the full bath in the hall.

First floor — 1,236 sq. ft.
Second floor — 1,120 sq. ft.

Total living area: 2,356 sq. ft.

Refer to **Pricing Schedule D** on the order form for pricing information

No materials list available

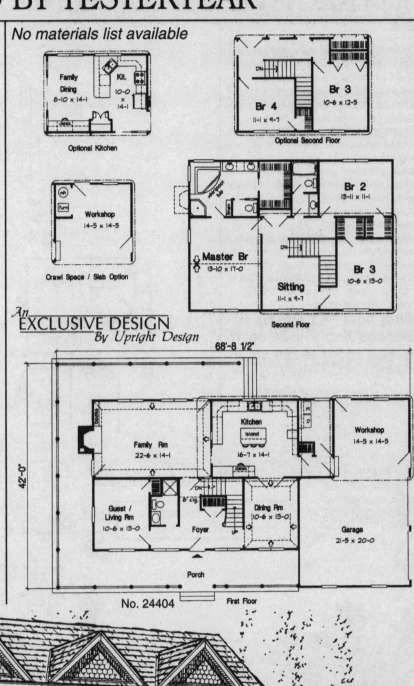

Optional Kitchen

Family Dining 8-10 x 14-1   Kit. 10-0 x 14-1

Br 4 11-1 x 9-7   Br 3 10-6 12-5

Optional Second Floor

Workshop 14-5 x 14-5

Crawl Space / Slab Option

Master Br 13-10 x 17-0

Br 2 13-11 x 11-1

Sitting 11-1 x 9-7   Br 3 10-6 x 13-0

Second Floor

An EXCLUSIVE DESIGN *By Upright Design*

68'-8 1/2"

42'-0"

Family Rm 22-6 x 14-1

Kitchen 16-7 x 14-1   Island

Workshop 14-5 x 14-5

Guest / Living Rm 10-6 x 13-0

Foyer

Dining Rm 10-6 x 13-0

Garage 21-5 x 20-0

Porch

No. 24404   First Floor

Design 91518

ATTRACTIVE USE OF WINDOWS

Vaulted ceilings and streaming natural light enhance the layout of this home. The living room is a prime example. Imagine sitting in this room with a glowing fireplace watching a snowy day through the gorgeous front window. Entertaining in the vaulted ceiling formal dining room is sure to be an elegant event. The huge efficient kitchen is every gourmet's dream with a center cooktop island and built-in pantry and planing desk. Family togetherness is easy because the family room flows from the eating nook. The second floor sleeping areas are arranged to give the master suite the most privacy. A master bath spoils its owner with spa tub, double vanity, step-in shower and large walk-in closet. There is also bonus space to decide on later.

First floor — 1,592 sq. ft.
Second floor — 958 sq. ft.
Bonus room — 194 sq. ft.

Total living area:
2,550 sq. ft.

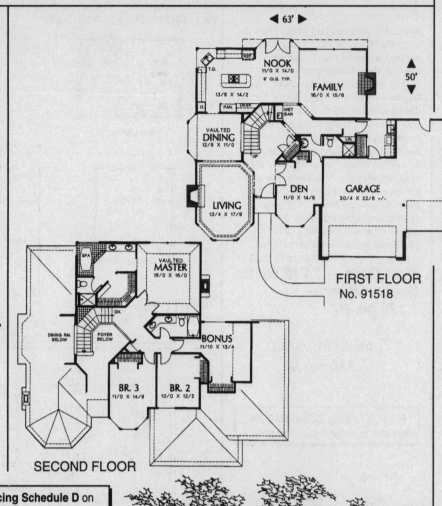

FIRST FLOOR
No. 91518

SECOND FLOOR

Refer to **Pricing Schedule D** on the order form for pricing information

SMALL YET SOPHISTICATED

The clean lines of this design afford a sophisticated appeal to the elevation. A spacious Great room welcomes guests into a cozy and elegant room highlighted by a fireplace and built-in shelving. The efficient kitchen is laid out in a U-shape with ample work and storage space. Flowing from the kitchen is the dining area, which is enhanced by a large bumped out window with a window seat. There is direct access to the covered patio from the dining area for increased living space. A vaulted ceiling tops the master suite's bedroom. An intimate sitting area allows for privacy and quiet moments. A sloped ceiling adds interest to the master bath. Two additional bedrooms share the full hall bath. This plan is available with a slab foundation only. No materials list is available with this plan.

Main floor — 1,360 sq. ft.
Garage — 380 sq. ft.

Total living area:
1,360 sq. ft.

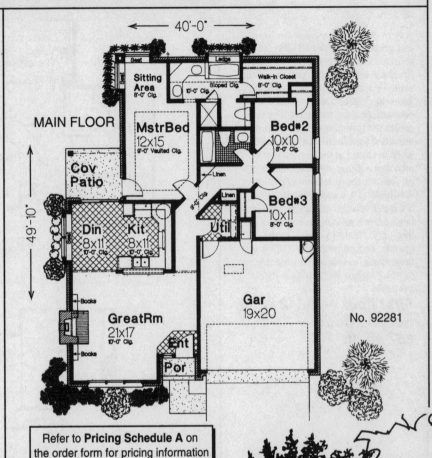

MAIN FLOOR

40'-0"

49'-10"

Sitting Area
8'-0" Clg.

MstrBed
12x15
9'-0" Vaulted Clg.

Walk-In Closet
8'-0" Clg.

Bed#2
10x10
8'-0" Clg.

Cov Patio

Linen

Bed#3
10x11
8'-0" Clg.

Din
8x11
10'-0" Clg.

Kit
8x11
10'-0" Clg.

Util

Books

GreatRm
21x17
10'-0" Clg.

Gar
19x20

Ent

Por

Books

No. 92281

Refer to **Pricing Schedule A** on the order form for pricing information

IN AN ELEGANT AND STYLISH MANNER

A high ceiling throughout the foyer and great room showcases the deluxe staircase, while the warmth of the fireplace and a built-in entertainment center makes the great room a favorite gathering place. Designed for convenience, the modern kitchen serves the formal dining room and breakfast area with equal efficiency. A walk-in pantry at the service entry provides additional storage space. A private master suite equipped with a whirlpool tub, a shower stall, his-n-her vanities and a spacious walk-in closet is a relaxing retreat after a busy day. Walk-in closets in the upstairs bedrooms and the option of a bonus room combine to create a very exciting home. No materials list available.

First floor — 1,542 sq. ft.
**Second floor —
667 sq. ft.**

*Total living area:
2,209 sq. ft.*

Refer to **Pricing Schedule D** on the order form for pricing information

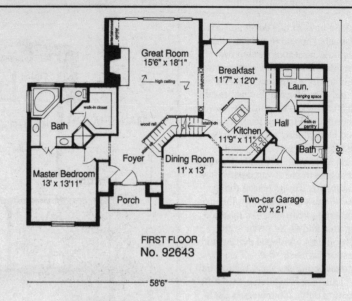

FIRST FLOOR
No. 92643

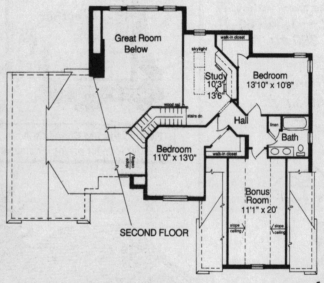

SECOND FLOOR

TAILORED FOR A SIDE VIEW

Tailored for a homesite with a view to the side, this design is perfect for entertaining and everyday living. The large entry foyer features a ceiling dome and French doors which lead to the private study or guest bedroom. The sunken Great room and large dining room feature high ceilings and are defined from the gallery by the use of columns and arched openings. The breakfast room has an optional planning desk and is open to the kitchen via the bar. A walk-in pantry adds to the storage space available. Two bedrooms share a bath with split vanity areas and the master suite features a bath with separate vanities and a closet which is accessible from both the bedroom and the bath. No materials list available for this plan.

Main floor — 2,579 sq. ft.
Garage — 536 sq. ft.

Total living area:
2,579 sq. ft.

Refer to **Pricing Schedule D** on the order form for pricing information

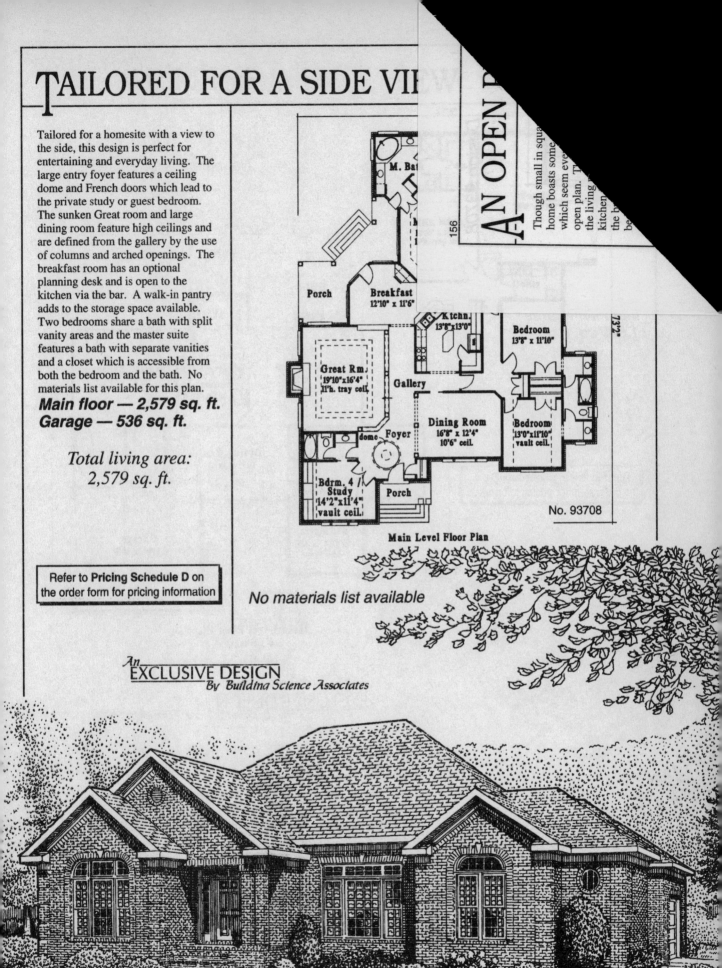

Porch

M. Bath

Breakfast
12'10" x 11'6"

Ktchn.
13'8"x13'0"

Bedroom
13'8" x 11'10"

Great Rm.
19'10"x16'4"
11'h. tray ceil.

Gallery

Dining Room
16'8" x 12'4"
10'6" ceil.

Bedroom
13'0"x11'10"
vault ceil.

dome   Foyer

Bdrm. 4 /
Study
14'2"x11'4"
vault ceil.

Porch

No. 93708

Main Level Floor Plan

No materials list available

An
EXCLUSIVE DESIGN
By Building Science Associates

PLAN

Design 93702

...re footage, this
...spacious rooms
...larger because of the
...here is a tray ceiling in
...room and the octagonal
...features a dining bar open to
...reakfast room. The large master
...droom has an oversized walk-in
closet and is isolated from the
bedrooms at the opposite end of the
house. The front bedroom would
make an excellent study or office with
its vaulted ceiling and a circle-topped
window.

**Main living area —
1,605 sq. ft.**

*Total living area:
1,605 sq. ft.*

Refer to **Pricing Schedule B** on
the order form for pricing information

No materials list available

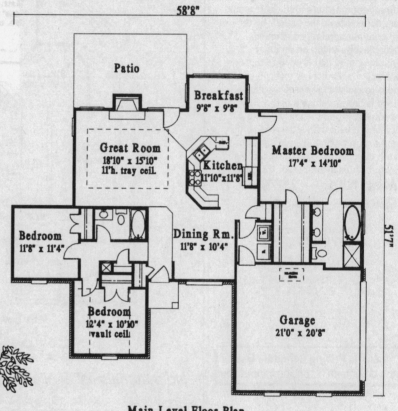

58'8"

51'7"

Patio

Breakfast
9'8" x 9'8"

Great Room
18'10" x 15'10"
11'h. tray ceil.

Kitchen
11'10"x11'8"

Master Bedroom
17'4" x 14'10"

Bedroom
11'8" x 11'4"

Dining Rm.
11'8" x 10'4"

Bedroom
12'4" x 10'10"
vault ceil.

Garage
21'0" x 20'8"

Main Level Floor Plan
8' Ceilings
No. 93702

An
EXCLUSIVE DESIGN
By Building Science Associates

CLASSIC STUCCO WITH A HIGH HIP ROOF

This classic stucco has a high hip roof and an angled three car garage all combining to give this house elegance. Bedrooms are offered at separate locations with a den located next to the master suite. The foyer adds columns and starts the elegant high ceiling trend throughout the house. Kitchen, nook and curved family room allow for spacious entertaining and views.

**Main living area —
2,598 sq. ft.
Garage — 828 sq. ft.**

*Total living area:
2,598 sq. ft.*

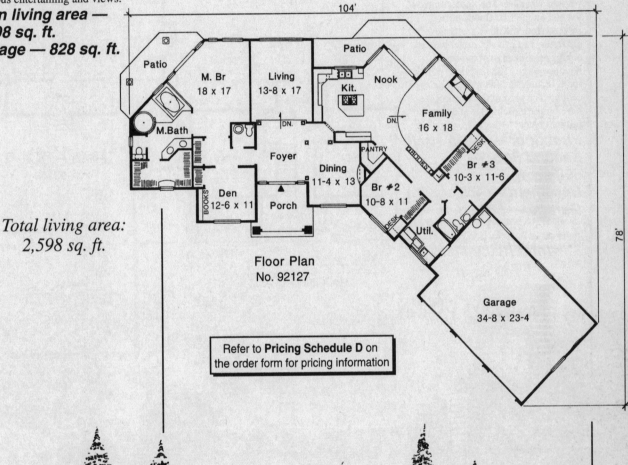

Floor Plan
No. 92127

Refer to **Pricing Schedule D** on
the order form for pricing information

COZY FRONT PORCH

Design 93269

From the cozy front porch, enter into an inviting living room with a large fireplace. The dining area is open to the living room, giving a spacious feeling to both rooms. An efficient kitchen includes ample counter and cabinet space as well as a double sink. A sunny breakfast area is available for informal eating. The sun deck expands your living area to the outdoors in the warmer weather. The master suite is located on the first floor insuring privacy from the other sleeping quarters. The private master bath is equipped with an oval tub and a double vanity. The first floor powder room includes a hide-away laundry center. The second floor bedrooms have ample closet space and share a full hall bath.

**First floor — 1,045 sq. ft.
Second floor — 690 sq. ft.
Basement — 465 sq. ft.
Garage — 580 sq. ft.**

Total living area: 1,735 sq. ft.

An **EXCLUSIVE DESIGN**
By Jannis Vann & Associates, Inc.

No materials list available

Refer to **Pricing Schedule B** on the order form for pricing information

SUNDECK 16'-0"X12'-0"

BREAKFAST 9'-0"X7'-8"

KIT. 9'-0"X9'-6"

DINING 10'-0"X11'-4"

LIVING AREA 18'-0"X13'-6"

M.BDRM. 15'-6"X13'-6"

PORCH

32'-0"

40'-4"

FIRST FLOOR
No. 93269

BATH 2
LIN.

BDRM.2 12'-2"X14'-4"

BDRM.3 13'-2"X14'-4"

SITTING AREA

SECOND FLOOR

UNIQUE SIDE ENTRY

This unique rambler is an excellent home for the first time home buyer, or empty-nester. The covered porch welcomes you to the side entry. Inside, you are greeted with architectural details, like columns welcoming you to the great room. The large great room, with a fireplace centered between two windows, is vaulted and open to the dining room, and angled serving bar from the kitchen. The efficient kitchen has ample counter space and double ovens. The master suite, with a double-door entry, is vaulted and features a separate access to the outside deck and very large walk-in closet. The master bath, with double vanity and large separate shower completes the suite. A second full bath and bedroom are conveniently located, as well as a third additional bedroom on the other side of the house. The double car garage can be accessed through the laundry room, complete with broom closet. The exterior of this home is enhanced with interesting roof lines and a unique side entry. This plan is available with a crawlspace foundation only. No materials list is available for this plan.

Total living area:
1,326 sq. ft.

Refer to **Pricing Schedule A** on the order form for pricing information

Main floor — 1,326 sq. ft.
Garage — 391 sq. ft.
Width — 49'-0"
Depth — 44'-0"

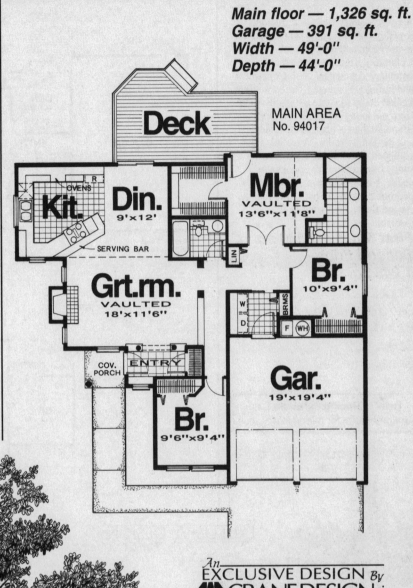

MAIN AREA
No. 94017

An
EXCLUSIVE DESIGN *By*
CRANE DESIGN inc.

Design 93339

WITH ROOM FOR ALL

A covered entry leads to a gracious foyer that is flanked by the formal living room and dining room. Columns define the dining room entrance. An elegant ceiling treatment and buffet area create a perfect setting. Pocket doors separate the family room from the living room. The cooktop island kitchen is open to the dinette and the family room. A secluded den, equipped with built-in shelves and a sunny bay window, overlooks the deck. A master suite, three additional bedrooms and a full bath complete the second floor. No materials list available.

First floor — 1,536 sq. ft.
Second floor — 1,245 sq. ft.

Total living area: 2,781 sq. ft.

Refer to **Pricing Schedule E** on the order form for pricing information

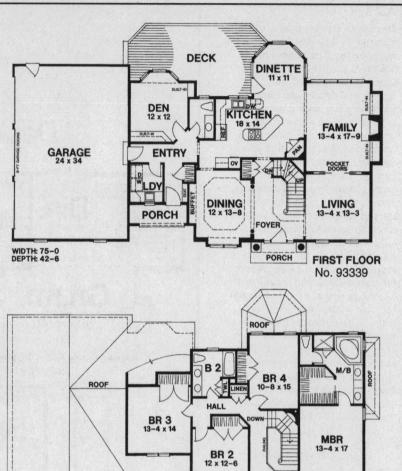

FIRST FLOOR
No. 93339

SECOND FLOOR

An EXCLUSIVE DESIGN
By Patrick Morabito, A.I.A. Architect

NEW ENGLAND CHARM

Refer to **Pricing Schedule B** on the order form for pricing information

The New England charm and warmth are expressed in this three bedroom Ranch house. It is basically divided into four parts: formal area, informal area, bedroom wing and service area. Featured are the master bedroom with its bath, the kitchen and the flowing spaces of living and dining rooms in the rear and the kitchen and family room/dinette in front. Each room is well defined. The combination of spaces fit well and give an impression of largeness. The spacious master bedroom has a dressing alcove off of it, and is adjacent to the other bedroom. It is equipped with a huge walk-in closet plus a linear one. Extras in the bathroom are two basins, shower stall and a 5'-6" whirlpool bathtub. The fully equipped kitchen is separated from the family room by a counter and high cabinets.

Terminating the family room is a pleasant bay suitable for a dinette table. Adjacent to the two-car garage is the service area, comprising a porch, family closet, laundry and lavatory.

Main living area — 1,686 sq. ft.
Basement — 1,609 sq. ft.
Garage and storage — 430 sq. ft.

74'-4"

41'-4"

TERR.

fence

D. R.
10' x 12'

L. R.
18 x 14'

shr.

t.v.

whirlpool tub

M. B. R.
15 x 16'

dress g

W.I.C.

SERVICE PORCH

cl.

D W

MUD RM

up

ptry

up

K.
10'x14'

FAM. RM
12'-8" x 15'

low wall

cl.

lin.

cl.

H.

STORAGE

dn.

ref.

dw

D'N'TTE

P.

B. R.
10'x 10'

cl.

cl.

B. R.
13' x 12'

TWO CAR GAR.
20' x 19'

FLOOR PLAN
No. 99643

Total living area:
1,686 sq. ft.

WITH ROOM FOR ALL

As a family matures, everyone needs his or her own space. This home provides enough living space for everyone. This attractive elevation promises wide open spaces inside. The large living area has a fireplace and built-in shelves on one wall, windows and access to the rear covered porch on another, with a decorative ceiling above it all. A U-shaped kitchen with a double sink, peninsula counter and an island is convieniently placed between the breakfast room and the laundry room. The garage entrance leads into the kitchen for ease in bringing in the groceries. A main floor master bedroom provides a private place for the owner to relax. Crowned by another decorative ceiling and equipped with a lavish bath and his-and-her walk-in closets, it is sure to please. The lower level's bedrooms have ample storage and one has a private bath. A lot of living space for everyone. No materials list available for this plan.

Refer to **Pricing Schedule E** on the order form for pricing information

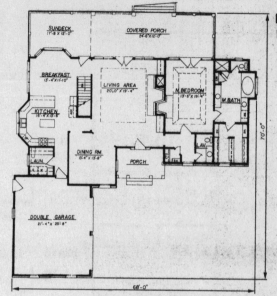

MAIN LEVEL
No. 93249

LOWER LEVEL

Main level — 1,871 sq. ft.
Lower level —
1,015 sq. ft.
Basement — 826 sq. ft.
Garage — 558 sq. ft.

Total living area:
2,886 sq. ft.

An **EXCLUSIVE DESIGN**
By Jannis Vann & Associates, Inc.

OUTSTANDING LUXURY

A balcony overlooks the foyer creating immediate interest upon entering this home. The formal dining room and the informal dinette area flank the gourmet kitchen. A cooktop work island, built-in pantry and an abundance of counter space help to make this well-appointed kitchen even more efficient. Sliding glass doors lead from the dinette to the large wooden deck. A coffered ceiling enhances the expansive family room that includes a fireplace. A spiral staircase to a loft above the library adds to this already cozy room, which includes another fireplace and built-in book shelves. The master suite on the second floor has access to the library's loft and a private deck. The private master bath offers luxuriant amenities. Three additional bedrooms have private access to full baths.

First floor — 2,277 sq. ft.
Second floor —
1,838 sq. ft.
Basement — 2,277 sq. ft.
Garage — 1,196 sq. ft.

Total living area:
4,115 sq. ft.

Refer to **Pricing Schedule F** on the order form for pricing information

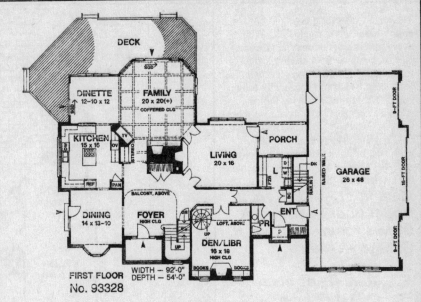

FIRST FLOOR
No. 93328

WIDTH — 92'-0"
DEPTH — 54'-0"

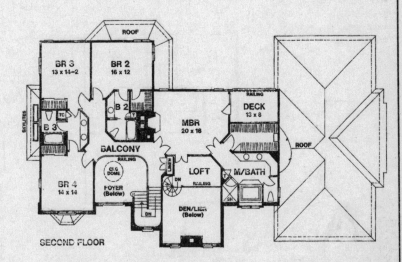

SECOND FLOOR

An
EXCLUSIVE DESIGN
By Patrick Morabito, A.I.A. Architect

MORE HOUSE FOR YOUR DOLLAR
Design 91672

This plan works for growing families, empty-nesters, and single folk. With every turn there is drama and function. Notice the upper floor economically tucked under the roof line. The great hall leads into the island kitchen with eating nook. The family and living rooms feature a fireplace. The master bedroom features a walk-in closet and master bath with spa tub. The two additional bedrooms upstairs feature walk-in closets and, they share a full bath. No materials list available for this plan.

Main floor — 1,928 sq. ft.
Upper floor — 504 sq. ft.
Bonus room — 335 sq. ft.
Garage — 440 sq. ft.

Total living area:
2,432 sq. ft.

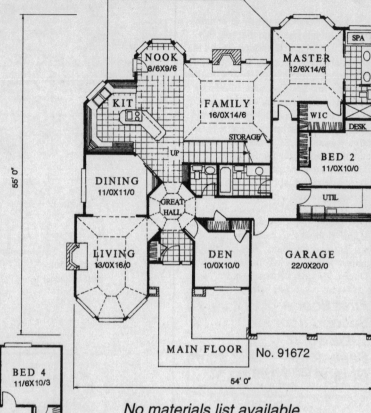

MAIN FLOOR   No. 91672

No materials list available

Refer to **Pricing Schedule D** on the order form for pricing information

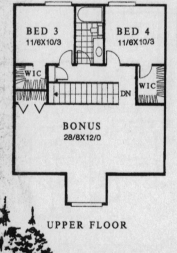

UPPER FLOOR

CAPE FOR MODERN LIVING

For those interested in both traditional charm and modern convenience, this Cape Cod fits the bill. Enter the foyer and find a quiet study to the left and a living room with a fireplace to the right. Straight ahead from the foyer is the kitchen and breakfast room. The island counter top affords lots of room for meal preparation. The service entry introduces a laundry and powder room. Look for three bedrooms upstairs and a pampering master bath.

First floor — 964 sq. ft.
Second floor — 783 sq. ft.

Total living area:
1,747 sq. ft.

Refer to **Pricing Schedule B** on the order form for pricing information

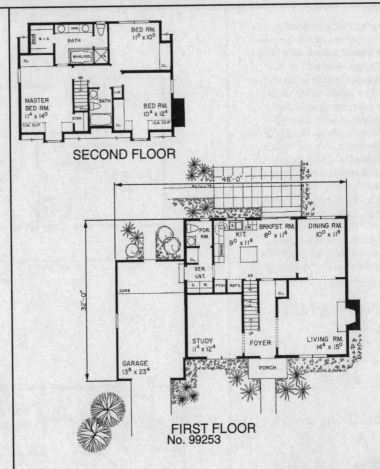

SECOND FLOOR

FIRST FLOOR
No. 99253

COUNTRY PORCH SHELTERS ENTRY

A country porch offers a warm welcome to visitors. Inside, the two-story foyer attains natural light from the arched window above. A convenient coat closet is to the right of the entry. The formal living room and dining room are adjoined through an arched opening. Another arched opening to the family room adds to the decor of this home. A gas fireplace is also featured in the family room. An island kitchen with a sunny breakfast bay, serves efficiently to both the formal and informal areas of the home. Sleeping quarters are located on the second floor. The master suite includes a lavish bath and a walk-in closet. Window seats are created by the country dormers on the front of the house. No materials list available for this plan.

First floor — 1,121 sq. ft.
Second floor — 748 sq. ft.
Width — 61'-0"
Depth — 32'-0"

Total living area:
1,869 sq. ft.

Refer to **Pricing Schedule C** on the order form for pricing information

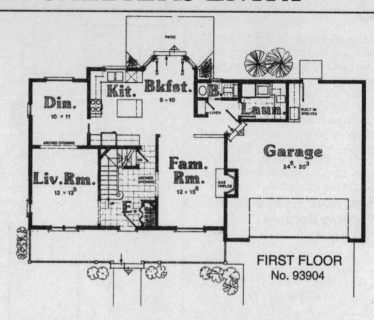

FIRST FLOOR
No. 93904

An
EXCLUSIVE DESIGN
By Independent Designs

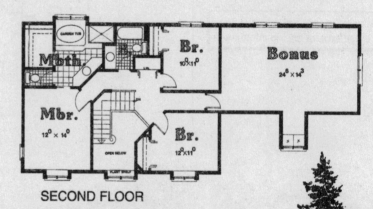

SECOND FLOOR

QUITE SPACIOUS FOR A SMALLER HOME

From the exterior, you can see that this is not a large home. This three bedroom home is only fifty-eight feet wide, so it will easily fit onto any standard lot. But when you step inside, the sense of spaciousness is surprising. The vaulted foyer is richly illuminated and presents three choices of direction. A door on the left opens into the luxurious master suite, and a hallway is on the right. What catches the eye, is the vaulted Great room, directly ahead. This comfortably large living area brings together the functions of kitchen, dining room, living room and family room. A bank of windows, running almost the entire length of the back wall, shower the room with light. A fireplace, tucked into the corner farthest from the windows, provides a colorful focal point when the sky outside turns gray. The kitchen is also much larger than one expects to find in a home this size. An eating bar adds to the work area and provides separation between the Great room and the kitchen. The location of the sink means the clean-up crew won't be left out of the activities. A central pantry allows handy access to canned goods and other supplies. Features in the master suite include a roomy walk-in closet, access to the back deck and a private bathroom. The toilet and shower area are separated from the twin basins and the mirror.

No materials list available

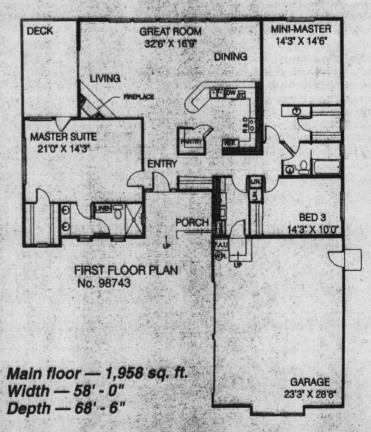

FIRST FLOOR PLAN
No. 98743

Main floor — 1,958 sq. ft.
Width — 58' - 0"
Depth — 68' - 6"

Total living area:
1,958 sq. ft.

Refer to **Pricing Schedule C** on the order form for pricing information

Design 84040

UNIQUE OPEN QUALITY IN EVERY ROOM

The angular windows and recessed ceilings separate the island kitchen from the formal dining and breakfast rooms. Twelve foot ceilings in the soaring, skylit living room add to its sophistication, along with a cozy fireplace and access to the outdoor deck. Separated from the active areas, the master suite boasts bump-out windows, a personal bath and a huge, walk-in closet. The two bedrooms off the foyer share a full, double-vanitied bath. No materials list available for this plan.

Main area — 2,026 sq. ft.
Garage — 545 sq. ft.

Total living area:
2,026 sq. ft.

Refer to **Pricing Schedule C** on the order form for pricing information

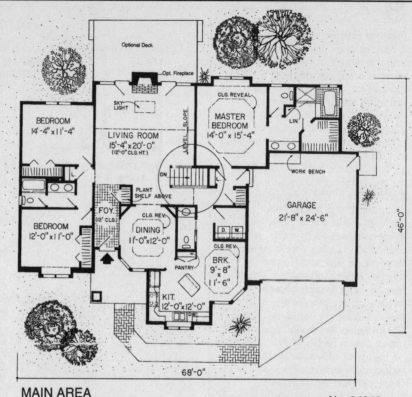

MAIN AREA

No materials list available

No. 84040

Slab/Crawlspace Option

PERFECT FOR A FIRST HOME

This traditional brick ranch features 1,564 sq. ft. of living space. Perfect for a first home, it has a spacious master suite as well as two additional bedrooms. The master suite features a luxurious master bath with separate garden tub and shower. The dining room and family room are highlighted by a vaulted ceiling. A fireplace is another nice feature in the family room. An oversized patio is accessible from the master suite, the family room and the breakfast room. Highlighting the breakfast room is a bay window. The well-planned kitchen measures 12' x 11'. Completing this plan are a laundry room and a hall bath. No materials list available.

Main area — 1,564 sq. ft.
Garage/Storage — 476 sq. ft.

Total living area: 1,564 sq. ft.

Refer to **Pricing Schedule B** on the order form for pricing information

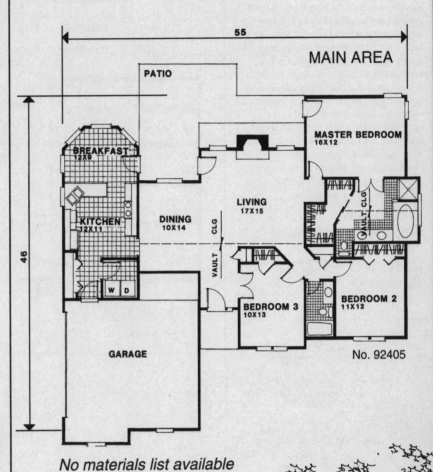

MAIN AREA

55

46

PATIO

BREAKFAST 12X9

KITCHEN 12X11

DINING 10X14

VAULT CLG

LIVING 17X15

MASTER BEDROOM 16X12

VAULT CLG

W D

GARAGE

BEDROOM 3 10X13

BEDROOM 2 11X12

No. 92405

No materials list available

FOR AN ESTABLISHED NEIGHBORHOOD

This home could fit in quite well in an established neighborhood. The large living room, which joins the dining room with ease, is perfect for entertaining. The galley-style kitchen is both efficient, well-appointed and convenient to both formal and informal dining areas. The layout of the home ensures privacy to the master suite, as it is situated at the opposite end of the house from the two additional bedrooms. The large master suite includes a master bath and a walk-in closet. The two additional bedrooms share the use of the full hall bath.

**Main living area —
1,276 sq. ft.
Finished staircase —
16 sq. ft.
Basement — 392 sq. ft.
Garage — 728 sq. ft.**

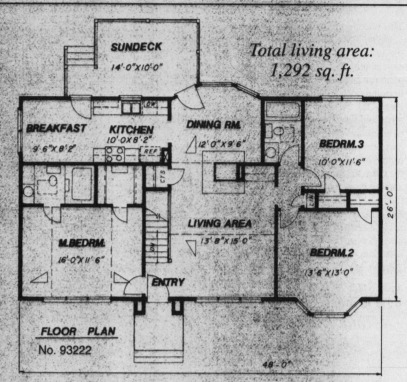

*Total living area:
1,292 sq. ft.*

SUNDECK
14'-0"X10'-0"

BREAKFAST
9'-6"X8'-2"

KITCHEN
10'-0X8'-2"

DINING RM.
12'-0"X9'-6"

BEDRM.3
10'-0"X11'-6"

M.BEDRM.
16'-0"X11'-6"

LIVING AREA
13'-8"X15'-0"

BEDRM.2
13'-6"X13'-0"

ENTRY

FLOOR PLAN
No. 93222

26'-0"

48'-0"

Refer to **Pricing Schedule A** on the order form for pricing information

An EXCLUSIVE DESIGN
By Jannis Vann & Associates, Inc.

STUCCO AND STONE

This appealing home features an elevation of stucco and stone with attention to detailing around the windows and entrance. The traffic pattern of the floor plan has been well thought-out. The large living room flows into the dining room. Both rooms enjoy the view through the large front window and the atmosphere created by an elegant fireplace. An efficient kitchen equipped with a double sink, peninsula counter and ample storage and work space is located between the formal and informal eating areas. The breakfast room has direct access to the deck. The master bedroom boasts a master bath with a double basin vanity and separate tub and shower. Two additional bedrooms share a full hall bath. There is a bonus room over the garage for future expansion.

Main floor — 831 sq. ft.
Second floor — 810 sq. ft.

An
EXCLUSIVE DESIGN
By *Jannis Vann & Associates, Inc.*

Bonus room — 280 sq. ft.
Basement — 816 sq. ft.
Garage — 484 sq. ft.

Total living area: 1,641 sq. ft.

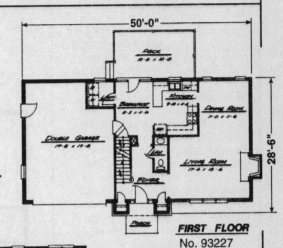

FIRST FLOOR
No. 93227

SECOND FLOOR

Refer to **Pricing Schedule B** on the order form for pricing information

CHARMING RANCH STYLE

The appeal of this ranch style home is not only in its charm and exterior style, but extends to the classic interior as well. Designed to provide an efficient floor plan, the real excitement lies in the amenities. Whether you enjoy formal entertaining, or a more casual lifestyle, this home can adapt to your needs. The Great room and dining room, accented by a sloped ceiling, columns and custom moldings, work together to create a spacious area for entertaining guests, or when centered around the corner fireplace, provides a place for family enjoyment. People will naturally want to gather in this outstanding breakfast area where the sloped ceiling continues, and light permeates through the rear windows and French doors, which lead to the spacious screened porch. Convenience was the order of the day when this kitchen was designed. Relaxing in the master bedroom suite is enhanced by the ultra bath with whirlpool tub, double vanity and a large walk-in closet. No materials list available for this plan.

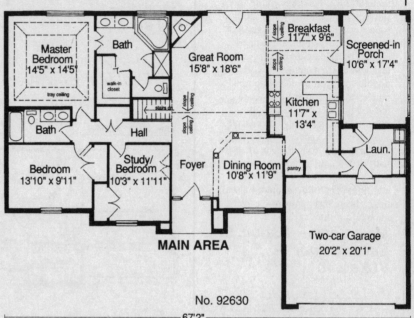

No. 92630

Main floor — 1,782 sq. ft.
Basement — 1,735 sq. ft.
Garage — 407 sq. ft.

Total living area:
1,782 sq. ft.

Refer to **Pricing Schedule B** on the order form for pricing information

BRICK HOME WITH EXQUISITE DETAILING

The detailing around the windows and door of this brick home set it apart from the rest. Upon entering, you will notice that the special touches continue. The dining room has an elegant ceiling treatment. The gourmet cooktop island kitchen flows easily through the breakfast room into the family room. The fireplace in the family room is flanked by built-in bookcases. The master suite has its own private master bath, two walk-in closets and direct access to the patio. The three additional bedrooms share the full hall bath. The second floor offers room to expand and added storage. No materials list available for this plan.

First floor — 2,577 sq. ft.
Bridge — 68 sq. ft.
Future rooms —
619 sq. ft.
Basement — 2,561 sq. ft.
Garage — 560 sq. ft.

Total living area:
2,645 sq. ft.

An
EXCLUSIVE DESIGN
By Jannis Vann & Associates, Inc.

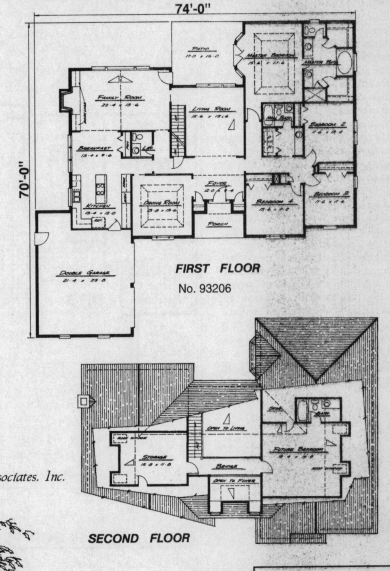

FIRST FLOOR

No. 93206

SECOND FLOOR

ECONOMICAL RANCH

This economical ranch plan with its contemporary exterior is easy-to-build with its affordable size and all the amenities. The impressive vaulted entry and hall serve as a buffer between the bedrooms on the left and the living areas on the right. To the left of the entry, a vaulted bedroom with beautiful arched windows at the front could substitute as a den or study. A second hall, left off the main hall, leads to a second bedroom on the right and a full bathroom on the left. The end of the hall leads to the deluxe master suite. The third bedroom has a large walk-in-closet, a linen closet, and a master bathroom with separate sinks for the dressing room and lavatory. The main hall stares directly into the oversized living room. This informal room features a raised-hearth fireplace, built-in bookshelves, vaulted ceilings and sliding glass doors to a rear deck. The vaulted kitchen offers plenty of counter space, a pantry, and an island with a stove.

Main area — 1,544 sq. ft.
Garage — 440 sq. ft.

Total living area:
1,544 sq. ft.

An
EXCLUSIVE DESIGN
By Gary Clayton

No materials list available

No. 92309

WOOD DECK

BLT-IS

MST
12/8 X 14/8

BR2
11/0 X 11/0

GR
26/8 X 13/6

KIT
10/2 X 13/2

DR
10/6 X 7/0

BR3
11/0 X 11/0

GAR
22/0 X 20/0

MAIN LEVEL FLOOR PLAN

Refer to **Pricing Schedule B** on the order form for pricing information

A LARGER FAMILY HOME

This is a larger home built with a growing family in mind. The formal areas are to the left side of the foyer. The dining room is crowned by a stepped ceiling, giving the room a touch of elegance. Family living areas are located to the rear of the home. The secluded study is equipped with built-in book shelves. The large family room includes built-in bookshelves and a fireplace. The open layout between the kitchen and dinette area give a feeling of spaciousness. A lavish master suite is on the second floor. There are three additional bedrooms, one with a private bath. No materials list available for this plan.

First floor — 1,965 sq. ft.
Second floor — 1,781 sq. ft.
Basement — 1,965 sq. ft.

Total living area: 3,746 sq. ft.

Refer to **Pricing Schedule F** on the order form for pricing information

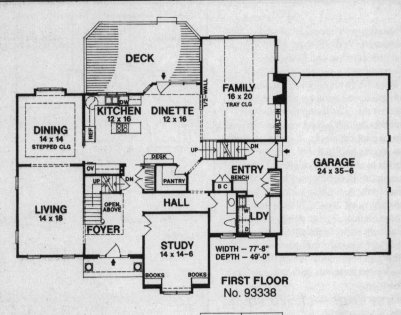

DECK

KITCHEN 12 x 16

DINETTE 12 x 16

FAMILY 16 x 20 TRAY CLG

DINING 14 x 14 STEPPED CLG

LIVING 14 x 18

FOYER

OPEN ABOVE

DESK

PANTRY

HALL

ENTRY BENCH

B C

LDY

STUDY 14 x 14-6

BOOKS   BOOKS

GARAGE 24 x 35-6

WIDTH — 77'-8"
DEPTH — 49'-0"

FIRST FLOOR
No. 93338

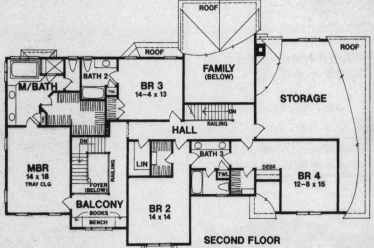

ROOF

ROOF

ROOF

M/BATH

BATH 2

BR 3 14-4 x 13

FAMILY (BELOW)

STORAGE

HALL

RAILING

MBR 14 x 18 TRAY CLG

FOYER (BELOW)

RAILING

LIN

BATH 3

DESK

BR 4 12-8 x 15

BALCONY

BOOKS

BENCH

BR 2 14 x 14

SECOND FLOOR

An EXCLUSIVE DESIGN
By Patrick Morabito, A.I.A. Architect

Design 98604

MANY WINDOWS AND ROOF LINES

Fantastic curb appeal is created by this elevation. A tiled foyer, adorned by a curved staircase and having a convenient coat closet, greets the visitor. A twelve-foot ceiling and a unique bayed window area are featured in the den. The living room includes another unique bayed window area and an elegant fireplace. A formal dining room adjoins the living room with direct access to a deck area. The large family room is enhanced by a cozy fireplace. A cooktop island in the kitchen/nook area adds even more convenience. An outstanding master bedroom suite, highlighted by a sitting area and a lavish bath, plus two additional bedrooms are on the second floor. No materials list available for this plan.

First floor — 1,570 sq. ft.
Second floor — 1,480 sq. ft.

Total living area: 3,050 sq. ft.

Refer to **Pricing Schedule E** on the order form for pricing information

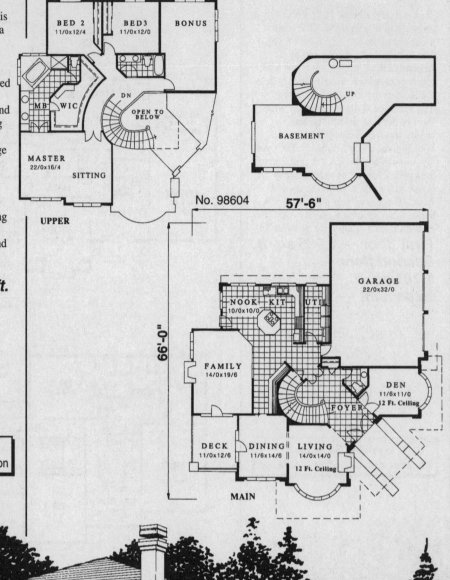

SOUTHERN TRADITION

An affordable, expandable house with a Southern Traditional flavor generates charm and warmth as one approaches the colonnaded front porch and enters the house. The foyer has a large coat closet and leads past the stairway to the second floor and to the main living space — a large living room with a 9-foot high ceiling. The living room flows gracefully into the dining room shaped by the angled pass-through into the kitchen. Two French doors lead from the dining room to a rear terrace. The kitchen, connecting to the left, provides another large space with plenty of countertop area, cabinet storage and bays out to form a dinette. Bedrooms flank both sides of the living room. On the left is the master suite that includes a large walk-in closet and master bath with a compartmentalized toilet, a separate stall shower, a whirlpool tub and two lavatories. Two identical bedrooms are located on the other side and share a full bath.

Refer to **Pricing Schedule B** on the order form for pricing information

First floor — 1,567 sq. ft.
Second floor —
338 sq. ft.
Basement — 1,567 sq. ft.
Garage — 504 sq. ft.
Front porch — 152 sq. ft.

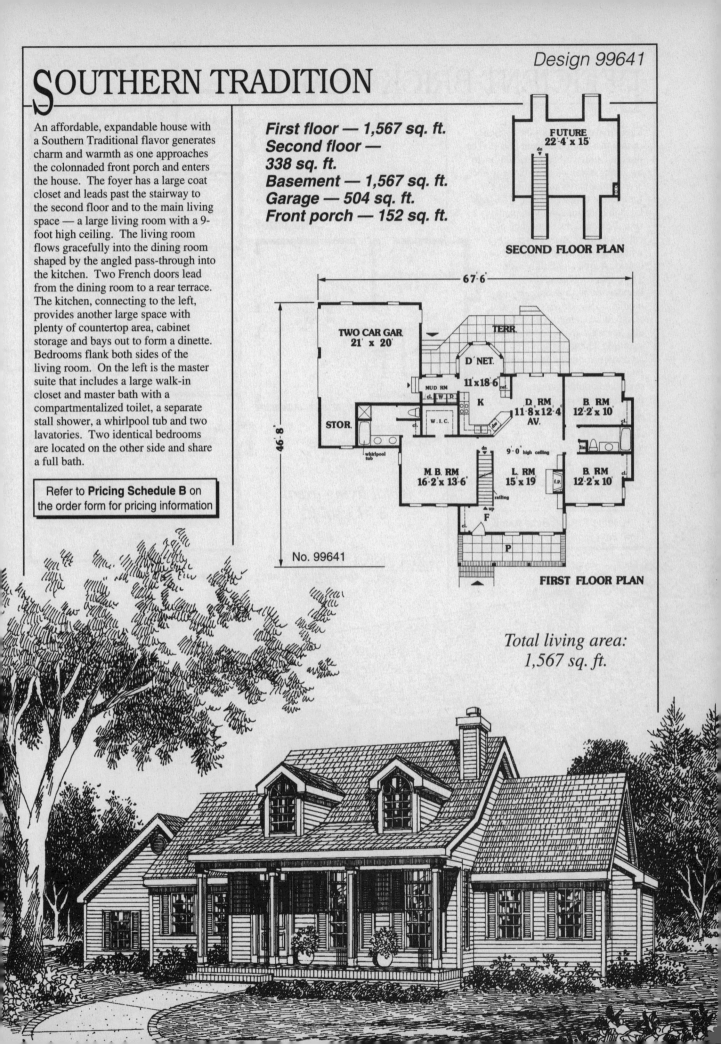

FUTURE
22'-4" x 15'

SECOND FLOOR PLAN

67'-6"

46'-8"

TWO CAR GAR.
21' x 20'

STOR.

MUD RM
cl. W D

K

W.I.C.

whirlpool tub

M. B. RM
16'-2" x 13'-6"

TERR.

D'NET.
11' x 18'-6"

ref.

D. RM
11'-8" x 12'-4"
AV.

B. RM
12'-2" x 10'

dn

9'-0" high ceiling

L. RM
15' x 19

up

railing

F

P

B. RM
12'-2" x 10'

No. 99641

FIRST FLOOR PLAN

Total living area:
1,567 sq. ft.

Design 93707

EFFICIENT BRICK BEAUTY

The rich exterior belies the effciency of this two story basement home. The dramatic entry porch leads visitors to the impressive two story foyer inside. The formal parlor can easily be used for a home office or study. The large kitchen contains a walk-in pantry, island/bar, and an abundance of cabinet storage and counter space, while opening to an expansive breakfast area and family room. The upper level contains a laundry room, to avoid carrying clothes up and down steps, and also features a master suite with his-and-her walk-in closets and separate vanities. The lower level has a recreation room, large enough for a pool table, a full bath and an oversized double garage. No materials list available for this plan.

**Main area —
1,210 sq. ft.
Upper level —
1,039 sq. ft.
Lower level — 464 sq. ft.**

Refer to **Pricing Schedule E** on the order form for pricing information

*Total living area:
2,713 sq. ft.*

An
EXCLUSIVE DESIGN
By Building Science Associates

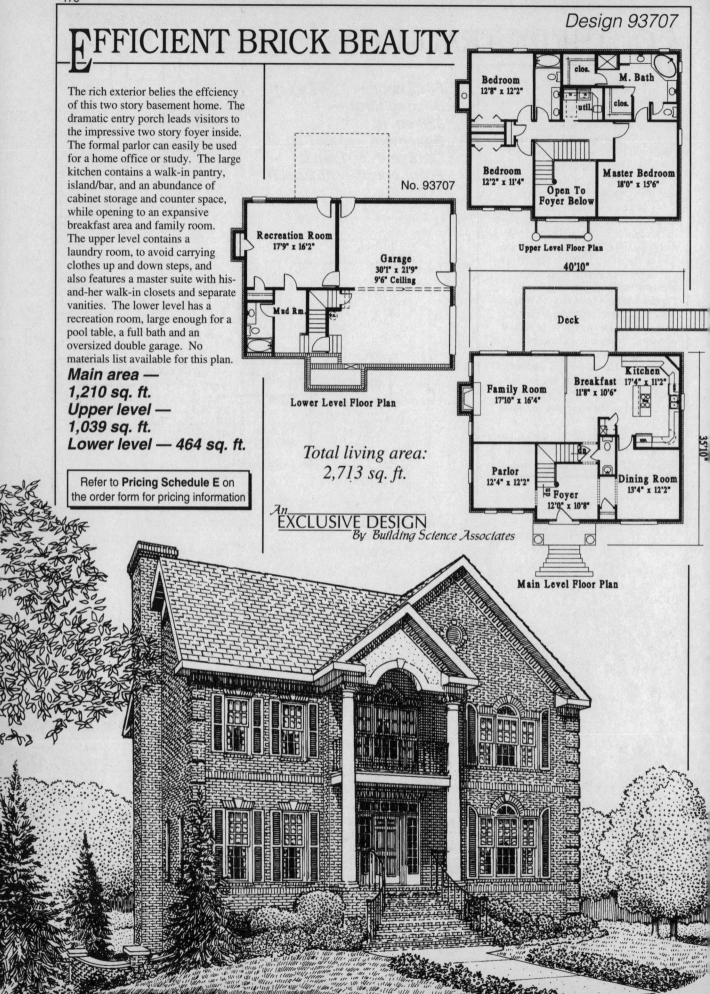

No. 93707

Recreation Room
17'9" x 16'2"

Garage
30'1" x 21'9"
9'6" Ceiling

Mud Rm.

Lower Level Floor Plan

Bedroom
12'8" x 12'2"

clos.

M. Bath

util.

clos.

Bedroom
12'2" x 11'4"

**Open To
Foyer Below**

Master Bedroom
18'0" x 15'6"

Upper Level Floor Plan

40'10"

Deck

Family Room
17'10" x 16'4"

Breakfast
11'8" x 10'6"

Kitchen
17'4" x 11'2"

Parlor
12'4" x 12'2"

Foyer
12'0" x 10'8"

Dining Room
13'4" x 12'2"

35'10"

Main Level Floor Plan

ROOM FOR FAMILY GATHERINGS

This classic Ranch features a large open Great room for family gatherings. The sunny kitchen sports a separate dining area. On the other side of the house three good-size bedrooms share two full bathrooms. A great hide-away laundry closet is located outside the large linen closet. A two-car optional garage attaches to this all inclusive home. This plan is available with a basement, slab or crawl space foundation. Please specify when ordering. No materials list available for this plan.

Main living area —
1,644 sq. ft.
Garage — 576 sq. ft.

Total living area:
1,644 sq. ft.

Refer to **Pricing Schedule B** on the order form for pricing information

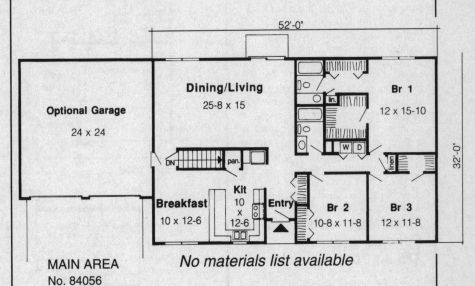

52'-0"

32'-0"

Optional Garage
24 x 24

Dining/Living
25-8 x 15

Br 1
12 x 15-10

lin.

W D

linen

DN

pan.

Kit
10 x 12-6

Breakfast
10 x 12-6

Entry

Br 2
10-8 x 11-8

Br 3
12 x 11-8

MAIN AREA
No. 84056

No materials list available

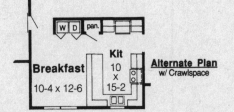

W D   pan.

Breakfast
10-4 x 12-6

Kit
10 x 15-2

Alternate Plan
w/ Crawlspace

A TOUCH OF OLD WORLD CHARM

Design 92646

There is a touch of old world charm in the authentic balustrade detail and open court yard, with plenty of modern amenities encapsulated into this unique package. From the foyer there is a panoramic view of the dramatic Great room and formal dining room. Features such as a fireplace, a high ceiling, french doors, a furniture alcove and a boxed window complement these two rooms. To aid in serving meals a butler's pantry is strategically located. French doors add light and style to the breakfast room while an abundance of counter space, a work top island and a walk-in pantry adds convenience and order to the kitchen. An upstairs balcony overlooks the Great room and continues to the outside. A materials list is not available for this plan.

First floor — 1,595 sq. ft.
Second floor — 725 sq. ft.

Total living area: 2,320 sq. ft.

Refer to **Pricing Schedule D** on the order form for pricing information

No. 92646

FIRST FLOOR

Laun. 9'10" x 8'5"
Bath
Hall
Kitchen
Breakfast 19'7" x 12' 3"
Great Room 15'8" x 16'5"
Master Bedroom 13'8" x 14'8"
Two-car Garage 19'10" x 21'4"
Dining Room 11' x 15'9"
Foyer
Hall
Dressing
Porch
Court Yard
walk-in closet
61'
41'8"

SECOND FLOOR

Bedroom 10'8" x 13'5"
Bedroom 10'9" x 10'
Great Room Below
Hall
Balcony
Bath
Bedroom 11' x 11'2"
Porch

INTERESTING ELEVATION

Interest is definitely created by this elevation on any street, because it is has a pronounced curb appeal. Once inside the home, modern family living has been planned out for more convenience and ease. The formal living room is enhanced by the large front windows. The formal dining room and a den occupy the rear of the first floor. The kitchen, nook and family room are open to each other creating a feeling of space and allowing for conversation from either room to continue. The second floor houses the sleeping quarters. The master suite includes a coved ceiling, walk-in closet and lavish bath with a spa tub. The two additional bedrooms share the use of the full hall bath. No materials list available for this plan.

First floor — 1,099 sq. ft.
Second floor — 722 sq. ft.
Lower level — 90 sq. ft.

Total living area: 1,911 sq. ft.

Refer to **Pricing Schedule C** on the order form for pricing information

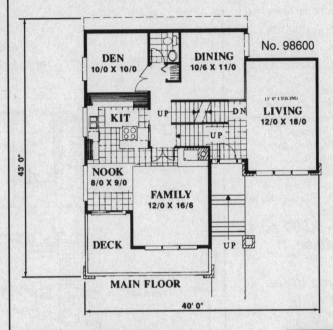

No. 98600

MAIN FLOOR

DEN 10/0 X 10/0
DINING 10/6 X 11/0
LIVING 12/0 X 18/0 — 13' 0" CEILING
KIT
UP
DN
NOOK 8/0 X 9/0
FAMILY 12/0 X 16/6
DECK
UP
43' 0"
40' 0"

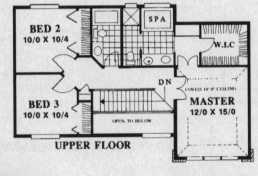

UPPER FLOOR

BED 2 10/0 X 10/4
SPA
W.I.C
BED 3 10/0 X 10/4
DN
COVED 10' 0" CEILING
MASTER 12/0 X 15/0
OPEN TO BELOW

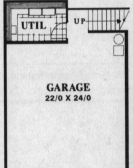

UTIL
UP
GARAGE 22/0 X 24/0

COMPACT AND EFFICIENT

This compact and efficient home has all the amenities you would find in a larger home, including a covered porch and skylight over the dining area. It is actually an economical home to build. A tiled entry leads to the living room, which is equipped with a vaulted ceiling and a fireplace. The large kitchen has an abundance of cabinets and counter space. There are two secondary bedrooms, one of these could be a den, that share a full bath. The master suite has a large walk-in closet and a private shower with a pocket door closure. No materials list available for this plan.

Main floor — 1,390 sq. ft.
Garage — 440 sq. ft.

Total living area:
1,390 sq. ft.

Refer to **Pricing Schedule A** on the order form for pricing information

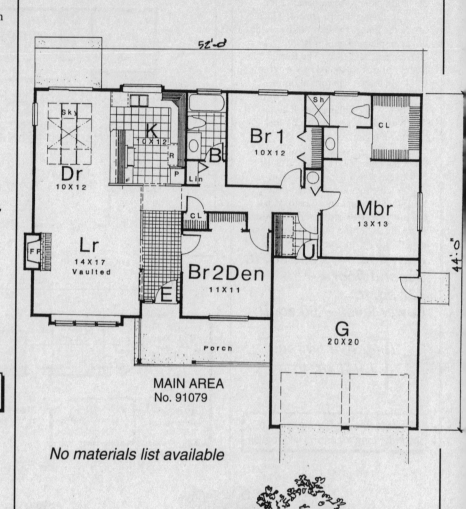

MAIN AREA
No. 91079

No materials list available

CHARMING TOUCHES OF COUNTRY

The living room of this country charmer is accented by a large front window. Adjoining the living room is the dining room, allowing for a smooth transition for entertaining. The U-shaped kitchen directly accesses the dining room. A breakfast bar/peninsula counter separates the kitchen from the spacious family room. A gas fireplace in the family room enhances this entire open living space. The master suite with all the amenities is on the second floor. There are two additional second floor bedrooms sharing the full bath in the hallway. A bonus area allows for future expansion. No materials list available for this plan.

First floor —
913 sq. ft.
Second floor —
771 sq. ft.

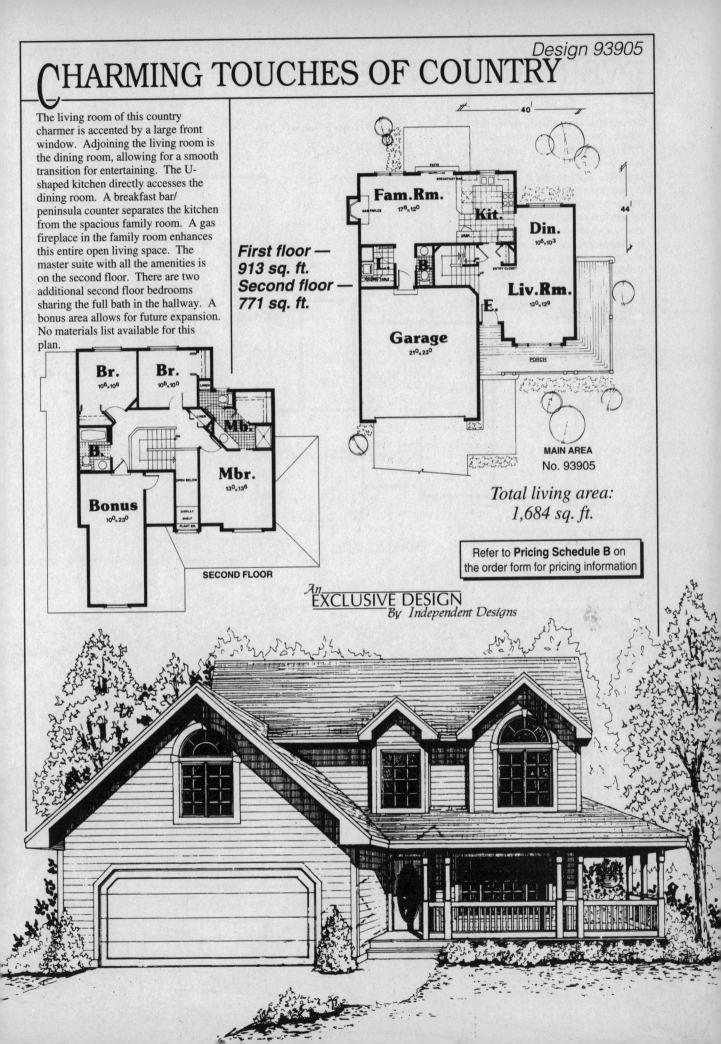

Fam. Rm.
17⁶×12⁰

GAS FIRPLCE

Kit.

Din.
10⁶×10³

Liv. Rm.
13⁰×12⁹

Garage
21⁰×23⁰

E.

ENTRY CLOSET

PORCH

PATIO

BREAKFAST BAR

40'

44'

MAIN AREA
No. 93905

Total living area:
1,684 sq. ft.

Br.
10⁶×10⁶

Br.
10⁶×10⁰

LINEN

LINEN

Mb.

Mbr.
13⁰×13⁶

B.

Bonus
10⁰×23⁰

OPEN BELOW

DISPLAY SHELF

PLANT BR.

SECOND FLOOR

Refer to **Pricing Schedule B** on the order form for pricing information

An
EXCLUSIVE DESIGN
By Independent Designs

EVERYTHING IN ITS PLACE

Not only is this plan attractive on the outside, it is pleasing on the inside. The central living area is equipped with a fireplace and access to the wood deck. The well-appointed, U-shaped kitchen flows efficiently into the dining room. The master suite is on the opposite side of the house from the secondary bedrooms to insure privacy. The secondary bedrooms have a full hall bath between them. Each bedroom has ample storage space, the master suite features a walk-in closet.

Main floor — 1,407 sq. ft.
Lower level — 40 sq. ft.
Basement — 950 sq. ft.
Garage — 400 sq. ft.

Total living area: 1,447 sq. ft.

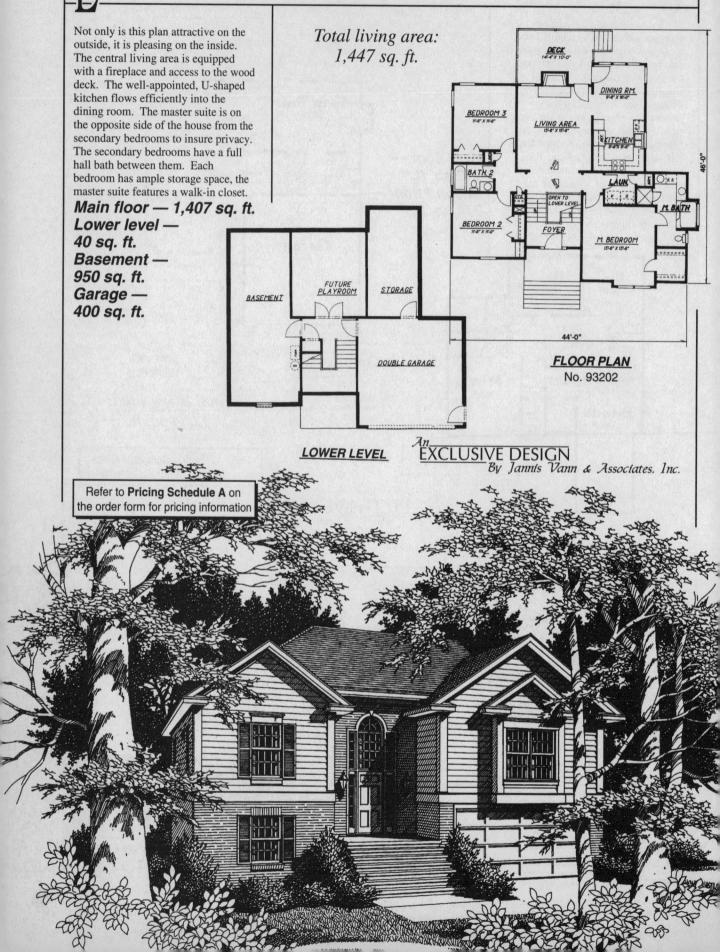

FLOOR PLAN
No. 93202

DECK
14'-4" X 10'-0"

DINING RM.
9'-6" X 10'-0"

BEDROOM 3
11'-6" X 11'-6"

LIVING AREA
13'-6" X 15'-6"

KITCHEN
9'-6" X 9'-6"

BATH 2

LAUN.

OPEN TO LOWER LEVEL

M. BATH

BEDROOM 2
11'-6" X 11'-0"

FOYER

M. BEDROOM
13'-6" X 13'-6"

46'-0"

44'-0"

BASEMENT

FUTURE PLAYROOM

STORAGE

DOUBLE GARAGE

LOWER LEVEL

An **EXCLUSIVE DESIGN**
By Jannis Vann & Associates, Inc.

Refer to **Pricing Schedule A** on the order form for pricing information

ONE-STORY COUNTRY HOME

The entrance to the house is sheltered by the front porch that leads into the living room with its imposing high ceiling that slopes down to a normal height of eight feet focusing on the decorative heat-circulating fireplace at the rear wall. Widely open to the living room is the dining room. Its front wall is windowed from side to side. The adjoining fully equipped kitchen is also a feature of the house.

The convenient dinette can comfortably seat six people and leads to the rear terrace through six foot sliding glass doors. The master suite is arranged with a large dressing area that has a walk-in closet plus two linear closets and space for a vanity. The main part of the bedroom contains a media wall designed for TV viewing with shelving and cabinets for a VCR, radio, speakers, records and CD player.

Main area — 1,367 sq. ft.
Garage — 431 sq. ft.
Basement — 1,267 sq. ft.

Total living area:
1,367 sq. ft.

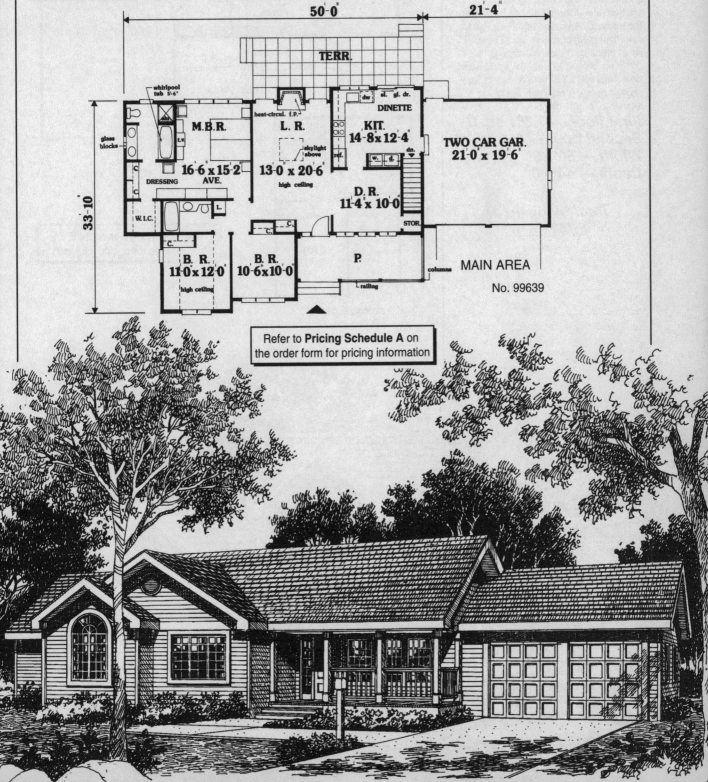

Refer to **Pricing Schedule A** on the order form for pricing information

STYLISH FAMILY LIVING

A sheltered porch entrance adds curb appeal to this elevation. A big first impression is achieved by the vaulted foyer with a staircase and a coat closet. The vaulted ceiling continues into the living room, accented by a large picture window and a fireplace. Adjoining the living room is the dining room conveniently close to the kitchen. A built-in pantry, an L-shaped counter and double sinks add efficiency to the kitchen. An informal dinette flows from the kitchen. A private first floor master suite will pamper the owner. The mud room entrance from the garage cuts down on tracked-in dirt. Two additional bedrooms and a full bath complete the second floor. A materials list is not available for this plan.

First floor — 1,281 sq. ft.
Second floor — 511 sq. ft.
Width — 58' - 0"
Depth — 44' - 0"

Total living area:
1,792 sq. ft.

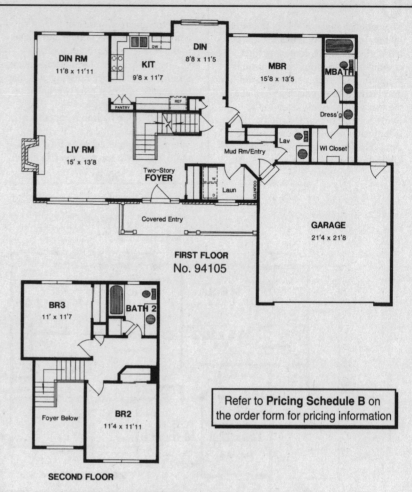

FIRST FLOOR
No. 94105

DIN RM
11'8 x 11'11

KIT
9'8 x 11'7

DIN
8'8 x 11'5

MBR
15'8 x 13'5

MBATH

PANTRY

REF

Dress'g

LIV RM
15' x 13'8

Lav

Mud Rm/Entry

WI Closet

Two-Story
FOYER

Laun

COUNTER

Covered Entry

GARAGE
21'4 x 21'8

BR3
11' x 11'7

BATH 2

Foyer Below

BR2
11'4 x 11'11

SECOND FLOOR

Refer to **Pricing Schedule B** on the order form for pricing information

VAULTED CEILINGS ADD SPACE

A sheltered entrance leads the visitor of this home into a large living room with a vaulted ceiling, large bay window and a fireplace. Arched openings lead to the formal dining room and to the family room. A large fireplace warms the mood as well as the temperature in the family room which is open to the kitchen and nook. A built-in entertainment center adds to the conveniences. The cook top island in the kitchen doubles as an eating bar. A walk-in pantry gives additional storage space. A private master suite awaits the owners pampering them in luxury. There are two walk-in closets, a skylit ultra bath that accesses the side porch which is equipped with a hot tub. A covered rear deck includes six skylights, a perfect place for outdoor entertaining. Two secondary bedrooms share a hall bath that includes two skylights.

**Main living area —
2,496 sq. ft.
Garage —
827 sq. ft.
Width — 96'-0"
Depth — 54'-0"**

*Total living area:
2,496 sq. ft.*

Refer to **Pricing Schedule D** on
the order form for pricing information

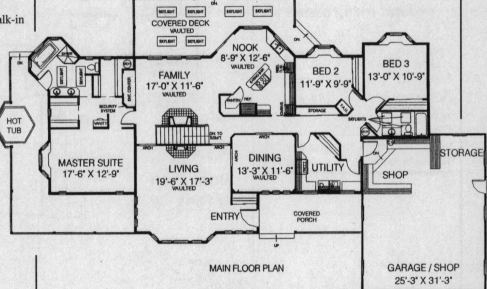

MAIN FLOOR PLAN

No. 98733

FRESH STYLE

This three bedroom ranch includes all the basics needed for that first home. The eat-in kitchen accesses the rear deck for easy outdoor entertaining. The dining room opens to the living room. The bay windows in the bedrooms give a cozy feeling to the rooms. The master suite has vaulted ceilings adding sophistication to the room.

Main living area — 1,146 sq. ft.

Total living area: 1,146 sq. ft.

Refer to **Pricing Schedule A** on the order form for pricing information

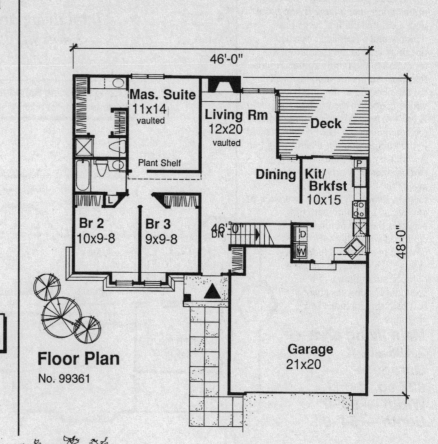

Floor Plan
No. 99361

COUNTRY-STYLE QUALITY LIVING

Windows and bays enhance this country-style home. The sunken living room and the master bedroom above are almost fully glazed in glamorous five-sided bays giving cheerfulness to these rooms and adding an interesting design element inside and out. A typical farmhouse front porch shelters the double-door entrance which opens to the spacious central foyer leading to all rooms and the second floor. Down two steps from the foyer is the formal living room whose focus is the decorative heat-circulating fireplace. The room terminates in the attractive, large windowed bay and is enhanced by a stepped ceiling. Adjacent, but separate is the formal dining room with its interior corners angled to form an octagon. The large fully-equipped kitchen has space for a table in the center. The informal area next to the kitchen flows together with the family room, creating one large space with a second decorative fireplace. Upstairs are four large bedrooms and two luxurious bathrooms around the central stair hall.

First floor — 1,217 sq. ft.
Second floor — 1,249 sq. ft.
Basement — 1,217 sq. ft.
Garage — 431 sq. ft.

Total living area:
2,466 sq. ft.

Refer to **Pricing Schedule D** on the order form for pricing information

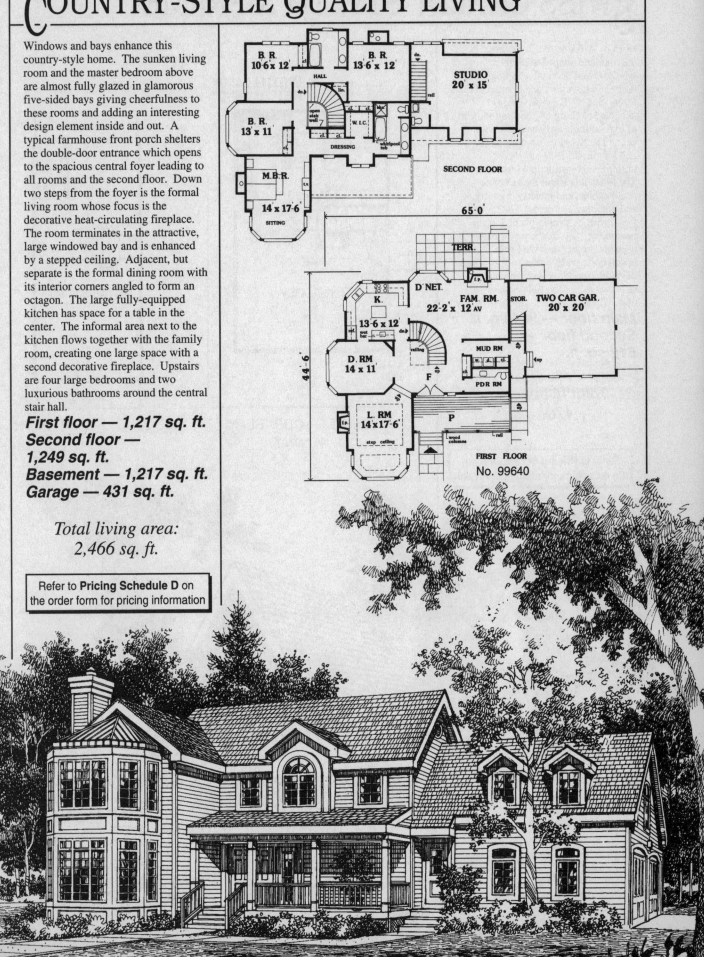

Design 99707

SWISS CHALET STYLED A-FRAME

With its A-frame roofline echoed in the diamond-shaped mullioned windows and decorative railings, this home instantly puts one in mind of the Swiss chalet. The steep roof is designed to shrug off the deep snowfall of high altitude environments with ease. The living room, dining room and kitchen all flow together, unimpaired by structural impediments. The kitchen is larger than in most small cabins, and includes a pantry, and a washer and dryer. The upper floor, with its steeply pitched, open-beamed ceiling, can be put to many uses. Narrower than the lower floor, it is still quite wide with a 16-foot width of usable space. A wide balcony stretches across the full width of the upper floor.

Main floor — 864 sq. ft.
Second floor — 612 sq. ft.

Total living area: 1,476 sq. ft.

Refer to **Pricing Schedule A** on the order form for pricing information

WIDTH 24'-0"
DEPTH 36'-0"

BEDROOM
9⁴ X 11⁶

DINING
9⁰ X 9⁰

LIVING AREA
23⁴ X 18⁰

FIREPLACE

DECK

FIRST FLOOR PLAN
No. 99707

BALCONY

HALF PARTITIONS

RECREATION AREA
16⁴ X 35⁴

BALCONY

SECOND FLOOR PLAN

AN ESTABLISHED FEELING

An established, stable feeling is created with this plan. The foyer is graced by a staircase with an attractive wooden rail. The formal living room uses a tray ceiling and pocket doors as accents. The family room is separated by a half wall from the informal dining room. An island kitchen, with a built-in pantry and ample storage, efficiently serves both formal and informal dining areas. A stepped ceiling tops the first floor master suite. Three additional bedrooms and a full bath are located on the second floor.

First floor — 1,788 sq. ft.
Second floor — 707 sq. ft.

Total living area: 2,495 sq. ft.

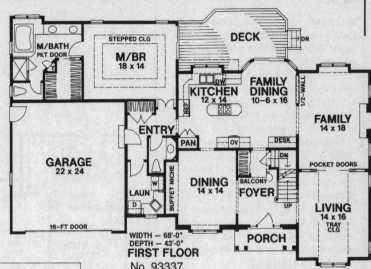

M/BATH PKT DOOR · STEPPED CLG · M/BR 18 x 14 · DECK · DN · KITCHEN 12 x 14 · DW · FAMILY DINING 10-6 x 16 · 1/2-WALL · FAMILY 14 x 18 · REF · ENTRY · PAN · OV · DESK · DN · POCKET DOORS · GARAGE 22 x 24 · DINING 14 x 14 · BALCONY · FOYER · UP · LIVING 14 x 16 TRAY CLG · LAUN · W · D · BUFFET NICHE · 16-FT DOOR · WIDTH — 68'-0" · DEPTH — 43'-0" · PORCH

FIRST FLOOR
No. 93337

BR 2 12 x 12 · ROOF · ROOF · B 2 · ROOF · BR 3 12 x 12 PLUS DORMER · BR 4 14 x 12 · DN · BALC · FOYER (BELOW) · ROOF

SECOND FLOOR

Refer to **Pricing Schedule D** on the order form for pricing information

An EXCLUSIVE DESIGN
By Patrick Morabito, A.I.A. Architect

A LOVELY SMALL HOME

A large living room with a ten foot ceiling is the focal point for this lovely small home. A dining room with a distinctive bay window provides a perfect place for formal dining. The breakfast room, located off the kitchen, is ideal for informal gatherings. The kitchen is designed with an angled eating bar to open the room to the living room beyond. The master bedroom is notable for a ceiling that vaults to ten feet. The master bath includes his-n-her vanities and a combination whirlpool tub and shower. The huge walk-in closet provides plenty of closet space. Bedroom two and three and a second bath complete this very livable plan. No materials list available for this plan.

Main floor — 1,402 sq. ft.
Garage — 437 sq. ft.

Total living area:
1,402 sq. ft.

Refer to **Pricing Schedule A** on the order form for pricing information

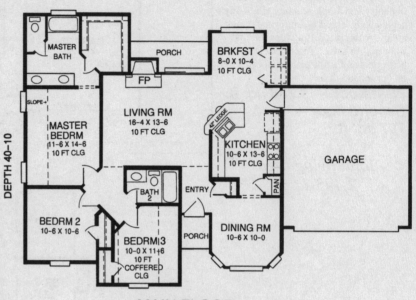

An
EXCLUSIVE DESIGN
By Belk Home Designs

WIDTH 59-10

MAIN FLOOR
No. 93026

TRADITIONAL RANCH

One of today's most popular features is a master suite which is isolated from the other bedrooms. This master suite measures 14'x18' and is highlighted by a trey ceiling. Spacious his-and-her closets flank the hallway which leads to the master bath. Separate vanities and a garden tub as well as a shower and a commode closet complete this area. Double French doors lead from the master suite to a deck. The 13'x13' living room features a cathedral ceiling while an angled trey ceiling highlights the 12'x13' dining room. Stair placement is shown if a basement foundation is desired. The 16'x18' family room is a spacious gathering area with vaulted ceiling and fireplace. The breakfast area leads into the 10'x10' kitchen which includes a snack bar. The two other bedrooms share a hall bath and each has a walk-in closet. Conveniently located in this bedroom wing is the laundry room. No materials list available.

Main area — 2,275 sq. ft.
Basement — 2,207 sq. ft.
Garage — 512 sq. ft.

Total living area:
2,275 sq. ft.

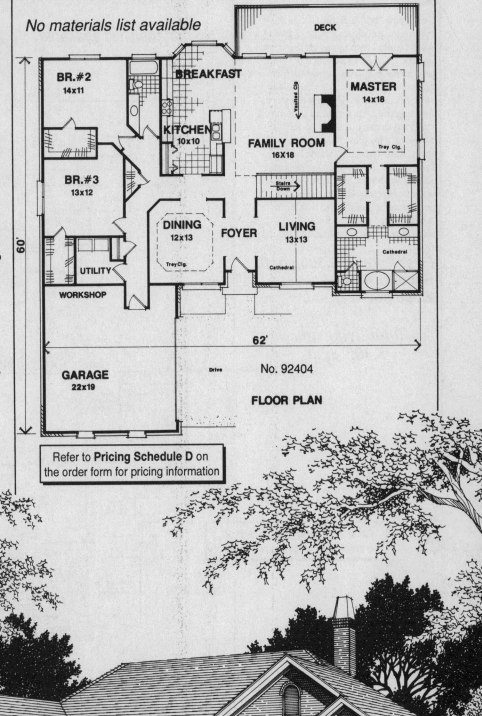

No materials list available

FLOOR PLAN

No. 92404

Refer to **Pricing Schedule D** on the order form for pricing information

SOUTHWEST STYLING

Southwest styling distinguishes this prestigious residence. A large two story family room opens off the central gallery. A video/audio area is provided along with a conveniently placed refreshment bar. The master suite features a see-through fireplace dividing the bedroom from an owner's study. A centerpiece whirlpool accented with glass block is located in front of the oversized shower. An in-law wing is designed on the opposite side of the home, and features a bath and kitchenette. Upstairs are three additional bedrooms and two baths. An oversized game room with a refreshment bar completes the second floor.

**First floor — 3,300 sq. ft.
Second floor —
2,005 sq. ft.**

*Total living area:
5,305 sq. ft.*

No materials list available

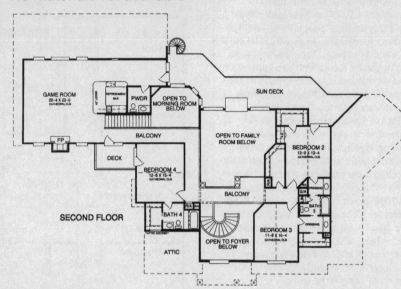

An **EXCLUSIVE DESIGN**
By Belk Home Designs

Refer to **Pricing Schedule F** on the order form for pricing information

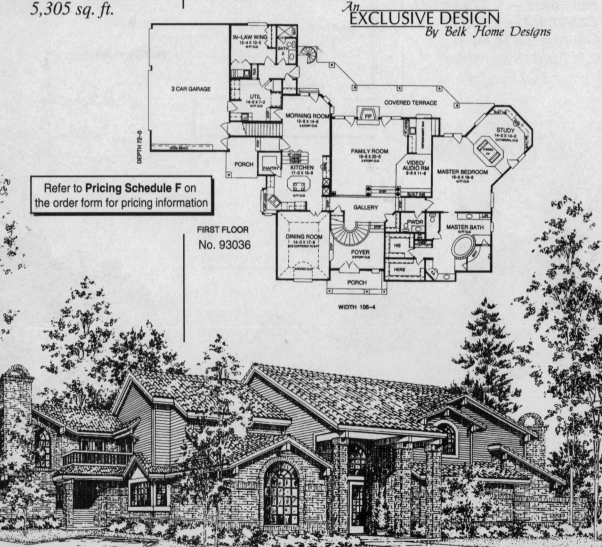

FIRST FLOOR
No. 93036

SPLENDOR AND DISTINCTION

The expansive kitchen in this home is sure to be a hub for activity. The cooktop island includes a convenient eating bar and a corner double sink looks out over the rear yard. The built-in pantry and planning desk add to its efficiency. The expansive family room is equipped with a built-in wetbar for convenience in serving your guests. The formal living room boasts a second fireplace and a view of the front yard. A bay window adds elegance to the formal dining room. The master suite is on the second floor and its private master bath will pamper the owner in luxury. Three additional bedrooms share a full hall bath. A balcony overlooks the family room and the foyer. No materials list available for this plan.

First floor — 1,720 sq. ft.
Second floor — 1,305 sq. ft.
Basement — 1,720 sq. ft.
Garage — 768 sq. ft.

Total living area: 3,025 sq. ft.

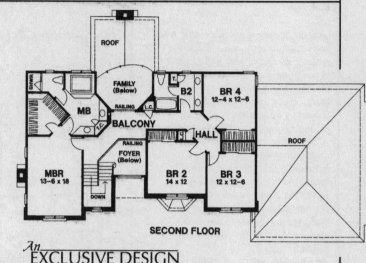

SECOND FLOOR

An EXCLUSIVE DESIGN
By Patrick Morabito, A.I.A. Architect

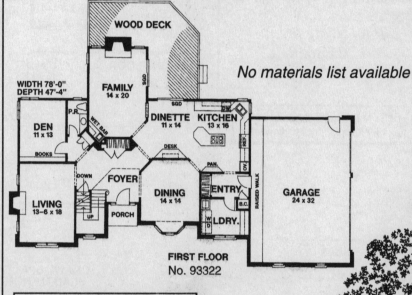

No materials list available

FIRST FLOOR
No. 93322

Refer to **Pricing Schedule E** on the order form for pricing information

EXTRA TOUCHES OF STYLE

Design 24700

You don't have to sacrifice style when buying a smaller home. Notice the palladian window with a fan light above at the front of the home. The entrance porch includes a turned post entry. Once inside, the living room is topped by an impressive vaulted ceiling. A fireplace accents the room. A decorative ceiling enhances both the master bedroom and the dining room. Efficiently designed, the kitchen includes a peninsula counter and serves the dining room with ease. A private bath and double closet highlight the master suite. Two additional bedrooms are served by a full hall bath.

Main floor — 1,312 sq. ft.
Basement — 1,293 sq. ft.

Total living area:
1,312 sq. ft.

Refer to **Pricing Schedule A** on the order form for pricing information

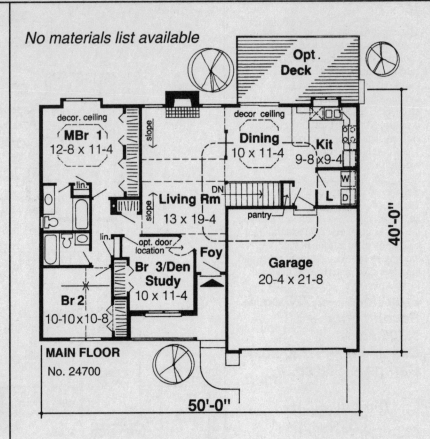

No materials list available

MAIN FLOOR
No. 24700

CRAWL SPACE/ SLAB OPTION

FOR THE DISCRIMINATING BUYER

A classic design and spacious interior make this home attractive and exciting to the discriminating buyer. Brick and wood trim, multiple gables, and wing walls enhance the outside; while the interior offers features that are designed for entertaining guests or family enjoyment. Sloped ceilings, a corner fireplace, windows across the rear of the Great room and a boxed window in the dining room area are immediately visible as you enter the open foyer. The extra large kitchen provides an abundance of counter space, and a pantry. The breakfast area is surrounded by windows that flood the room with natural light. In the master bedroom suite there is an ultra bath with whirlpool tub, a double sink, a shower and a walk-in closet. This three bedroom Ranch can be expanded to twice its original size by accessing the full basement. No materials list available for this plan.

**Main living area —
1,710 sq. ft.
Basement — 1,560 sq. ft.
Garage — 455 sq. ft.
Width — 65'-10"
Depth — 56'-0"**

*Total living area:
1,710 sq. ft.*

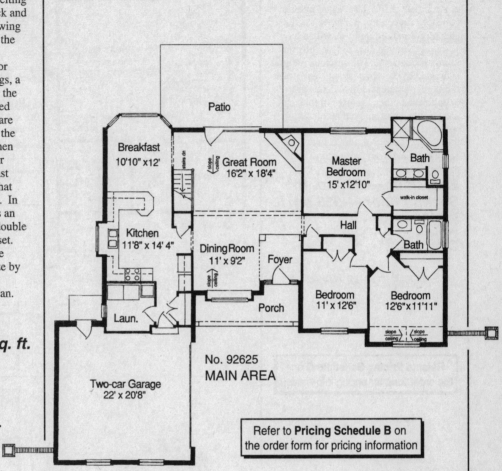

No. 92625
MAIN AREA

Refer to **Pricing Schedule B** on the order form for pricing information

OPEN LAYOUT IN FAMILY LIVING AREA

A covered porch creates a welcoming environment at the start. Enter into the two story foyer area. To the left is the elegant formal dining room with a bay window. Straight ahead is the informal family living area. The spacious feeling is created by the open layout. The great room, the dinette and the kitchen are open to each other. A large fireplace in the great room is enjoyed in this living space. Three bedrooms are located on the second floor. An ultra master bath and a walk-in closet enhance the large master suite.

First floor — 961 sq. ft.
Second floor — 926 sq. ft.
Width — 52' - 8"
Depth — 40' - 0"

Total living area:
1,887 sq. ft.

Refer to **Pricing Schedule C** on the order form for pricing information

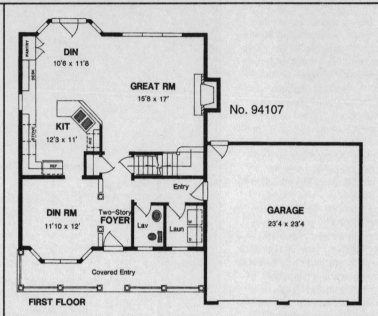

No. 94107

FIRST FLOOR

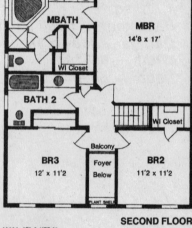

SECOND FLOOR

WARM AND INVITING

The stone and siding exterior with a covered porch and a boxed window combine to create a warm and an inviting home. Family activities will center around the sunken Great room, a wood-burning fireplace and an entertainment center, and can be easily expanded to the outdoors. Across the rear wall of the Great room is a series of double hung windows which are repeated in the breakfast area, providing a bright and cherry place for everyday living. A pass through is featured at the kitchen sink and an expanded counter space, handy for serving quick meals. Steps away is the dining room which adds formality to those special occasions. Split stairs trimmed with wood rails lead to the second floor. A master suite, featuring an ultra bath and a sloped ceiling and two additional bedrooms are included on the second floor. No materials list available.

First floor — 1,065 sq. ft.
Second floor — 833 sq. ft.

Total living area:
1,898 sq. ft.

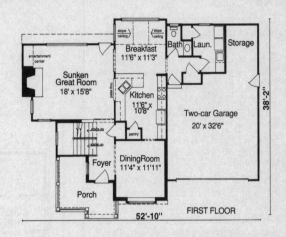

No. 92647

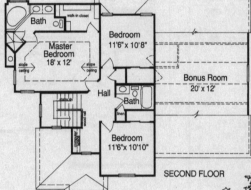

Refer to **Pricing Schedule C** on the order form for pricing information

ONE-LEVEL LIVIING

Entering the foyer from the covered porch of this elegant European design we find the coat closet to the right and the living room to the rear. This grand living area features a four-way vaulted ceiling a fireplace with built-in cabinets on each side. The rear wall is virtually all glass and is covered by the back porch. The gourmet kitchen is very large and features built-in ovens, cook-top, dishwasher and pantry. To the left of the foyer, we find three bedrooms. The large master bedroom has a raised ceiling and features a compartmentalized bath with a whirlpool tub and separate shower stall and an oversized walk-in closet. This room also has French doors which open onto the covered rear porch. This plan packs everything you need on one level.

Main area — 1,887 sq. ft.
Porch — 196 sq. ft.
Garage & Storage — 524 sq. ft.

Total living area:
1,887 sq. ft.

Refer to **Pricing Schedule C** on the order form for pricing information

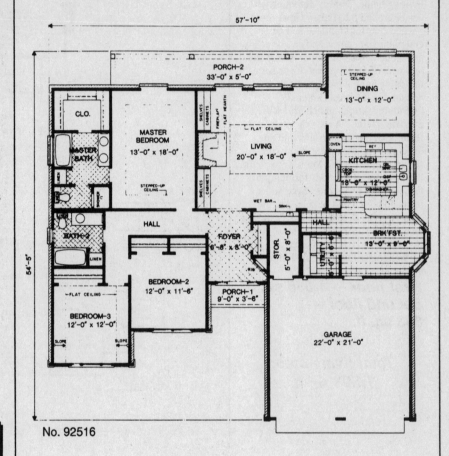

No. 92516

TRIPLE TANDEM GARAGE

The large foyer of this gracious ranch leads you back to the bright and spacious living room. The large open kitchen features a central work island with lots of extra storage space and there is also a handy laundry room with pantry and garage access. The master suite features a private master bath with oversized tub, corner shower, room-sized walk-in closet, as well as a bay shared sitting area and French doors. The two front bedrooms share a full bath. The lower level has plenty of open space for future expansion. The triple tandem garage provides space for a third car, boat, or just plenty of storage and work space. No materials list available for this plan.

Main area — 1,761 sq. ft.
Basement — 1,761 sq. ft.
Garage — 658 sq. ft.

Total living area:
1,761 sq. ft.

Refer to **Pricing Schedule B** on the order form for pricing information

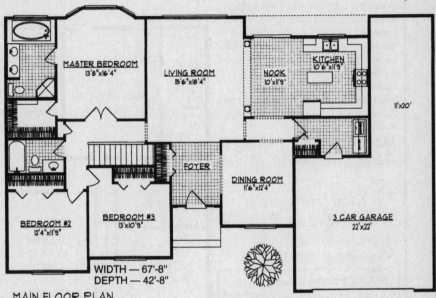

An
EXCLUSIVE DESIGN
By Ahmann Design Inc.

MASTER BEDROOM
13'8"x16'4"

LIVING ROOM
15'6"x18'4"

NOOK
10'x11'9"

KITCHEN
10'6"x11'9"

11'x20'

FOYER

DINING ROOM
11'6"x12'4"

BEDROOM #2
12'4"x11'9"

BEDROOM #3
13'x10'9"

3 CAR GARAGE
22'x22'

WIDTH — 67'-8"
DEPTH — 42'-8"

MAIN FLOOR PLAN
No. 93133

A COMPACT HOME

Siding with brick wainscoting distinguish the elevation of this compact plan. A large family room with a corner fireplace is the centerpiece for this small, but livable home. An arched opening leads to the breakfast area with bay window and the efficiently designed kitchen. The master bath is designed with a separate vanity area for privacy and convenience. Two additional bedrooms and a full bath complete this compact home. No materials list available for this plan.

Main floor — 1,142 sq. ft.
Garage — 428 sq. ft.

Total living area:
1,142 sq. ft.

Refer to **Pricing Schedule A** on the order form for pricing information

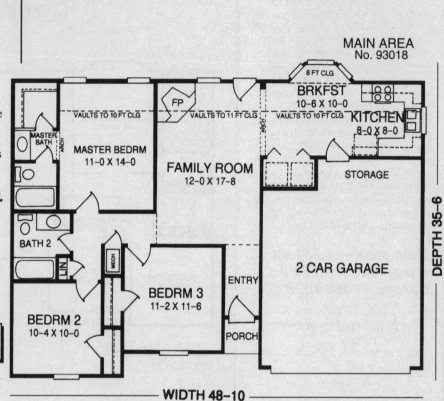

MAIN AREA
No. 93018

8 FT CLG

VAULTS TO 10 FT CLG

FP

VAULTS TO 11 FT CLG

VAULTS TO 10 FT CLG

BRKFST
10-6 X 10-0

KITCHEN
8-0 X 8-0

MASTER BATH

MASTER BEDRM
11-0 X 14-0

FAMILY ROOM
12-0 X 17-8

STORAGE

BATH 2

MECH

LIN

2 CAR GARAGE

BEDRM 3
11-2 X 11-6

ENTRY

BEDRM 2
10-4 X 10-0

PORCH

DEPTH 35-6

WIDTH 48-10

An
EXCLUSIVE DESIGN
By Belk Home Designs

STUCCO AND BRICK

The unique character of this home is evident judging from the arched top windows, copper roof over the two-story bay, and the elegantly detailed mixture of stucco and brick. The grand foyer has a wide and open staircase, two-story ceiling and magnificent balcony which also overlooks the den. It is surrounded by a large and spacious living room and dining room with it's own bay window. As you enter the den from the foyer, you pass the large round columns which extend up two full floors through the balcony. This large den features a built in wetbar, cabinets, shelves and a full two-story fireplace. This room defines elegance and sophistication. The master suite is located to the right of the den and features a sitting room with a vaulted ceiling. The master bath has his-n-her walk-in closets, separate vanities and linen closets. The gourmet kitchen is to the left of the den and a breakfast bar opens to the breakfast room with a vaulted ceiling. The upstairs has three large bedrooms with walk-in closets.

**Main area —
2,442 sq. ft.
Second floor —
1,062 sq. ft.
Garage — 565 sq. ft.**

*Total living area:
3,504 sq. ft.*

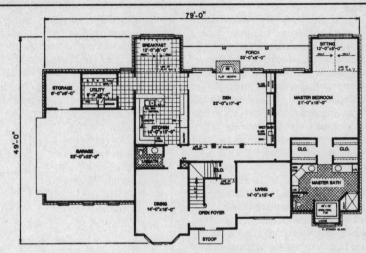

FIRST FLOOR PLAN
No. 92505

Refer to **Pricing Schedule F** on the order form for pricing information

SECOND FLOOR PLAN

EUROPEAN CLASSIC

Multiple gables, a box window and easy maintenance combine to create a dramatic appearance to the 2-story European Classic home. Excitement abounds in the Great room beginning with a wall of windows across the rear, a sloped ceiling, and an entertainment center nestled in the corner set to one side of the columned fireplace. The kitchen offers an island with sink and looks directly through French doors onto the patio and an oversized breakfast room. The dining room ceiling has a raised center section with molding and a furniture alcove is added for extra roominess around the table. The luxury and convenience of the first floor master bedroom suite is highlighted by his and her vanities, a shower and whirlpool tub. The second floor provides a private retreat for a guest suite or for a family with teenagers. A bonus room over the garage offers the option of a fourth bedroom. A balcony provides a view of the Great room and foyer. The rear of this home is stepped for privacy and ultimate use of windows for an infusion of light. No materials list available for this plan.

Refer to **Pricing Schedule E** on the order form for pricing information

FIRST FLOOR
No. 92613

Porch

Patio

Breakfast
13' x 10'5"

Laun.

Bath

Hall

Kitchen
17' x 13'2"

butler's pantry

Garage
21'10" x 32'4"

Great Room
19'4" x 17'9"

entertainment center

Master Bedroom
13'8" x 17'9"

Dining Room
13' x 12'9"

tray ceiling

Foyer

Hall

Bath

Porch

Bath

Dressing

walk-in closet

WIDTH 74'-4"
DEPTH 69'-11"

SECOND FLOOR

Bedroom
13' x 13'11"

Bath

Bonus Room
16'8" x 15

Balcony

Great Room Below

Bedroom
13' x 13'4"

First floor — 2,192 sq. ft.
Second floor —
654 sq. ft.
Total living area:
2,846 sq. ft.

Design 93041

TWO-STORY ENTRY ADDS GRACE

A stucco design is used to accent the arched, two-story entry of this pleasing design. Inside, all major living areas are located with views to the rear grounds, which makes this plan a winner for a golf course, pool or lake site. The kitchen, breakfast room and family room are adjacent and open to one another. The master suite has all the extras with an angled whirlpool tub, separate shower and his-n-her vanities. The second floor includes three bedrooms, an in-home office or bedroom and a bath.

**First floor —
1,974 sq. ft.
Second floor —
1,060 sq. ft.
Garage — 51 sq. ft.**

An
EXCLUSIVE DESIGN
By Belk Home Designs

Refer to **Pricing Schedule E** on
the order form for pricing information

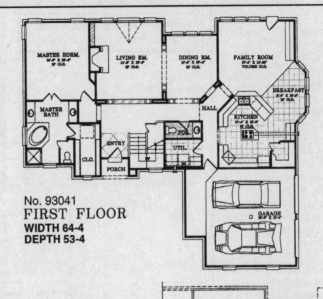

No. 93041
FIRST FLOOR
WIDTH 64-4
DEPTH 53-4

SECOND FLOOR
No materials list available

*Total living area:
3,034 sq. ft.*

Design 93219

OLD-FASHIONED COUNTRY PORCH

The old-fashioned country porch on the front of this home warmly welcomes all who visit. As you enter the home, the warm glow of the fireplace in the living room encourages you to move further into the home. The dining room is close at hand for an elegant dinner party or an intimate evening. The U-shaped kitchen efficiently services both the formal dining room and the informal breakfast area. A first floor master suite ensures privacy for parents by sending the children to bed on the second floor. The master suite includes a luxurious master bath with a double vanity, walk-in closet, oval tub, and step-in shower. A convenient half-bath with a laundry center is located on the first floor. On the second floor the full hall bath is flanked by the two additional bedrooms. The second floor bedrooms are large and have ample closet space.

First floor — 1,057 sq. ft.
Second floor — 611 sq. ft.
Basement — 511 sq. ft.
Garage — 546 sq. ft.

An
EXCLUSIVE DESIGN
By Jannis Vann & Associates, Inc.

Refer to **Pricing Schedule B** on the order form for pricing information

Total living area: 1,668 sq. ft.

SUNDECK
16'-0" X 12'-0"

BREAKFAST
9'-0" X 18'-0"

KITCHEN
9'-0" X 9'-6"

DINING RM.
9'-10" X 11'-4"

LIVING AREA
18'-0" X 13'-6"

MASTER BEDROOM
15'-6" X 13'-6"

38'-0"

36'-0"

FIRST FLOOR
No. 93219

BEDROOM-2
15'-8" X 13'-4"

BEDROOM-3
15'-6" X 11'-0"

SECOND FLOOR

ADDED PIZZAZZ

Tall ceilings, large windows, and custom trims and moldings give added pizzazz to this four bedroom, two-story home. A sunken family room with a tray ceiling is large enough for real family enjoyment and provides a spectacular view of the yard through a wall of windows. A fireplace is located on the far wall and can be viewed from the breakfast area or the cooking area of the kitchen. An oversized island brings added counter space and a pantry combines to create an abundance of kitchen storage. The living room and dining room on either side of the foyer opens the front of the house, creating a formal area to welcome visitors. A first floor den provides a private retreat or a spacious guest room. Four bedrooms on the second floor maximizes the use of living space. The master bedroom suite, with all the luxurious amenities, keeps the parents close at hand for the junior members of the family. No materials list available for this plan.

*First floor —
1,516 sq. ft.
Second floor —
1,148 sq. ft.
Garage —
440 sq. ft.*

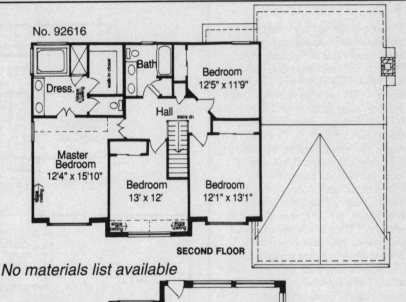

No. 92616

SECOND FLOOR

Bath
Dress.
walk-in closet
Bedroom 12'5" x 11'9"
Hall
stairs dn
Master Bedroom 12'4" x 15'10"
Bedroom 13' x 12'
Bedroom 12'1" x 13'1"
slope ceiling

No materials list available

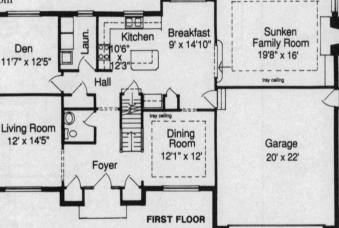

Den 11'7" x 12'5"
Laun.
Kitchen 10'6" x 12'3"
Breakfast 9' x 14'10"
Sunken Family Room 19'8" x 16'
tray ceiling
Hall
Living Room 12' x 14'5"
tray ceiling
Dining Room 12'1" x 12'
Garage 20' x 22'
Foyer

FIRST FLOOR

*Total living area :
2,664 sq. ft.*

**WIDTH 59'-6"
DEPTH 40'-0"**

Refer to **Pricing Schedule E** on the order form for pricing information

TURN-OF-THE-CENTURY STYLE

The turn-of-the-century country style exterior of this home gives way to living spaces that are brighter, more spacious and less formal than builders made them way back when. When you first enter the house the entryway has a vaulted ceiling to the second floor and is brightened by a window at the top of the upstairs landing. To the right is a huge Great room separated by nothing more than a fireplace. The kitchen is large and includes a central work island, pantry and access to one of two decks. There are skylights in the eating nook, providing a sunny start to your day. There is a luxurious master suite with a vaulted ceiling, a large walk-in closet, spa and separate vanity. The utility room, with its pullman bed tucked into a recessed wall, doubles as a guest room. Upstairs are two bedrooms, one is slightly larger than the other, and a bath.

First floor — 1,472 sq. ft.
Second floor —
478 sq. ft.
Garage — 558 sq. ft.
Width — 62'-0"
Depth — 51'-0"

Total living area:
1,950 sq. ft.

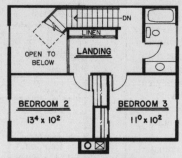

SECOND FLOOR PLAN

No. 99757

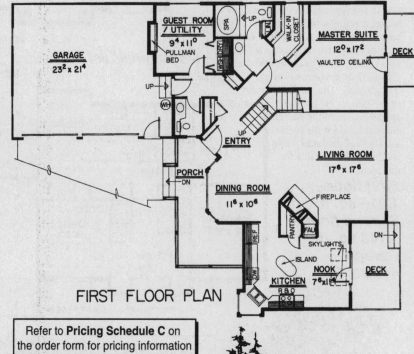

FIRST FLOOR PLAN

Refer to **Pricing Schedule C** on the order form for pricing information

AN ENERGY EFFICIENT HOME

The money you save on your utility costs on this home may help you pay for the mortgage. Beyond being energy efficient, this home includes the amenities that every modern family requires. The well-appointed kitchen with double sink, peninsula counter that doubles as an eating bar and ample storage space, is sure to please the cook of your family. The dining area and family room open into each other making all three rooms, kitchen, dining, and family rooms, appear more spacious than they actually are. The bedrooms are all located on the right wing of the home. The master suite includes a private bath with a shower and a walk-in closet. The two additional bedrooms share a full bath.

Main floor — 1,605 sq. ft.
Garage — 2-car

Total living area:
1,605 sq. ft.

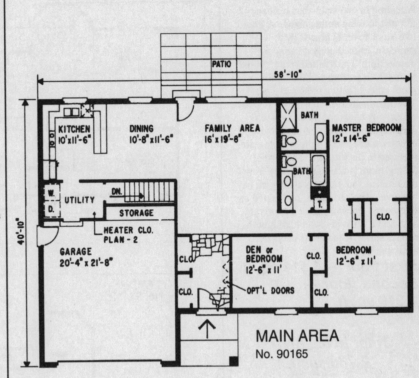

MAIN AREA
No. 90165

Refer to **Pricing Schedule B** on the order form for pricing information

DISTINGUISHED DWELLING

A feeling of an established residency is felt just looking at this home. A grand two-story foyer is graced by a staircase, immediately creating a impression. The vaulted ceiling in the formal living room and the family room adds a feeling of spaciousness. The dinette area is topped by a stepped ceiling. A cooktop island, a double sink, an abundance of storage and counter space and a built-in pantry are featured in the kitchen. The formal dining room is accessed directly from the kitchen and includes an elegant bay window. The bedrooms are located on the second floor. A luxurious private bath and a walk-in closet highlight the master suite. A materials list is not available with this plan.

First floor — 1,514 sq. ft.
Second floor — 1,219 sq. ft.

Total living area: 2,733 sq. ft.

Refer to **Pricing Schedule E** on the order form for pricing information

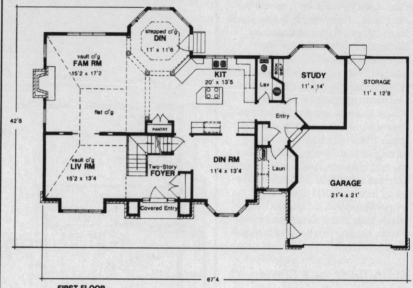

FIRST FLOOR
No. 94112

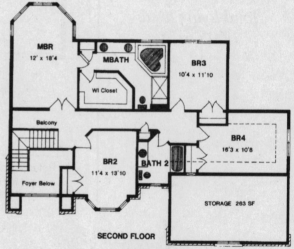

SECOND FLOOR

COUNTRY RANCH

A railed and covered wrap-around porch adds charm to this country Ranch styled home. This home is as compact and efficient as it is attractive. Wide bay windows over-arched by another window set high in the front wall, under the gabled arch outside, give a bright, open feel to the vaulted living room. Despite its small size, the kitchen has ample cupboard and counter space and is augmented by a large pantry. The master suite has all the amenities, including a double walk-in closet and an oversized tub. There is a formal living room and an informal family room. Bedrooms two and three share a hall bath. The full deck at the rear of the house is accessed from both the master suite and the family room. Charm and convenience abound in this house.

**Main living area —
1,485 sq. ft.
Garage — 701 sq. ft.
Width — 51'-6"
Depth —63'-0"**

*Total living area:
1,485 sq. ft.*

Refer to **Pricing Schedule A** on the order form for pricing information

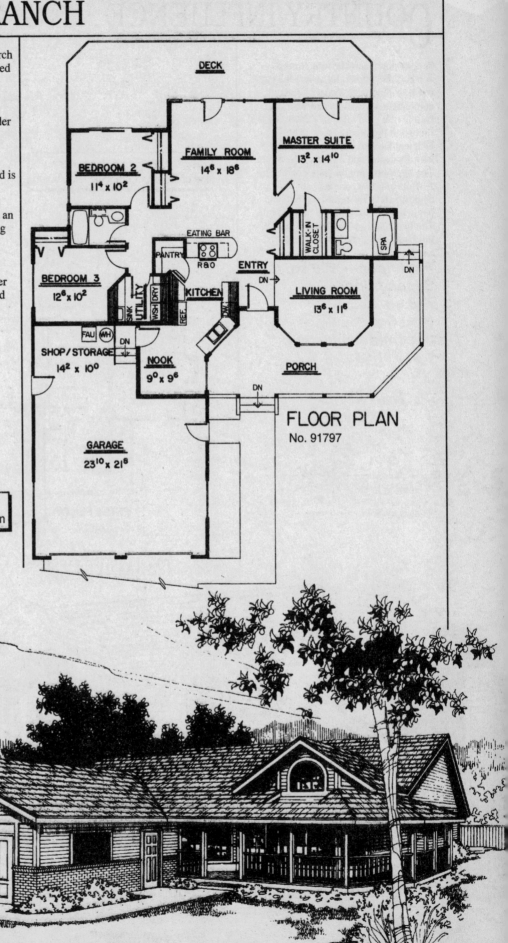

FLOOR PLAN
No. 91797

COUNTRY INFLUENCE

A cozy porch sets the tone for this comfortable home. Enter into the sun room that includes a coat closet and convenient access to a half bath. A simple half wall separates the living room and the dining room. The efficient kitchen is equipped with a laundry center and a sunny bayed area. The bedrooms are on the second floor. A walk-in closet, private bath with an oval tub and a decorative ceiling and bay window highlight the master suite. The two additional bedrooms share a full bath. No materials list available for this plan.

First floor — 806 sq. ft.
Second floor — 748 sq. ft.

Total living area:
1,554 sq. ft.

Refer to **Pricing Schedule B** on the order form for pricing information

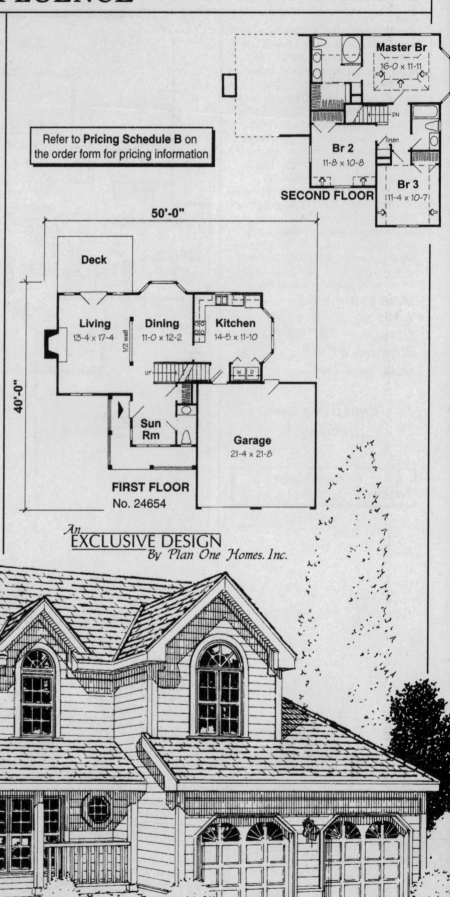

SECOND FLOOR

Master Br
16-0 x 11-11

Br 2
11-8 x 10-8

Br 3
11-4 x 10-7

linen

DN

50'-0"

40'-0"

Deck

Living
13-4 x 17-4

1/2 wall

Dining
11-0 x 12-2

Kitchen
14-5 x 11-10

UP

W D

Sun Rm

Garage
21-4 x 21-8

FIRST FLOOR
No. 24654

An
EXCLUSIVE DESIGN
By Plan One Homes, Inc.

A SPLIT BEDROOM PLAN

This split bedroom plan features a traditional elevation coupled with an up-to-date, efficiently designed floor plan. Upon entering, an angled foyer opens the home to a large Great room with a fireplace. A formal dining room is defined with a series of columns that give the home an elegant feel. The master suite is entered through double doors and is privately located away from the other bedrooms. The master bath features all the luxuries with an angled whirlpool tub, separate shower and double vanities. An enormous walk-in closet complete the arrangement. The kitchen features a pantry and has plenty of cabinet and counter space. A coffered ceiling treatment adds character to the breakfast room located on the rear of the home. Bedrooms two and three are arranged nearby with convenient access to the second bath. No materials list available for this plan.

Main floor — 1,955 sq. ft.
Garage — 561 sq. ft.

Total living area:
1,955 sq. ft.

Refer to **Pricing Schedule C** on the order form for pricing information

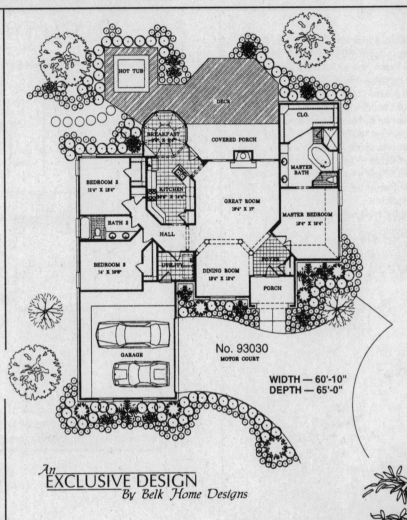

No. 93030
MOTOR COURT

WIDTH — 60'-10"
DEPTH — 65'-0"

An **EXCLUSIVE DESIGN**
By Belk Home Designs

IDEAL RANCH

This three bedroom ranch offers all the things your family will need. The spacious living room will catch your eye as you enter, and the open floor plan makes staying in touch easy. The master bedroom is separate from the other two bedrooms, this insures privacy for the owner. The other two bedrooms share a main floor bath. The stairs off the foyer lead to a lower level, where you'll find plenty of room for future expansion. No materials list is available.

**Main living area —
1,508 sq. ft.
Basement — 1,508 sq. ft.
Garage — 400 sq. ft.**

*Total living area:
1,508 sq. ft.*

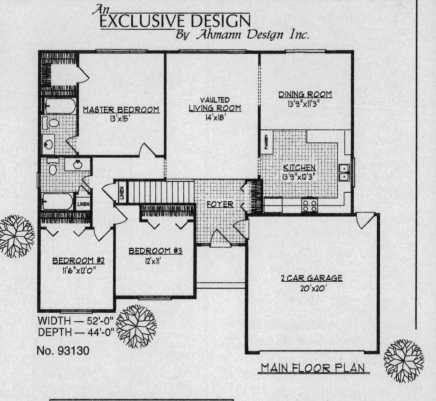

An
EXCLUSIVE DESIGN
By Ahmann Design Inc.

MASTER BEDROOM
13'x15'

VAULTED
LIVING ROOM
14'x18'

DINING ROOM
13'9"x11'3"

KITCHEN
13'9"x12'3"

FOYER

LINEN

BEDROOM #2
11'6"x12'0"

BEDROOM #3
12'x11'

2 CAR GARAGE
20'x20'

WIDTH — 52'-0"
DEPTH — 44'-0"

No. 93130

MAIN FLOOR PLAN

Refer to **Pricing Schedule B** on the order form for pricing information

CONTEMPORARY DRAMA

Special dramatics focused on the grand stairway and balcony above the great room. A columned arcade directs traffic from the vestibule to the master suite and the library wing on the left; the family and kitchen areas are on the right. The entrance offers impressive view of the double height great room with a detailed fireplace wall. The vast master suite has a walk-in closet and whirlpool tub with twin vanities in the master bath. There is private access through the master suite allows intimate evenings relaxing in the hot tub on the deck. The dining room is open, yet in its own alcove. The L-shaped kitchen opens to the breakfast area with sliding glass doors to the second deck. Three additional bedrooms on the second level each sport personal baths and plenty of closet space.

First floor — 3,900 sq. ft.
**Second floor —
1,720 sq. ft.**
Basement — 2,500 sq. ft.
Garage — 836 sq. ft.

*Total living area:
5,620 sq. ft.*

Refer to **Pricing Schedule F** on the order form for pricing information

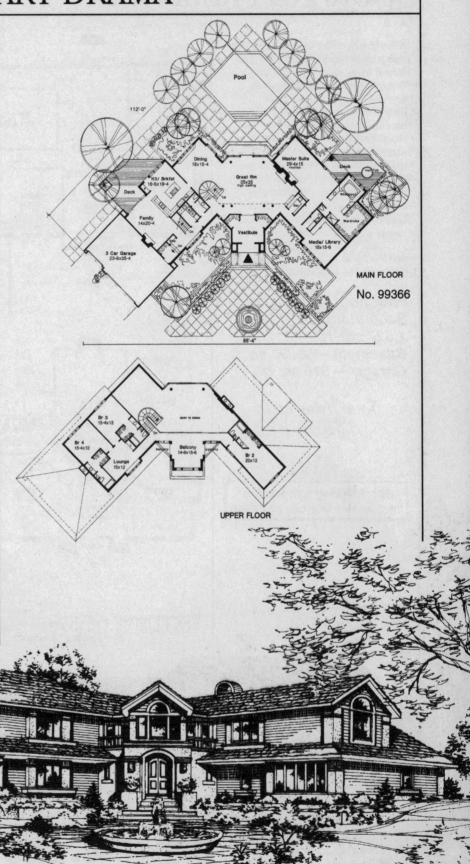

MAIN FLOOR

No. 99366

UPPER FLOOR

A GRAND PRESENCE

A foyer with a high ceiling greets your guests upon entering this home. The formal living room has a fantastic fireplace that can be seen from the foyer. The formal dining room includes intriguing pocket doors between it and the dinette area. The island kitchen includes a built-in pantry and planning desk, as well as more than ample counter and cabinet space. A tray ceiling crowns the family room, equipped with a cozy fireplace and a built-in entertainment center. A luxury bath highlights the master suite that also includes a walk-in closet. Three additional bedrooms, two having walk-in closets, share a full hall bath. No materials list available for this plan.

**First floor — 2,093 sq. ft.
Second floor —
1,527 sq.. ft.
Basement — 2,093 sq. ft.
Garage — 816 sq. ft.**

*Total living area:
3,620 sq. ft.*

Refer to **Pricing Schedule F** on the order form for pricing information

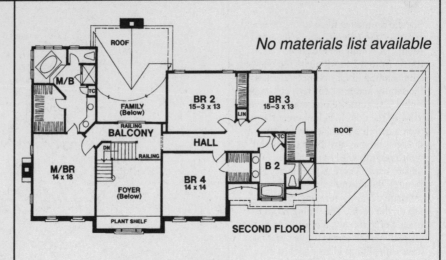

No materials list available

SECOND FLOOR

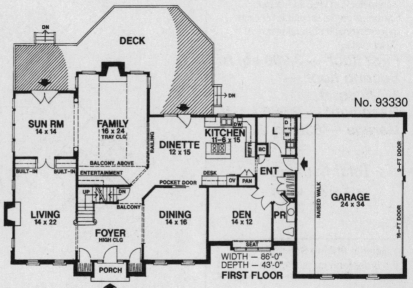

No. 93330

WIDTH — 86'-0"
DEPTH — 43'-0"
FIRST FLOOR

An
EXCLUSIVE DESIGN
By Patrick Morabito, A.I.A. Architect

CHARMING YET DIGNIFIED

Spacious rooms arranged around a central foyer, with many features, plus a charming, warm and dignified exterior result in a home for quality family living. There is a large all purpose room and bath at the top level. It can be used as a fifth bedroom, a studio, office or whatever suits the family. An oversized master bedroom boasts a huge double loaded walk-in closet 12 feet 6 inches long, a roomy bath with double vanity, whirlpool tub, stall shower and a decorative window. The efficient "U" shaped kitchen is equipped with a pantry and adjacent planning desk. You enter the house through a welcoming wrap-around porch into an imposing two-story foyer. In front are the formal living and dining rooms on each side of the foyer. Rooms for the informal activities are placed in the rear; the family room merges with the dinette separated by a wet bar. The dinette is enhanced with a fully glazed bay that gives access to a terrace that stretches across the rear and is pleasantly decorated with a circular reflecting pool. Lots of windows are a key to the exterior design. It is a strong statement that builds up from the lower floor to the apex of a triangular pediment.

First floor —
1,293 sq. ft.
Second floor —
1,138 sq. ft.
Third floor —
575 sq. ft.
Basement —
1,293 sq. ft.

Total living area:
3,006 sq. ft.

Refer to **Pricing Schedule E** on the order form for pricing information

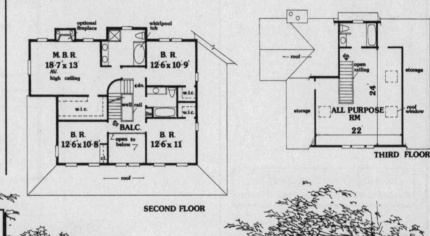

FIRST FLOOR
No. 99649

63'-4"
53'-4"

optional reflecting pool
TERRACE
2-CAR GAR. 20' x 20'
heat-circ. f.p.
FAM. RM 19'-6 x 13
wet bar
DINETTE 9'-8 x 11
KIT. 12'-6 x 15'-8
dw
ref.
D W
LAUN
cl.
pan.
dn.
L. R. 12'-6 x 16'-8
up
2-STOR. FOYER
cl.
D. R. 12'-6 x 14

SECOND FLOOR

optional fireplace
whirlpool tub
M. B. R. 18'-7 x 13 AV. high ceiling
B. R. 12'-6 x 10'-9
dn.
w.i.c.
w.i.c.
w.i.c.
lin.
well rail
up
BALC.
open to below
B. R. 12'-6 x 10'-8
cl.
B. R. 12'-6 x 11
roof

THIRD FLOOR

roof
dn.
open railing
storage
24
storage
ALL PURPOSE RM
22
roof window

Design 94109

A TRADITIONAL STANCE

A covered entry leads to a two story foyer. Flanking the foyer are the formal living room and the dining room. To the rear of the home are the informal living spaces. The well-appointed kitchen has direct access to the garage. A bayed dinette area provides a bright, informal eating place. An expansive family room is highlighted by a large fireplace. All the sleeping quarters are on the second floor. The roomy master suite includes a private bath and a walk-in closet. Three additional bedrooms share the full hall bath. A materials list is not available for this plan.

First floor — 1,025 sq. ft.
Second floor — 988 sq. ft.

Total living area: 2,013 sq. ft.

Refer to **Pricing Schedule C** on the order form for pricing information

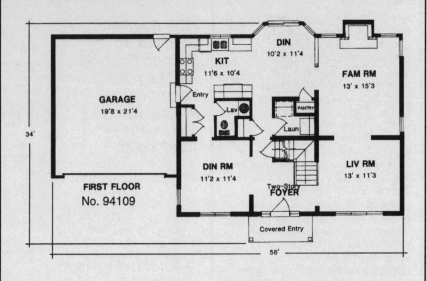

FIRST FLOOR
No. 94109

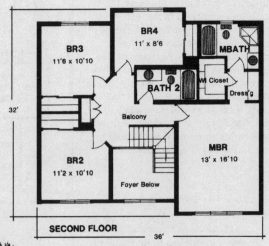

SECOND FLOOR

COZY AND UNIQUE RANCH

The mixture of brick and shaker siding gives this cozy Ranch a unique look sure to please your family as well as guests. The foyer opens into a large family room with a tall, vaulted ceiling. The unique kitchen, sure to please any chef, includes a desk area and breakfast bar which overlooks a sunny dining room perfect for entertaining. The large master suite with walk-in closet and generous bath area offers plenty of privacy. No materials list available for this plan.

**Main living area —
1,756 sq. ft.
Basement — 1,756 sq. ft.
Garage — 536 sq. ft.
Width — 50'-0"
Depth — 60'-0"**

*Total living area:
1,756 sq. ft.*

**Width — 58' - 0"
Depth — 55' - 0"**

Refer to **Pricing Schedule B** on the order form for pricing information

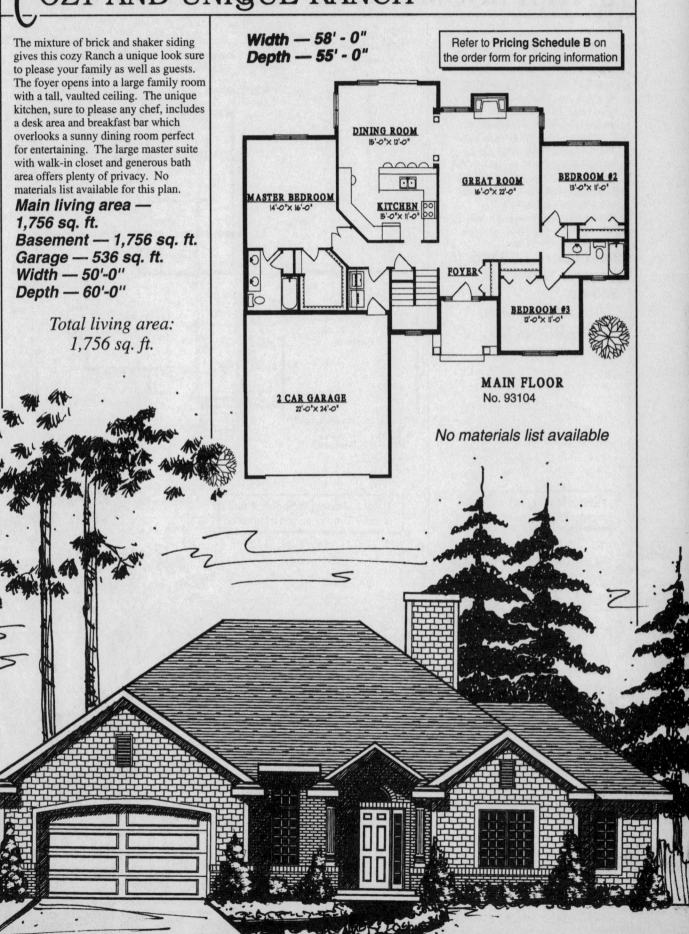

DINING ROOM
15'-0" x 12'-0"

GREAT ROOM
16'-0" x 22'-0"

BEDROOM #2
13'-0" x 11'-0"

MASTER BEDROOM
14'-0" x 16'-0"

KITCHEN
15'-0" x 11'-0"

FOYER

BEDROOM #3
12'-0" x 11'-0"

2 CAR GARAGE
22'-0" x 24'-0"

MAIN FLOOR
No. 93104

No materials list available

Design 93025

WITH A ROOMY WRAP-AROUND PORCH

A roomy wrap-around porch accents this farmhouse-style elevation, Inside, ten foot ceilings in the Great room, kitchen, and dining room give this home a spacious look. The efficiently designed kitchen includes a large pantry and plenty of cabinet and counter space. The dining room is nearby, and perfect for either family gatherings or formal entertaining. The master bedroom is located at the back of the home and features a functional master bath with double vanities. Bedrooms two and three and a second full bath complete this compact plan.

Main floor — 1,302 sq. ft.
Garage — 484 sq. ft.

Total living area:
1,302 sq. ft.

An
EXCLUSIVE DESIGN
By Belk Home Designs

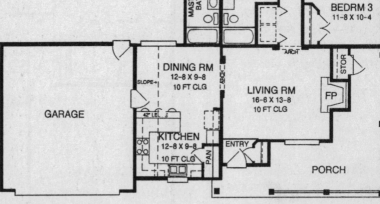

WIDTH 58–10

DEPTH 46–0

MASTER BEDRM
13-8 X 12-6

BEDRM 2
11-8 X 12-6

LIN

MASTER BATH

BATH 2

BEDRM 3
11-8 X 10-4

GARAGE

DINING RM
12-8 X 9-8
10 FT CLG

STOR

LIVING RM
16-6 X 13-8
10 FT CLG

FP

KITCHEN
12-8 X 9-8
10 FT CLG

PAN

ENTRY

PORCH

MAIN FLOOR
No. 93025

Refer to **Pricing Schedule A** on the order form for pricing information

IMPRESSIVE BALCONY OVERLOOK

The foyer of this home makes a grand first impression. Two-story in height, with streaming natural light and a balcony overlooking it all. The living room and the dining room are in an open layout making a spacious feel to both rooms. The efficient kitchen is U-shaped, and includes a corner double sink and a built-in pantry. The breakfast room has a coat closet and is easily accessible to the double garage. The family room is equipped with a pleasant fireplace to cuddle around on a stormy evening. The bedrooms are located on the second floor. The master suite has a walk-in closet, private master bath and its own linen closet. The two additional bedrooms have ample closet space and share a full hall bath. There is an area set aside for either a fourth bedroom, or whatever your family's needs determine in the future. A convenient second floor laundry room is located right outside the master suite.

Refer to **Pricing Schedule D** on the order form for pricing information

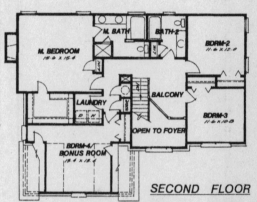

No. 93215

FIRST FLOOR

First floor — 949 sq. ft.
Second floor — 1,038 sq. ft.
Bonus room — 232 sq. ft.
Basement — 949 sq. ft.
Garage — 484 sq. ft.
Deck — 192 sq. ft.

SECOND FLOOR

Total living area: 2,219 sq. ft.

An EXCLUSIVE DESIGN
By Jannis Vann & Associates, Inc.

A COZY FRONT PORCH

An enchanting one level home with grand openings between rooms creates a spacious effect. The functional kitchen provides an abundance of counter space. Additional room for quick meals or serving an oversized crowd is provided at the breakfast bar. Double hung windows and angles add light and dimension to the dining area. The bright and cheery Great room with a sloped ceiling and a wood burning fireplace opens to the dining area and the foyer, making this three bedroom ranch look and feel much larger than its actual size. No materials list available.

Main floor — 1,508 sq. ft.

*Total living area:
1,508 sq. ft.*

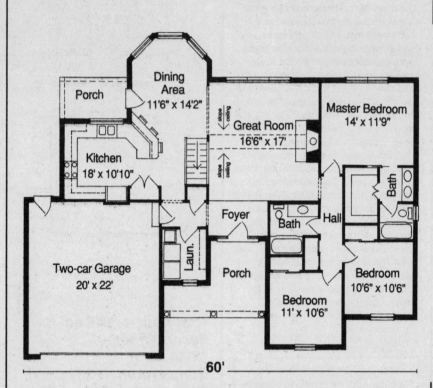

MAIN FLOOR
No. 92649

Refer to **Pricing Schedule B** on the order form for pricing information

CONVENIENT AND EFFICIENT RANCH

The one floor convenience of a ranch cannot be matched. The floor plan of this home keeps the private areas—the bedrooms—to one side and the high traffic areas to the other. The foyer features a barrel vault ceiling. Turning left from the foyer into the dinette, one can't help but notice another decorative ceiling, a stepped ceiling. There is also a stepped ceiling in the formal dining room. The kitchen features a work island and built-in pantry. An expansive gathering room has a tray ceiling and a large fireplace. The master suite affords the owner the luxury of privacy. A private master bath features separate shower and tub as well as a double vanity. The walk-in closet provides more than adequate storage space. Two additional bedrooms share the full hall bath. No materials list available for this plan.

Main living area — 1,810 sq. ft.
Garage — 528 sq. ft.

Total living area: 1,810 sq. ft.

Refer to **Pricing Schedule C** on the order form for pricing information

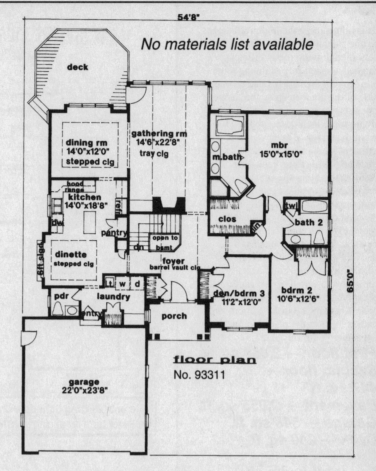

No materials list available

54'8"

65'0"

deck

dining rm
14'0"x12'0"
stepped clg

gathering rm
14'6"x22'8"
tray clg

m.bath

mbr
15'0"x15'0"

hood
range
kitchen
14'0"x18'8"

ref

clos

twl

bath 2

pantry

open to bsmt

dn

dinette
stepped clg

foyer
barrel vault clg

pdr

lt w d
laundry

entry

porch

den/bdrm 3
11'2"x12'0"

bdrm 2
10'6"x12'6"

floor plan
No. 93311

garage
22'0"x23'8"

An EXCLUSIVE DESIGN
By Patrick Morabito, A.I.A. Architect

SPECTACULAR STUCCO

This home keeps the high traffic areas to one side of the house. The sensational living room, efficient kitchen, elegant formal dining room and laundry area are located on one side of the home keeping the sleeping quarters private and quiet. The large living room includes a fireplace for warmth and mood enhancement. The efficient kitchen has a cooktop island that can double as an eating bar. There is informal eating space in the breakfast area and elegant formal entertaining space in the dining room. A wood deck, located off the living room, expands your living space outside. The master suite has a decorative ceiling and a private master bath with oval tub, double vanity and separate shower. The two additional bedrooms on this floor share a full hall bath. Upstairs a fourth bedroom and bath completes the plan. No materials list available for this plan.

First floor — 2,068 sq. ft.
Second floor —
447 sq. ft.
Basement — 2,055 sq. ft.
Garage — 548 sq. ft.
Deck — 240 sq. ft.

Total living area:
2,515 sq. ft.

An
EXCLUSIVE DESIGN
By Jannis Vann & Associates, Inc.

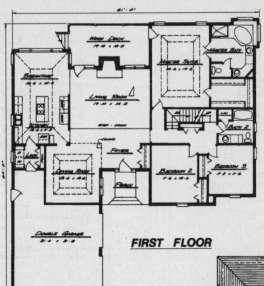

FIRST FLOOR

Refer to **Pricing Schedule D** on the order form for pricing information

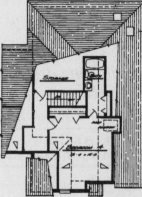

SECOND FLOOR

AN OPEN CONCEPT HOME

An angled entry creates the illusion of space and makes this split bedroom home feel larger. Two square columns flank the bar separating the kitchen from the living room and add detail to this open concept home. A dining room located off the kitchen services both formal and informal occasions. The master bedroom has a large walk-in closet and functional master bath with double vanities, linen closet and whirlpool tub/shower combination. Two additional bedrooms and a full bath area located on the opposite side of the home and complete the layout. No materials list available for this plan.

**Main living area —
1,282 sq. ft.
Garage — 501 sq. ft.**

*Total living area:
1,282 sq. ft.*

Refer to **Pricing Schedule A** on the order form for pricing information

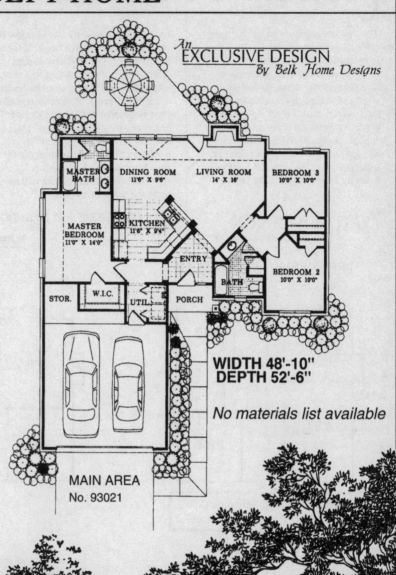

An EXCLUSIVE DESIGN
By Belk Home Designs

MASTER BATH

DINING ROOM 11'6" X 9'6"

LIVING ROOM 14' X 16'

BEDROOM 3 10'0" X 10'0"

MASTER BEDROOM 11'0" X 14'0"

KITCHEN 11'6" X 9'4"

ENTRY

BATH

BEDROOM 2 10'0" X 10'0"

STOR.

W.I.C.

UTIL.

PORCH

**WIDTH 48'-10"
DEPTH 52'-6"**

No materials list available

MAIN AREA
No. 93021

CHARMING COLONIAL

This two-story plan with its charming colonial exterior and family-friendly interior offers both formal and informal rooms in an economical size. The shutters and detail around the windows, the elliptical window, and the covered entry are all aspects of this home that give it wonderful street appeal. A formal living room is located to the left of the entry and is separated from the informal family room by French doors. The family room features a sunny bay window to the rear and a fireplace on the left end of the room. The spacious dinette offers atrium doors leading to a rear wood deck and access to stairs leading to the lower level. A luxurious master suite is isolated from the other three bedrooms by a large walk-in closet on one end and a master bath with whirlpool and linen closet on the other. An additional full bathroom is conveniently located off the hall to serve the other bedrooms.

An
EXCLUSIVE DESIGN
By Gary Clayton

No materials list available

First floor — 1,030 sq. ft.
Second floor (3 bdrms.)
— 1,022 sq. ft.
Second floor (4 bdrms.)
— 1,088 sq. ft.
Garage — 498 sq. ft.

Total living area:
2,052 sq. ft. (3 bdrms.)
2,118 sq. ft. (4 bdrms.)

UPPER LEVEL FLOOR PLAN

MAIN LEVEL FLOOR PLAN

BR3

MST

BR2

FR

D

KIT

GAR

LR

DR

Refer to **Pricing Schedule C** on the order form for pricing information

No. 92308

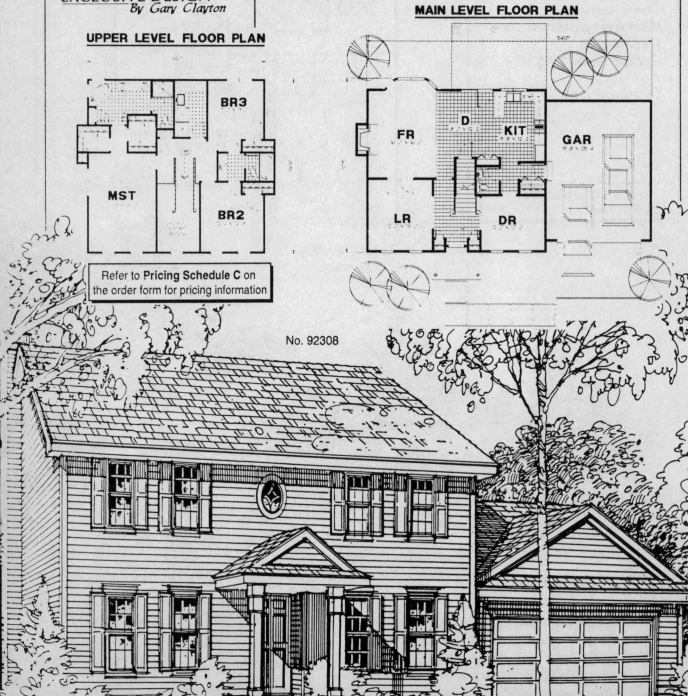

AN AFFORDABLE FLOOR PL

The living room of this home is enhanced by a vaulted ceiling and a fireplace with an old-fashioned hearth. The vaulted ceiling also enhances the dining room which opens out onto the patio. The kitchen is accessible from the dining area and features a U-shaped counter with all the amenities that any homeowner can ask for. The master bedroom is located away from the active areas of the home and has a large walk-in closet with its own private bath. Please specify foundation option, crawl space or slab, when ordering.

Main living area — 1,410 sq. ft.
Garage — 484 sq. ft.

Total living area: 1,410 sq. ft.

Refer to **Pricing Schedule A** on the order form for pricing information

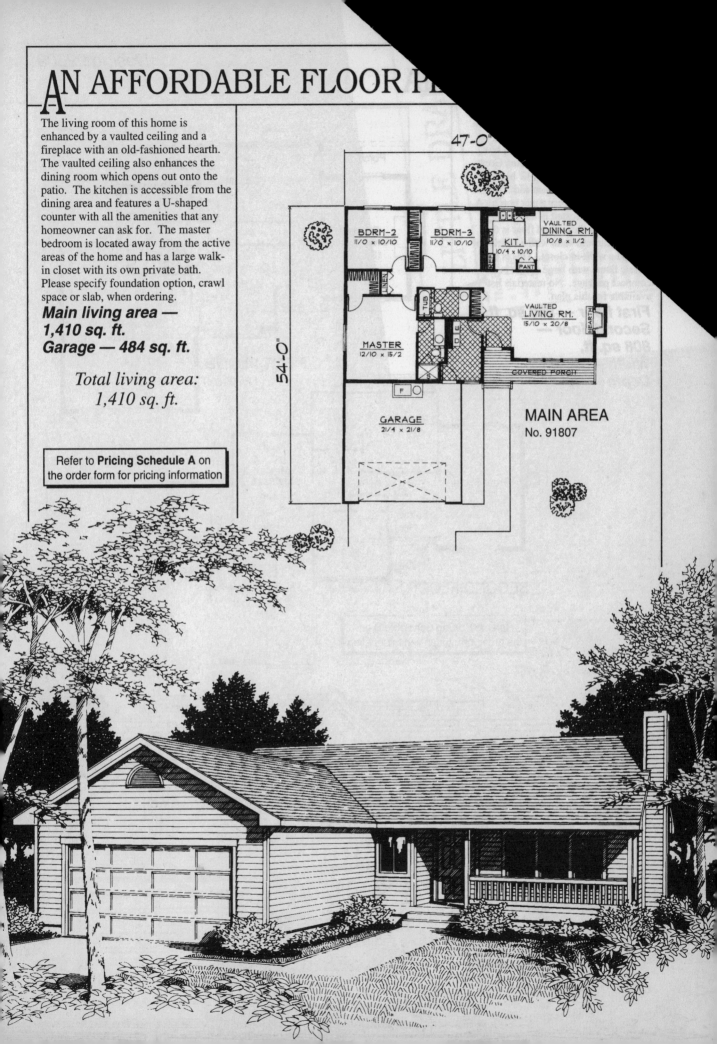

47'-0"

54'-0"

BDRM-2
11/0 x 10/10

BDRM-3
11/0 x 10/10

KIT.
10/4 x 10/10

PANT.

VAULTED
DINING RM.
10/8 x 11/2

LINEN

TUB

VAULTED
LIVING RM.
15/10 x 20/8

HEARTH

MASTER
12/10 x 15/2

COVERED PORCH

F

GARAGE
21/4 x 21/8

MAIN AREA
No. 91807

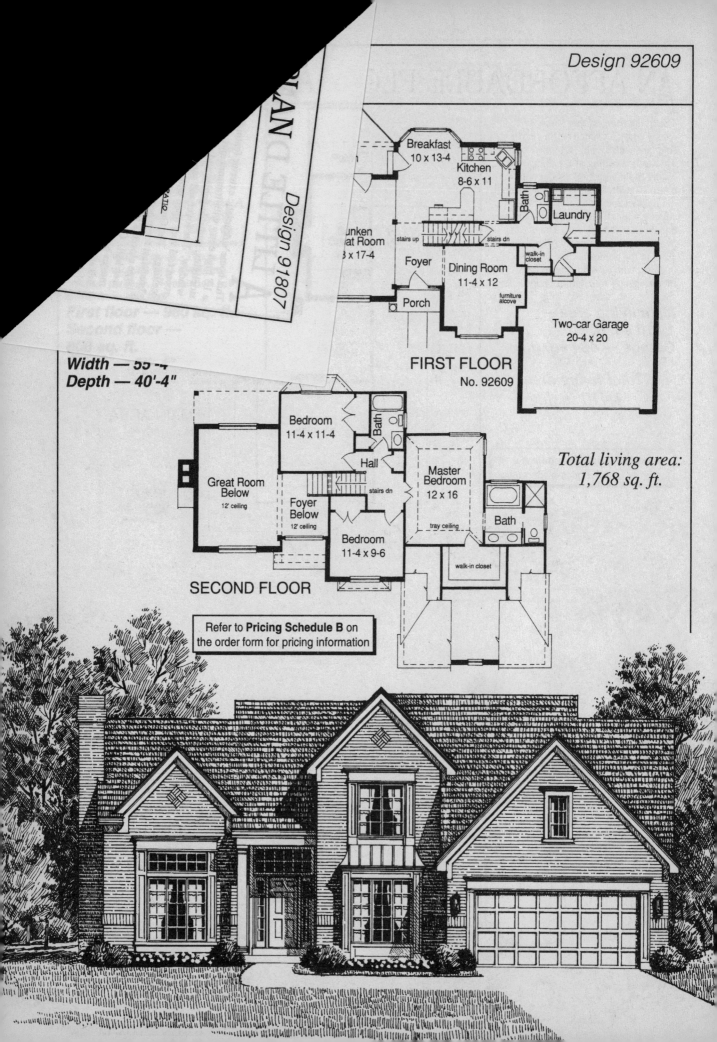

Design 92609

Breakfast
10 x 13-4

Kitchen
8-6 x 11

Bath

Laundry

Sunken
Great Room
8 x 17-4

stairs up   stairs dn

walk-in
closet

Foyer

Dining Room
11-4 x 12

Porch

furniture
alcove

Two-car Garage
20-4 x 20

FIRST FLOOR

No. 92609

PLAN

Design 91807

PATIO

First floor —
Second floor —

Width — 55'-4"
Depth — 40'-4"

Bedroom
11-4 x 11-4

Bath

Hall

stairs dn

Master
Bedroom
12 x 16

Bath

Great Room
Below
12' ceiling

Foyer
Below
12' ceiling

Bedroom
11-4 x 9-6

tray ceiling

walk-in closet

SECOND FLOOR

Total living area:
1,768 sq. ft.

Refer to **Pricing Schedule B** on
the order form for pricing information

Design 93240

TWO-STORY FOYER ADDS ELEGANCE

As you enter this magnificent home the two-story entrance captures your attention. There is a cascading curved staircase directly in front of you. The foyer is flanked by the formal dining room and the formal living room, both enjoy the view of the front yard through large windows. The family room is enhanced by a fireplace and has access to a sundeck. A sunny breakfast area is directly off of the well-appointed kitchen. Upstairs, the master suite has a decorative ceiling and a large master bath. Three additonal bedrooms share the full hall bath. A bonus room is provided to accommodate your future needs. No materials list available for this plan.

Main floor — 1,277 sq. ft.
Second floor — 1,177 sq. ft.
Bonus room — 392 sq. ft.
Basement — 1,261 sq. ft.
Garage — 572 sq. ft.
Deck — 192 sq. ft.

Total living area:
2,454 sq. ft.

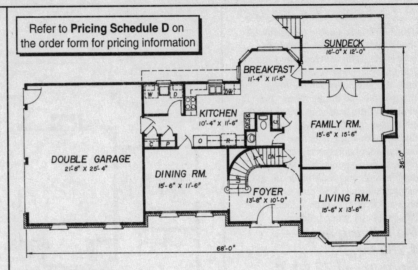

Refer to **Pricing Schedule D** on the order form for pricing information

FIRST FLOOR
No. 93240

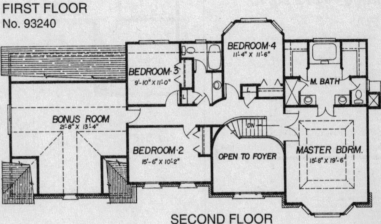

SECOND FLOOR

An
EXCLUSIVE DESIGN
By Jannis Vann & Associates, Inc.

Design 91814

WHEELCHAIR ACCESSIBLE

This home is adaptable for barrier free living. All rooms are wheelchair accessible. The covered porch and patio have decorative columns and half-round windows in the foyer, living room and dining room. The ceilings in the bedrooms are 8' but the ceilings in the foyer, living room, dining room and kitchen are 11'. The large master bedroom features access to the patio and dressing area with double sinks and walk-in closet, spa, tub and shower. This plan is available with a slab or crawl space foundation. Please specify when ordering.

Main living area — 1,785 sq. ft.
Garage — 672 sq. ft.

Total living area: 1,785 sq. ft.

Refer to **Pricing Schedule B** on the order form for pricing information

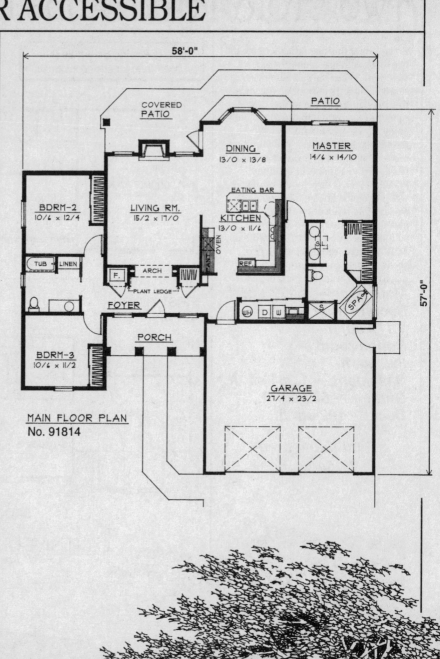

MAIN FLOOR PLAN
No. 91814

COLONIAL CHARMER

This charming Colonial gives you four bedrooms in only 1,920 sq. ft. The oversized family room opens onto the kitchen/nook area to create a feeling of openness. The family room features a large fireplace and access to the patio. A peninsula counter in the kitchen doubles as an eating bar. There is a formal living room and dining room for entertaining. The master suite has two closets and a private master bath with a jacuzzi and double vanity. The three additional bedrooms, one with a walk-in closet, share a full hall bath.

First floor — 970 sq. ft.
Second floor —
950 sq. ft.
Basement — 970 sq. ft.

Total living area: 1,920 sq. ft.

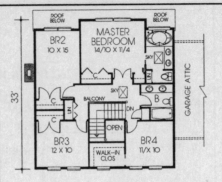

SECOND FLOOR

Refer to **Pricing Schedule C** on the order form for pricing information

OPTIONAL BASEMENT

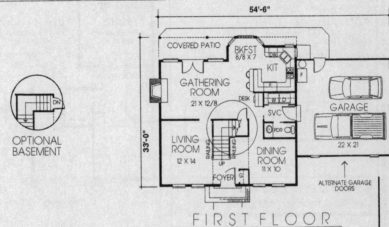

FIRST FLOOR

No. 93523

TURRET ADDS APPEAL

Make yourself at home in this delightful one story home. Volume ceilings highlight the main living areas which include a formal dining room and a Great room with access to one of the verandas. In the turreted study, quiet time is assured with double doors closing off the rest of the house. Nearby, the master bedroom suite features a luxury bath. The secondary bedrooms reside on the other side of the house.

Main floor — 2,214 sq. ft.
Garage — 652 sq. ft.

Total living area:
2,214 sq. ft.

Refer to **Pricing Schedule D** on the order form for pricing information

No materials list available

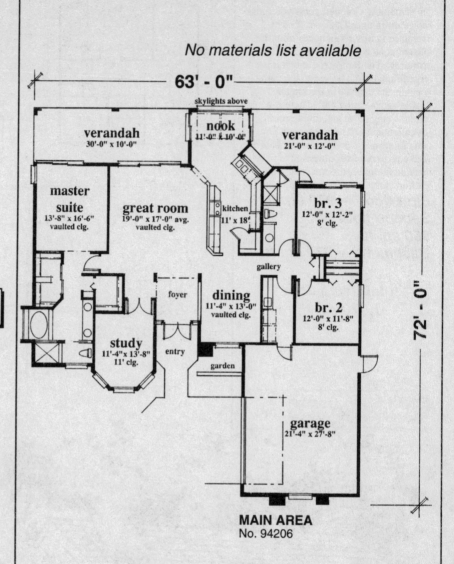

MAIN AREA
No. 94206

SKYLIGHTS ADD WARMTH

A partial stone veneer front makes this large ranch design very inviting. Inside, a vestibule entry serves as an airlock. A large library/den next to the foyer shares a two-way fireplace with the living room, and has a sloped ceiling, as does the living room. The living room leads to a deck or screened porch. A very large kitchen has a hexagonal island with a connecting dining room. The dining room also has skylights adding warmth and additional lighting to the room. Also in the dining room, a door leads out to the veranda. This spacious design has four bedrooms and ample closet space.

Main area — 2,450 sq. ft.
Basement — 2,450 sq. ft.
Garage — 739 sq. ft.

Total living area: 2,450 sq. ft.

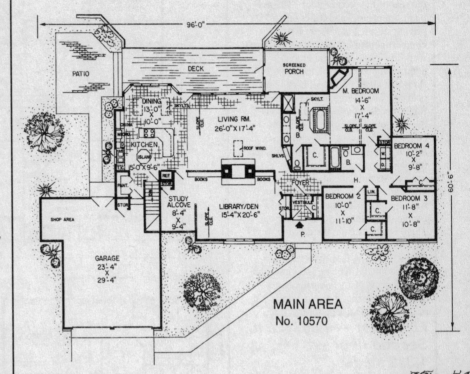

MAIN AREA
No. 10570

Refer to **Pricing Schedule D** on the order form for pricing information

EXPANSIVE MASTER SUITE

The master suite of this home takes up the rear of the second floor. The main bedroom is large and flows into a private sitting area. There is a compartmented master bath and a large walk-in closet. There are three additional bedrooms on the second floor that share a full hall bath. There is even a bonus area to answer to your future needs. As you enter the house, the spacious foyer gives you three choices in direction. To your left is the formal living room, to your right is the formal dining room or you may proceed straight ahead into the kitchen/breakfast area. The kitchen is well-appointed and has a peninsula counter that doubles as an eating bar. There is a door from the garage into the kitchen with a closet directly to the door's left. The family room is enhanced by a fireplace and views the rear sundeck. This home has been designed with the family in mind. No materials list available for this plan.

First floor — 1,307 sq. ft.
Second floor — 1,333 sq. ft.
Bonus room — 308 sq. ft.
Basement — 1,307 sq. ft.
Garage — 528 sq. ft.
Deck — 168 sq. ft.

Total living area:
2,640 sq. ft.

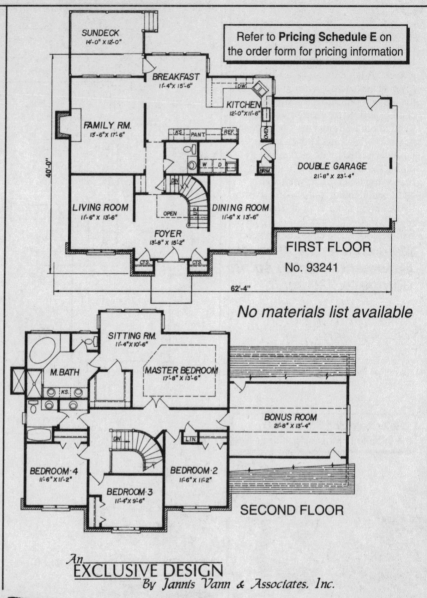

Refer to **Pricing Schedule E** on the order form for pricing information

FIRST FLOOR
No. 93241

No materials list available

SECOND FLOOR

An
EXCLUSIVE DESIGN
By *Jannis Vann & Associates, Inc.*

PACKED WITH EFFICIENCY

A modest-sized two-story home with consideration for cost-efficient construction and the value-oriented consumer. This home features an open plan with minimum circulation. The kitchen is large enough for an informal eating area. The entry views the spacious living room. The master suite has a large walk-in closet and private bath. The secondary bedrooms are conveniently equipped with an upper level laundry area. No materials list available for this plan.

First floor — 684 sq. ft.
Second floor — 727 sq. ft.
Garage — 400 sq. ft.
Basement — 684 sq. ft.

Total living area:
1,411 sq. ft.

No materials list available

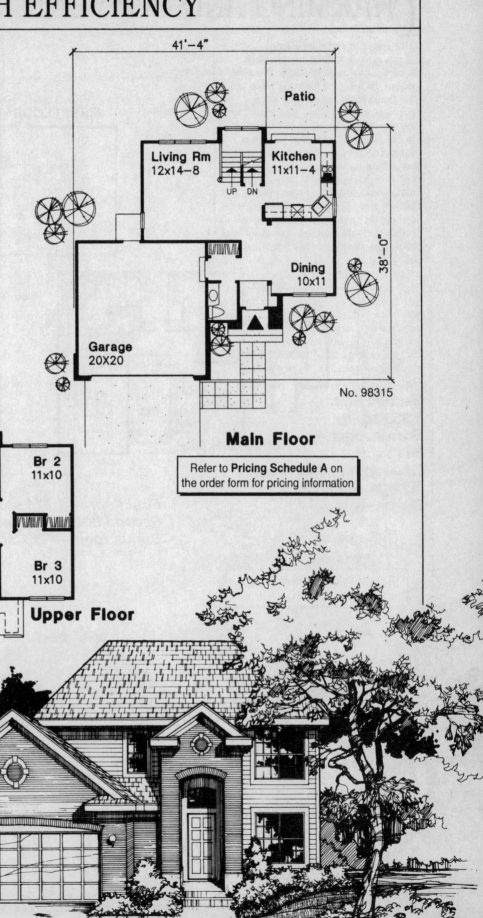

Main Floor

No. 98315

Refer to **Pricing Schedule A** on the order form for pricing information

Upper Floor

CHARMING AND CONVENIENT

This attractive elevation offers a charming style and the conveniences needed for the modern family. To either side of the foyer are the living room and the dining room in their traditional positions. A convenient garage entry into the laundry room, cuts down on tracked-in dirt. The well-appointed kitchen is equipped with a peninsula counter/eating bar, a built-in pantry and a planning desk and a bright eating nook. A cozy family room with a fireplace is open to the kitchen area. Crowned by a vaulted ceiling, the master suite includes an ultra bath and a walk-in closet. Two additional bedrooms share the double vanity hall bath.

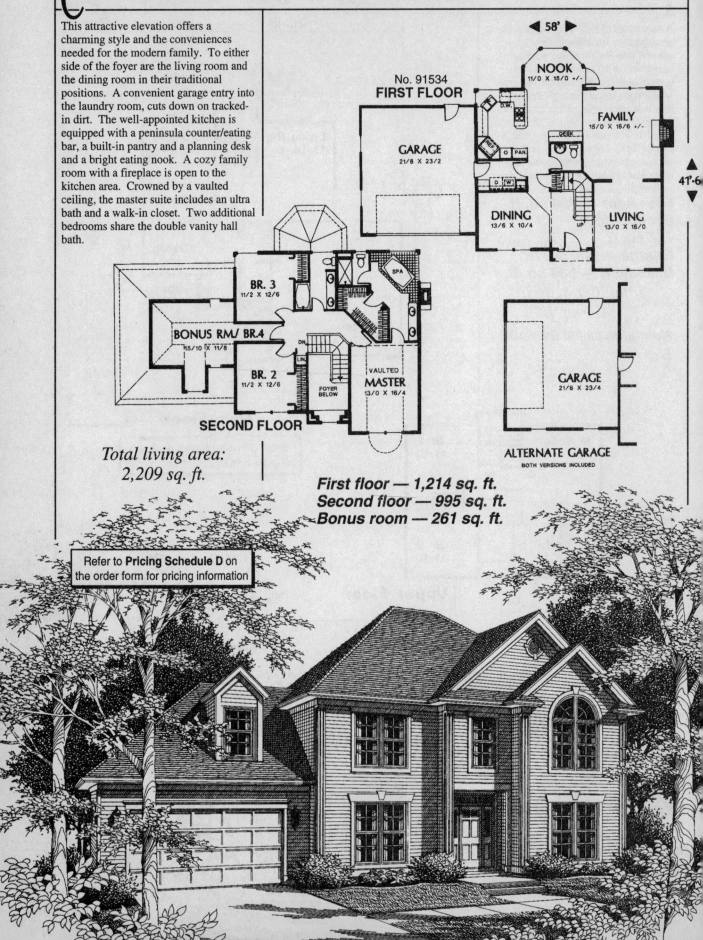

◄ 58' ►

No. 91534
FIRST FLOOR

NOOK
11/0 X 15/0 +/-

GARAGE
21/8 X 23/2

FAMILY
15/0 X 18/6 +/-

DESK

REF.

O PAN.

D.W.

D W

DINING
13/6 X 10/4

LIVING
13/0 X 16/0

UP

47'-6

BR. 3
11/2 X 12/6

SPA

BONUS RM./ BR.4
15/10 X 11/8

BR. 2
11/2 X 12/6

LIN.

DN.

FOYER BELOW

VAULTED
MASTER
13/0 X 16/4

SECOND FLOOR

GARAGE
21/8 X 23/4

ALTERNATE GARAGE
BOTH VERSIONS INCLUDED

Total living area: 2,209 sq. ft.

**First floor — 1,214 sq. ft.
Second floor — 995 sq. ft.
Bonus room — 261 sq. ft.**

Refer to **Pricing Schedule D** on the order form for pricing information

FOR MODERN FAMILY LIVING

Design 93310

A two-story foyer greets you as you enter this home. The spacious living room flows easily into the formal dining room adding to the comfort and convenience in entertaining. A large island kitchen includes a pantry, double sink and ample storage and counter space, while the expansive family room has a cozy fireplace and a stepped ceiling. The sleeping quarters are located on the second floor; the master suite is equipped with a private bath and walk-in closet, and the two family bedrooms share a full hall bath. A bonus room with a sloped ceiling will add to your family's living space. Today's lifestyle requires this modern, convenient house. No materials list available for this plan.

First floor — 1,166 sq. ft.
Second floor — 863 sq. ft.
Bonus room — 208 sq. ft.
Basement — 1,166 sq. ft.
Garage — 462 sq. ft.

Total living area:
2,029 sq. ft.

Refer to **Pricing Schedule C** on the order form for pricing information

An EXCLUSIVE DESIGN
By Patrick Morabito, A.I.A. Architect

FIRST FLOOR
No. 93310

49'0"

42'8"

WOOD DECK
12X18'6"

DINETTE
8'6"X11'6"

KITCHEN
18'6"x11'6"

DINING RM
11X14

FAMILY RM
17X14
STEPPED CLG

REFR PANTRY

P.R.

FLR ABOVE

LIVING RM
13X16

LAUND
D. W.

ENTRY

FOYER
HIGH CLG

PORC
shelf

STEP

UP

PORCH

GARAGE
22X21

BRICK VENEER

18FT. DOOR

SECOND FLOOR

B.R.#2
11X11

BATH

M.BATH

CLOSET

B.R.#3
12'8"X11

BALCONY

FOYER,
BELOW

M.B.R.
13X15

PORCH,
BELOW

DN

BONUS RM
15'6"X17'6"
SLOPED CLG

BRICK VENEER

BAY WINDOWS ADD APPEAL

The sheltered entrance, leads to an entry hall that is graced by a staircase, coat closet and a half bath. The formal living room/dining room combination includes a bay window adding natural illumination and a decorative touch to the room. Ample counter space is augmented by the peninsula counter/eating bar in the kitchen. Informal eating is accommodated in the nook area. A warm fireplace highlights the relaxed atmosphere of the family room. The second bay window provides the view from the master suite which is equipped with a private compartmented bath and walk-in closet. Two additional bedrooms and a bonus room share the full bath in the hall.

First floor — 972 sq. ft.
**Second floor —
843 sq. ft.**
**Bonus room —
180 sq. ft.**

Total living area:
1,815 sq. ft.

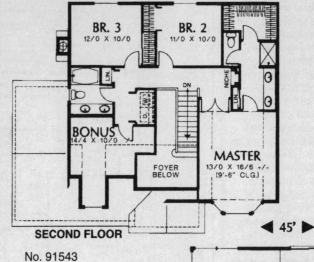

SECOND FLOOR

No. 91543

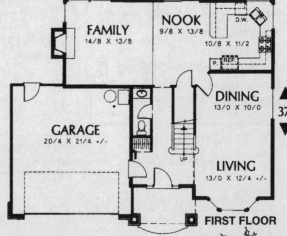

FIRST FLOOR

Refer to **Pricing Schedule C** on
the order form for pricing information

VICTORIAN TOUCHES

A little nostalgia flavors this plan. The "steeple" and porch bring back memories of another era. Don't let the exterior fool you. Inside is a thoroughly modern home. The kitchen has an island, corner double sink, built-in planning desk and breakfast nook. A large family room with a fireplace includes French doors to the side porch and to the rear sun deck. A master suite on the second floor includes a sitting area created by the "steeple" and a private balcony. The master bath includes an oval tub, separate shower, compartment toilet and a walk-in closet. There is also a walk-in closet in the master bedroom. Three additional bedrooms share a full hall bath. A convenient second floor laundry center is located in the hall.

An **EXCLUSIVE DESIGN**
By Jannis Vann & Associates. Inc.

FIRST FLOOR

46'-0"

36'-8"

SUNDECK 18'7 x 12'0

BREAKFAST 10 x 15'6

KITCHEN 9'6 x 13'6

LAV.

FAMILY RM. 19'6 x 13'6

DINING RM. 13'6 x 14'6 W/BAY

LIVING RM. 13'6 x 11'6

FOYER 10 x 9'6

PORCH

First floor —
1,155 sq. ft.
Second floor —
1,209 sq. ft.
Basement — 549 sq. ft.
Garage — 576 sq. ft.

Total living area:
2,364 sq. ft.

No. 93283

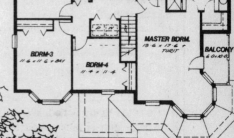

BDRM-2 11'6 x 11'2

BATH-2

M. BATH

BDRM-3 11'6 x 11'6 + BAY

BDRM-4 11'4 x 11'4

MASTER BDRM. 13'6 x 17'6 + TURRIT

BALCONY 6'0 x 10'0

SECOND FLOOR

Refer to **Pricing Schedule D** on the order form for pricing information

INTRIGUING, EYE-CATCHING DETAILS

The eye-catching details used around the arched entrance and windows of this home demand attention. From the varied roofline to the wonderful use of glass around the front door, this is a home that says style. Upon entering the foyer, the curved staircase may catch your attention. The living room and dining areas flow beautifully into each other for ease in entertaining. A lot of thought went into the efficient layout of the kitchen. The ample counter and cabinet space is sure to please the gourmet of your household. Notice, too, the easy access to both the nook and the dining area from the kitchen. The family room, sure to be the hub of activity for your family, boasts a fireplace for added atmosphere and warmth. Upstairs, the master suite provides a luxurious retreat. Walk-in closet, whirlpool bath and double vanities are just a few of the amenities offered. Two secondary bedrooms, a bonus room, loft and full bath complete the second floor. Efficient, stylish, and full of the amenities you're looking for......this house is for you. No materials list is available for this plan.

Refer to **Pricing Schedule D** on the order form for pricing information

First floor —1,383 sq. ft.
Second floor —
1,181 sq. ft.
Bonus — 172 sq. ft.
Total living area:
2,564 sq. ft.

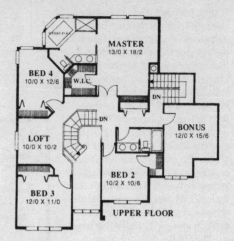

No. 91691

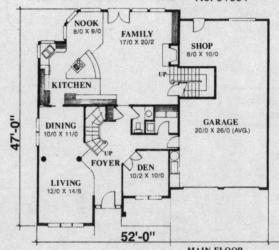

DECORATIVE QUIONS

This attractive elevation uses brick detailing and arched windows to achieve an eye-catching home. A covered entry leads into the gallery area. A spacious living room looms in front of the visitor highlighted by a fireplace centered in the rear wall. Cathedral ceilings top the family room and the formal dining rooms. The spacious kitchen/breakfast area includes an island and L-shaped counter space. Sloping ceilings add interest to the front bedroom and the master suite. A covered patio extends living area to the outside.

Main floor — 2,470 sq. ft.

Total living area: 2,470 sq. ft.

Refer to **Pricing Schedule D** on the order form for pricing information

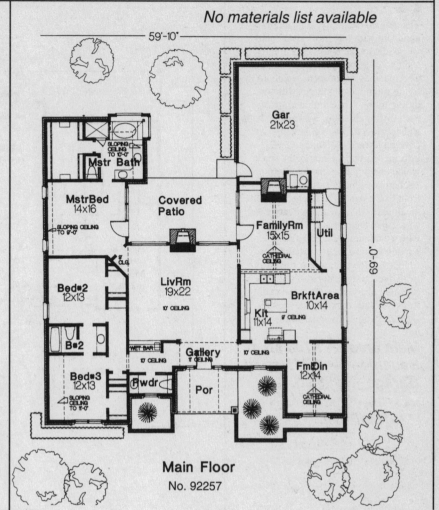

Main Floor
No. 92257

ANGLED CONTEMPORARY

This angled one story Contemporary is abundant with features. The angled shape allows the house to be rotated on a site to give the optimum orientation. The spacious foyer opens widely to the living room which merges with the dining room. The combined space, each distinguishable, is enhanced with sliding glass doors to a partially covered terrace. Moving to the informal part of the house, the space which encompasses the family room, kitchen and dinette flows from the front to the rear. The kitchen separates the dinette which features a large window in the rear and a family room with a cathedral ceiling, large windows, and a heat-circulating fireplace. The bedroom wing, away from the action, features a large master bedroom also with a cathedral ceiling. Its lavish bathroom includes a stall shower, two basins and a whirlpool tub.

Main area — 1,798 sq. ft.
Basement — 1,715 sq. ft.
Garage — 456 sq. ft.

Total living area:
1,798 sq. ft.

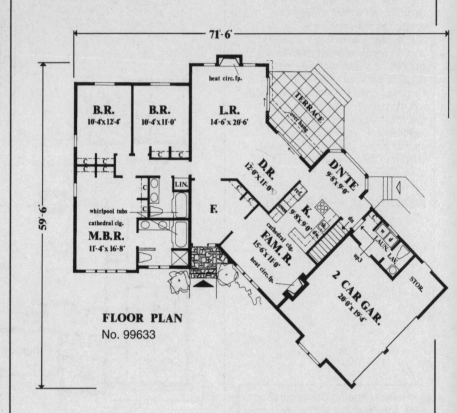

FLOOR PLAN
No. 99633

Refer to **Pricing Schedule B** on the order form for pricing information

HIGH IMPACT TWO-STORY

Gracious living abounds in this four bedroom upscale 1-1/2 story home, where the family room becomes the focus of intersecting activities. Its high impact effect comes from its two story entry with double doors and transom. As you enter you see the firplace/window walls of the large two story family room. The master suite is quite spacious and unique with curved glass block behind the tub in the master bath. The sitting area in the master suite has a semi-circular window wall and see-thru fireplace, perfect for romantic, cozy evenings. Entertaining is a joy in the gourmet kitchen and breakfast area that opens to a covered lanai. If your guest decides to stay the night, the guest suite is more than accomodating. It is not only spacious, but features a private deck and walk-in closet. The secondary bedrooms share a bath.

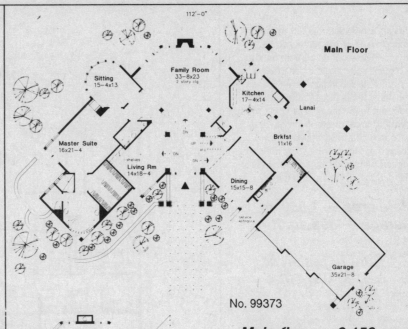

Main Floor

No. 99373

Main floor — 3,158 sq. ft.
Upper floor —
1,374 sq. ft.

Total living area:
4,532 sq. ft.

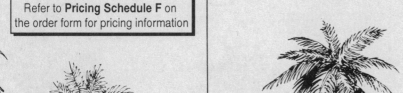

Upper Floor

Refer to **Pricing Schedule F** on the order form for pricing information

FOR THE EMPTY-NESTER

This stylish Ranch markets to the empty-nester or the second home buyer. The second bedroom doubles as a guest suite and the den offers a comfortable secondary living space. The entry looks through the Great room out to the lanai. The Great room, breakfast area, master bedroom and the bathroom all access the lanai, for covered outdoor living. The high 10' flat ceilings are throughout the house. The den may function as a third bedroom.

Main area — 1,859 sq. ft.
Garage — 393 sq. ft.

Total living area:
1,859 sq. ft.

Refer to **Pricing Schedule C** on the order form for pricing information

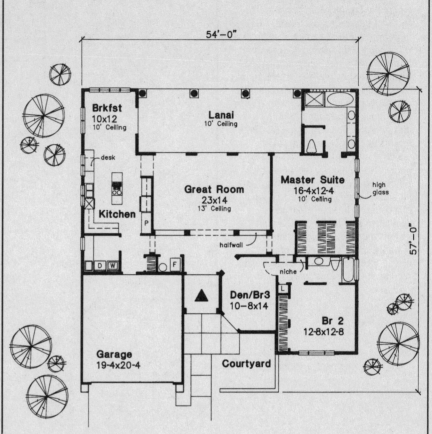

Floor Plan
No. 98316

THREE BEDROOM TRADITIONAL CAPE

This three bedroom traditional Cape design, has a welcoming full-length country porch. Although this home is classified as small, it has a lot of potential for a growing family. The master suite has its own master bath with mirrored vanity, stall shower and step-up whirlpool spa. Upstairs the secondary bedrooms share a full bath. Completing the first floor is the U-shaped kitchen, the powder room, dining room and the living room with a log burning, brick faced fireplace.

First floor — 913 sq. ft.
Second floor — 581 sq. ft.

Total living area: 1,494 sq. ft.

Refer to **Pricing Schedule A** on the order form for pricing information

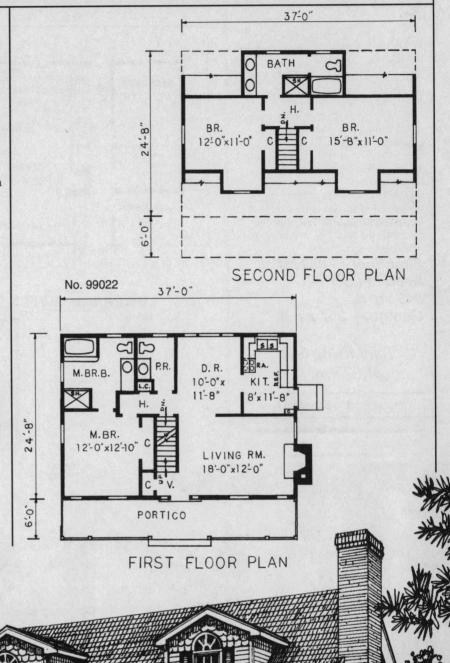

SECOND FLOOR PLAN

FIRST FLOOR PLAN

CONTEMPORARY STYLING

This plan offers a contemporary look on an A-frame design. The spa deck pampers you while you enjoy the surrounding vistas. A second deck is located off of the living room. A cozy fireplace adds warmth and atmosphere, enhancing the entire open living area of the living room, and kitchen. A peninsula counter/eating bar, double sink and ample storage and workspace are featured in the kitchen. The first floor bedroom is located in close proximity to the three quarter bath in the hall. A spacious master suite is located on the second floor providing the owner the luxury of privacy. No materials list available

First floor — 680 sq. ft.
Second floor —
345 sq. ft.
Garage — 357 sq. ft.

Total living area:
1,025 sq. ft.

Refer to **Pricing Schedule A** on
the order form for pricing information

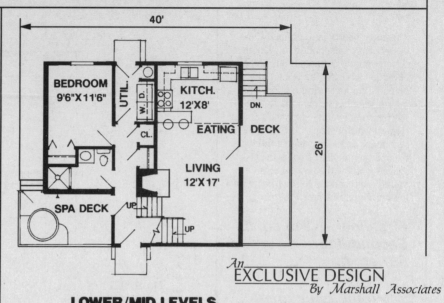

An
EXCLUSIVE DESIGN
By Marshall Associates

LOWER/MID LEVELS
No. 94305

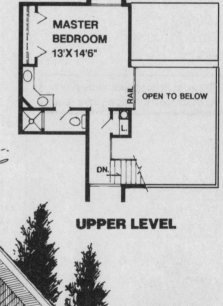

UPPER LEVEL

COUNTRY STYLE FOR TODAY

The spacious foyer of this design features a graceful, curved stair and an elegant columned entrance to the living room. Additional features are the heat-circulating fireplace, two bay windows in the living room and family-sized dining room with its bay window. In the rear the octagonal shaped dinette is defined by columns, dropped beams and the bay window. Although there is a flowing of space between the kitchen, dinette and family room, each is well defined. The second floor features four spacious bedrooms and two baths. The luxurious master bathroom is equipped with a large whirlpool tub plus two basins. The same equipment is in the second bathroom.

First floor — 1,132 sq. ft.
Second floor — 1,020 sq. ft.
Lndry/mudroom — 60 sq. ft.
Garage & Storage — 469 sq. ft
Basement — 1,026 sq. ft.

Total living area:
2,212 sq. ft.

Refer to **Pricing Schedule D** on the order form for pricing information

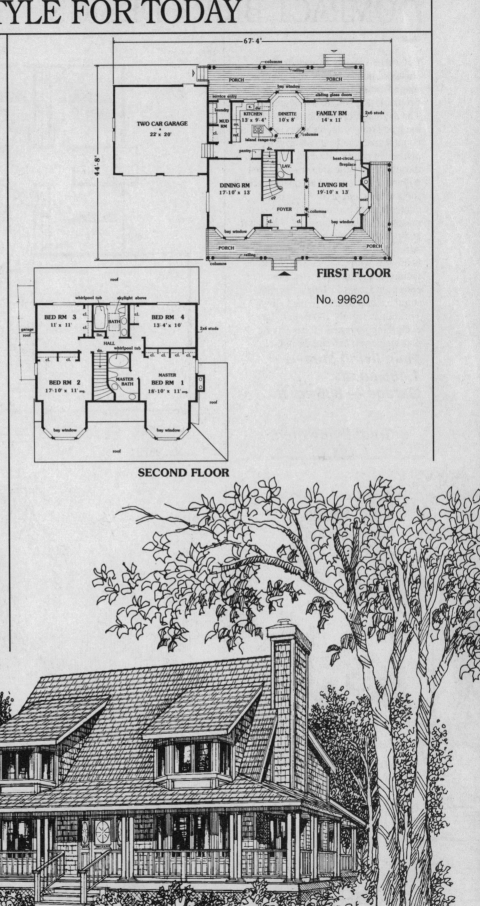

FIRST FLOOR

No. 99620

SECOND FLOOR

Design 98721

COMPACT BRICK DESIGN

Enter this home by its welcoming sheltered porch, and move right to a magnificent Great room, with a cozy fireplace, that adjoins a dining area. The angular kitchen contains a center oven and range, double sinks, plenty of counter space and a good-sized concealed pantry. Reach a large deck through the dining area or utility area with a handy sink and adequate space for a washer and dryer. This plan contains three bedrooms, one being the master suite with a large walk-in closet and private bath with a separate vanity. A full hall bath serves the other two bedrooms with ease. A two-car, front-facing garage contains a back outdoor entrance. Extras include a linen and storage closet located in the hallway. This home, at only 1,485 sq. ft. has everything you need for easy living plus an elegant exterior design.

**Main living area —
1,485 sq. ft.
Garage — 685 sq. ft.**

*Total living area:
1,485 sq. ft.*

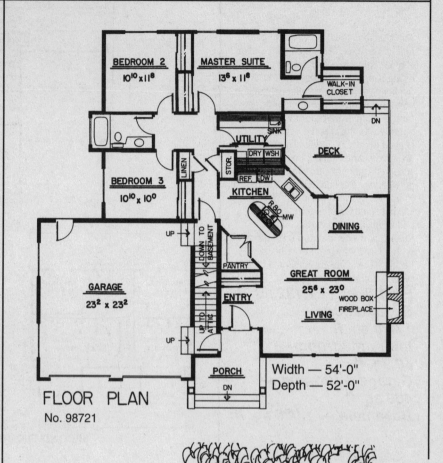

FLOOR PLAN
No. 98721

Width — 54'-0"
Depth — 52'-0"

Refer to **Pricing Schedule A** on the order form for pricing information

SPACIOUS, ELEGANT VICTORIAN

Dominating the second floor of this large two-story home, the master suite has a sleeping area equal in size to the living room. A wide bay window, which could easily accommodate a couch and/or a couple of easy chairs, bathes one end of the room in natural light, and a fireplace. The rest of the suite includes a huge walk-in closet, a dressing room and a private bath. Two more bedrooms share another skylit bathroom. The living room, like the master bedroom has a wide bay window and fireplace. Built-in bookcases fill part of the back wall here, as well as part of one wall in the den/office. Amenities in the comfortable country kitchen include a central work center, a garden window and an eating nook with double glass doors that open onto a deck. A closet provides extra storage in the vaulted entryway and the two-car garage has space for a work area.

Main floor — 1,315 sq. ft.
Upper floor — 1,066 sq. ft.
Garage — 649 sq. ft.
Width — 72'-0"
Depth — 34'-0"

Total living area: 2,381 sq. ft.

Refer to **Pricing Schedule D** on the order form for pricing information

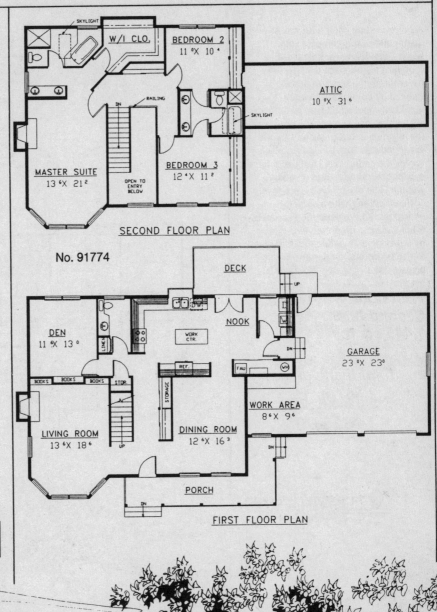

SECOND FLOOR PLAN

No. 91774

FIRST FLOOR PLAN

COMPACT STUCCO HOME

A commanding entry with lots of glass distinguishes this compact stucco home. The living room and dining room are visible from the two story foyer through a series of arches flanked by columns. The kitchen, breakfast room and keeping room are adjacent to one another and are great for informal entertaining and family get-togethers. A two sided fireplace serves the entire area. Upstairs, a large master bedroom features a vaulted ceiling. The master bath has a lovely coffered ceiling with a corner whirlpool tub, separate shower and his-n-her vanities. Bedroom two is served by a private bath, while the third and fourth bedrooms are designed with private dressing areas. No materials list available.

**First floor — 1,421 sq. ft.
Second floor —
1,446 sq. ft.**

*Total living area:
2,867 sq. ft.*

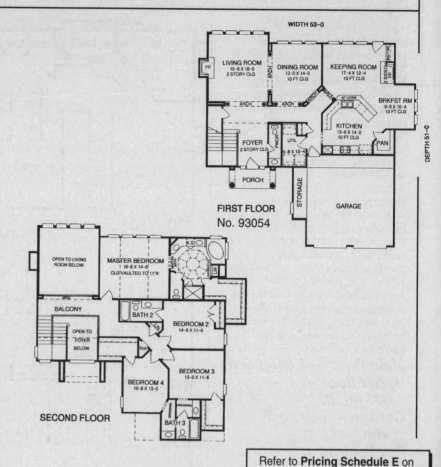

**FIRST FLOOR
No. 93054**

SECOND FLOOR

Refer to **Pricing Schedule E** on the order form for pricing information

An
EXCLUSIVE DESIGN
By Belk Home Designs

Ignoring Copyright Laws Can Be A $1,000,000 Mistake

Recent changes in the US copyright laws allow for statutory penalties of up to **$100,000** per incident for copyright infringement involving any of the copyrighted plans found in this publication. The law can be confusing. So, for your own protection, take the time to understand what you can and cannot do when it comes to home plans.

—— What You Cannot Do ——

You Cannot Duplicate Home Plans

Purchasing a set of blueprints and making additional sets by reproducing the original is *illegal*. If you need multiple sets of a particular home plan, then you must purchase them.

You Cannot Copy Any Part of a Home Plan to Create Another

Creating your own plan by copying even part of a home design found in this publication is called "creating a derivative work" and is *illegal* unless you have permission to do so.

You Cannot Build a Home Without a License

You must have specific permission or license to build a home from a copyrighted design, even if the finished home has been changed from the original plan. It is *illegal* to build one of the homes found in this publication without a license.

What Garlinghouse Offers

Home Plan Blueprint Package

By purchasing a single or multiple set package of blueprints from Garlinghouse, you not only receive the physical blueprint documents necessary for construction, but you are also granted a license to build one, and only one, home. You can also make any changes to our design that you wish, as long as these changes are made directly on the blueprints purchased from Garlinghouse and no additional copies are made.

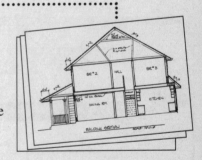

Home Plan Vellums

By purchasing vellums for one of our home plans, you receive the same construction drawings found in the blueprints, but printed on vellum paper. Vellums can be erased and are perfect for making design changes. They are also semi-transparent making them easy to duplicate. But most importantly, the purchase of home plan vellums comes with a broader license that allows you to make changes to the design (ie, create a hand drawn or CAD derivative work), to make an unlimited number of copies of the plan, and to build up to three homes from the plan.

License To Build Additional Homes

With the purchase of a blueprint package or vellums you automatically receive a license to build one home or three homes, respectively. If you want to build more homes than you are licensed to build through your purchase of a plan, then additional licenses may be purchased at reasonable costs from Garlinghouse. Inquire for more information.

You've Picked Your Dream Home!

You can already see it standing on your lot... you can see yourselves in your new home... enjoying family, entertaining guests, celebrating holidays. All that remains ahead are the details. That's where we can help. Whether you plan to build-it-yourself, be your own contractor, or hand your plans over to an outside contractor, your Garlinghouse blueprints provide the perfect beginning for putting yourself in your dream home right away.

We even make it simple for you to make professional design modifications. We can also provide a materials list for greater economy.

My grandfather, L.F. Garlinghouse, started a tradition of quality when he founded this company in 1907. For over 85 years, homeowners and builders have relied on us for accurate, complete, professional blueprints. Our plans help you get results fast... and save money, too! These pages will give you all the information you need to order. So get started now... I know you'll love your new Garlinghouse home!

Sincerely,

TYPICAL WALL SECTION

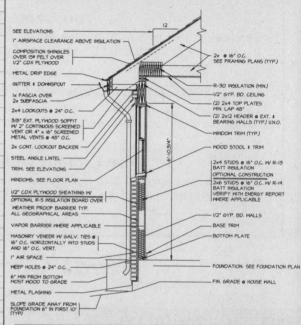

This section is provided to help your builder understand the structural components and materials used to construct the exterior walls of your home. This section will address insulation, roof components, and interior and exterior wall finishes. Your plans will be designed with either 2x4 or 2x6 exterior walls, but most professional contractors can easily adapt the plans to the wall thickness you require.

EXTERIOR ELEVATIONS

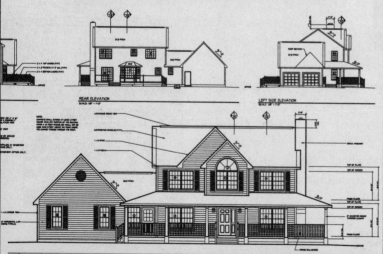

Elevations are scaled drawings of the front, rear, left and right sides of a home. All of the necessary information pertaining to the exterior finish materials, roof pitches and exterior height dimensions of your home are defined.

CABINET PLANS

KITCHEN CABINET PLAN
SCALE: 3/8" = 1'-0"

These plans, or in some cases elevations, will detail the layout of the kitchen and bathroom cabinets at a larger scale. This gives you an accurate layout for your cabinets or an ideal starting point for a modified custom cabinet design.

ke Your Dream Come True!

or home designs by respected professionals.

FIREPLACE DETAILS

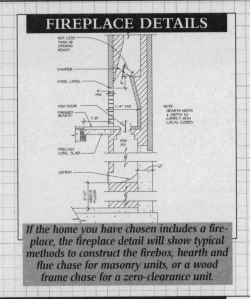

If the home you have chosen includes a fire-place, the fireplace detail will show typical methods to construct the firebox, hearth and flue chase for masonry units, or a wood frame chase for a zero-clearance unit.

TYPICAL CROSS SECTION

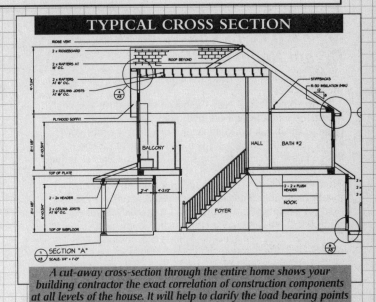

A cut-away cross-section through the entire home shows your building contractor the exact correlation of construction components at all levels of the house. It will help to clarify the load bearing points from the roof all the way down to the basement.

FOUNDATION PLAN

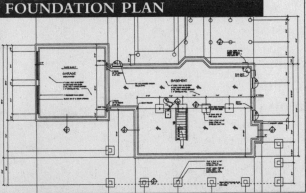

These plans will accurately dimension the footprint of your home including load bearing points and beam placement if applicable. The foundation style will vary from plan to plan. Your local climatic conditions will dictate whether a basement, slab or crawlspace is best suited for your area. In most cases, if your plan comes with one foundation style, a professional contractor can easily adapt the foundation plan to an alternate style.

DETAILED FLOOR PLANS

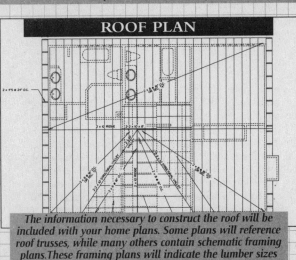

The floor plans of your home accurately dimension the positioning of all walls, doors, windows, stairs and permanent fixtures. They will show you the relationship and dimensions of rooms, closets and traffic patterns. Included is the schematic of the electrical layout. This layout is clearly represented and does not hinder the clarity of other pertinent information shown. All these details will help your builder properly construct your new home.

ROOF PLAN

The information necessary to construct the roof will be included with your home plans. Some plans will reference roof trusses, while many others contain schematic framing plans.These framing plans will indicate the lumber sizes necessary for the rafters and ridgeboards based on the designated roof loads.

STAIR DETAILS

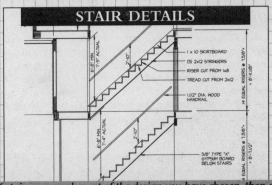

If stairs are an element of the design you have chosen, then a cross-section of the stairs will be included in your home plans. This gives your builders the essential reference points that they need for headroom clearance, and riser and tread dimensions.

GARLINGHOUSE OPTIONS & EXTRAS
MAKE THE DREAM TRULY YOURS.

Reversed Plans Can Make Your Dream Home Just Right!

"That's our dream home... if only the garage were on the other side!"

You could have exactly the home you want by flipping it end-for-end. Check it out by holding your dream home page of this book up to a mirror. Then simply order your plans "reversed". We'll send you one full set of mirror-image plans (with the writing backwards) as a master guide for you and your builder.

The remaining sets of your order will come as shown in this book so the dimensions and specifications are easily read on the job site... but they will be specially stamped "REVERSED" so there is no construction confusion.

We can only send reversed plans with multiple-set orders. But, there is no extra charge for this service.

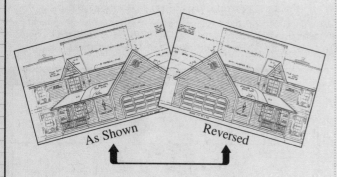

As Shown   Reversed

Modifying Your Garlinghouse Home Plan

Easy modifications to your dream home such as minor non-structural changes and simple material substitutions, can be made between you and your builder and marked directly on your blueprints. However, if you are considering making major changes to your design, we strongly recommend that you purchase our reproducible vellums and use the services of a professional designer or architect. For additional information call us at 1-860-343-5977.

Our Reproducible Vellums Make Modifications Easier

With a vellum copy of our plans, a design professional can alter the drawings just the way you want, then you can print as many copies of the modified plans as you need. And, since you have already started with our complete detailed plans, the cost of those expensive professional services will be significantly less. Refer to the price schedule for vellum costs. Call for vellum availability for plan numbers 90,000 and above.

Reproducible vellum copies of our home plans are only sold under the terms of a license agreement that you will receive with your order. Should you not agree to the terms, then the vellums may be returned unopened for a full refund.

Yours FREE With Your Order
FREE
SPECIFICATIONS AND CONTRACT FORM

provides the perfect way for you and your builder to agree on the exact materials to use in building and finishing your home before you start construction. A must for homeowner's peace of mind.

Remember To Order Your Materials List

It'll help you save money. Available at a modest additional charge, the Materials List gives the quantity, dimensions, and specifications for the major materials needed to build your home. You will get faster, more accurate bids from your contractors and building suppliers — and avoid paying for unused materials and waste. Materials Lists are available for all home plans except as otherwise indicated, but can only be ordered with a set of home plans. Due to differences in regional requirements and homeowner or builder preferences... electrical, plumbing and heating/air conditioning equipment specifications are not designed specifically for each plan. However, non plan specific detailed typical prints of residential electrical, plumbing and construction guidelines can be provided. Please see next page for additional information.

Questions?

Call our customer service number at 1-860-343-5977.

How Many Sets Of Plans Will You Need?

The Standard 8-Set Construction Package

Our experience shows that you'll speed every step of construction and avoid costly building errors by ordering enough sets to go around. Each tradesperson wants a set — the general contractor and all subcontractors; foundation, electrical, plumbing, heating/air conditioning, drywall, finish carpenters, and cabinet shop. Don't forget your lending institution, building department and, of course, a set for yourself.

The Minimum 5-Set Construction Package

If you're comfortable with arduous follow-up, this package can save you a few dollars by giving you the option of passing down plan sets as work progresses. You might have enough copies to go around if work goes exactly as scheduled and no plans are lost or damaged. But for only $50 more, the 8-set package eliminates these worries.

The Single-Set Decision-Maker Package

We offer this set so you can study the blueprints to plan your dream home in detail. But remember... one set is never enough to build your home... and they're copyrighted.

New Plan Details For The Home Builder

Because local codes and requirements vary greatly, we recommend that you obtain drawings and bids from licensed contractors to do your mechanical plans. However, if you want to know more about techniques — and deal more confidently with subcontractors — we offer these remarkably useful detail sheets. Each is an excellent tool that will enhance your understanding of these technical subjects.

Residential Construction Details

Eight sheets that cover the essentials of stick-built residential home construction. Details foundation options - poured concrete basement, concrete block, or monolithic concrete slab. Shows all aspects of floor, wall, and roof framing. Provides details for roof dormers, eaves, and skylights. Conforms to requirements of Uniform Building code or BOCA code. Includes a quick index.

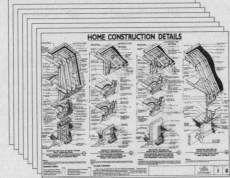

$14.95 per set

Residential Plumbing Details

Nine sheets packed with information detailing pipe connection methods, fittings, and sizes. Shows sump-pump and water softener hookups, and septic system construction. Conforms to requirements of National Plumbing Code. Color coded with a glossary of terms and quick index.

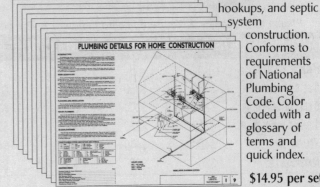

$14.95 per set

Residential Electrical Details

Nine sheets that cover all aspects of residential wiring, from simple switch wiring to the complexities of three-phase and service entrance connection. Explains service load calculations and distribution panel wiring. Shows you how to create a floor-plan wiring diagram. Conforms to requirements of National Electrical Code. Color coded with a glossary of terms and a quick index.

$14.95 per set

Important Shipping Information

Please refer to the shipping charts on the order form for service availability for your specific plan number. Our delivery service must have a street address or Rural Route Box number — never a post office box. Use a work address if no one is home during the day.

Orders being shipped to APO, FPO or Post Office Boxes must go via First Class Mail. Please include the proper postage.

For our International Customers, only Certified bank checks and money orders are accepted and must be payable in U.S. currency. For speed, we ship international orders Air Parcel Post. Please refer to the chart for the correct shipping cost.

An important note:

All plans are drawn to conform to one or more of the industry's major national building standards. However, due to the variety of local building regulations, your plan may need to be modified to comply with local requirements — snow loads, energy loads, seismic zones, etc. Do check them fully and consult your local building officials.

A few states require that all building plans used be drawn by an architect registered in that state. While having your plans reviewed and stamped by such an architect may be prudent, laws requiring non-conforming plans like ours to be completely redrawn forces you to unnecessarily pay very large fees. If your state has such a law, we strongly recommend you contact your state representative to protest.

VISA BEFORE ORDERING PLEASE READ ALL ORDERING INFORMATION **MasterCard**

Please submit all Canadian plan orders to:
Garlinghouse Company
60 Baffin Place, Unit #5, Waterloo, Ontario N2V 1Z7
Canadian Customers Only: 1-800-561-4169/Fax #: 1-800-719-3291
Customer Service #: 1-519-746-4169

ORDER TOLL FREE— 1-800-235-5700
Monday-Friday 8:00 a.m. to 5:00 p.m. Eastern Time
or FAX your Credit Card order to 1-860-343-5984
All foreign residents call 1-860-343-5977

Please have ready: 1. Your credit card number 2. The plan number 3. The order code number ⇨ H6NH1

GARLINGHOUSE BLUEPRINT PRICE CODE SCHEDULE:
Additional sets with original order $25

PRICE CODE	A	B	C	D	E	F	G	H
8 SETS OF SAME PLAN	$330	$350	$375	$400	$430	$470	$510	$555
5 SETS OF SAME PLAN	$280	$300	$325	$350	$380	$420	$460	$505
1 SINGLE SET OF PLANS	$210	$230	$255	$280	$310	$350	$390	$435
VELLUMS	$420	$440	$465	$490	$520	$560	$600	$645
MATERIALS LIST	$25	$25	$30	$30	$35	$40	$40	$45

SHIPPING & HANDLING ALL PLANS

	1-3 Sets	4-6 Sets	7+ & Vellums
First Class Mail(5-7 Days)*P.O. Boxes Only	$9.00	$18.00	$20.00
Regular Delivery Canada(7-10 Days)	$14.00	$17.00	$20.00
Express Delivery Canada(5-6 Days)	$35.00	$40.00	$45.00
Overseas Delivery Airmail(2-3 Weeks)	$45.00	$52.00	$60.00

SHIPPING (Plans 1-89999)

	1-3 Sets	4-6 Sets	7+ & Vellums
Standard Delivery(UPS 2-Day)	$15.00	$20.00	$25.00
Overnight Delivery	$30.00	$35.00	$40.00

SHIPPING (Plans 90000-99000)

	1-3 Sets	4-6 Sets	7+ & Vellums
Ground Delivery(7-10 Days)	$9.00	$18.00	$20.00
Express Delivery(3-5 Days)	$15.00	$20.00	$25.00

Canadian Orders and Shipping: To our friends in Canada, we have a plan design affiliate in Kitchener, Ontario. This relationship will help you avoid the delays and charges associated with shipments from the United States. Moreover, our affiliate is familiar with the building requirements in your community and country. We prefer payments in U.S. Currency. If you, however, are sending Canadian funds please add 40% to the prices of the plans and shipping fees.

GARLINGHOUSE ——— *B l u e p r i n t   O r d e r   F o r m* ——— Order Code No. **H6NH1**

Plan No. _____

☐ As Shown   ☐ Reversed *(mult. set pkgs. only)*

	Each	Amount
8 set pkg.		$
5 set pkg.		$
1 set pkg. (no reverses)		$
____ (qty.) Add'l. sets @		$
Vellums		$
Materials List (with plan order only)		$
Residential Builder Plans		
____ set(s) Construction	@ $14.95	$
____ set(s) Plumbing	@ $14.95	$
____ set(s) Electrical	@ $14.95	$
Shipping		$
Subtotal		$
Sales Tax (CT residents add 6% sales tax, KS residents add 6.15% sales tax) (Not required for other states)		$
Total Amount Enclosed		**$**

Plan prices guaranteed until 8-1-97
Payment must be made in U.S. funds
Foreign Mail Orders: Certified bank checks in U.S. funds only

Credit Card Information

Charge To: ☐ Visa   ☐ Mastercard

Card # |_|_|_|_|_|_|_|_|_|_|_|_|_|_|_|_|

Signature _____ Exp. ____/____

Send your check, money order or credit card information to:
(No C.O.D.'s Please)

Please Submit all United States & Other Nations plan orders to:
Garlinghouse Company
P.O. Box 1717
Middletown, CT 06457

Please Submit all Canadian plan orders to:
Garlinghouse Company
60 Baffin Place, Unit #5
Waterloo, Ontario N2V 1Z7

Bill To: (address must be as it appears on credit card statement)

Name _____

Address _____

City/State _____   Zip _____

Daytime Phone (____) _____

Ship To (if different from Bill to):

Name _____

Address _____

City/State _____   Zip _____

TERMS OF SALE FOR HOME PLANS:

All home plans sold through this publication are copyright protected. Reproduction of these home plans, either in whole or in part, including any direct copying and/or preparation of derivative works thereof, for any reason without the prior written permission of The L.F. Garlinghouse Co., Inc., is strictly prohibited. The purchase of a set of home plans in no way transfers any copyright or other ownership interest in it to the buyer except for a limited license to use that set of home plans for the construction of one, and only one, dwelling unit. The purchase of additional sets of that home plan at a reduced price from the original set or as a part of a multiple set package does not entitle the buyer with a license to construct more than one dwelling unit.